Claiming Citizenship
Rights, Participation and Accountability
Series editor • John Gaventa

Around the world, a growing crisis of legitimacy characterises the relationship between citizens and the institutions that affect their lives. In both north and south, citizens speak of mounting disillusionment with government, based on concerns about corruption, lack of responsiveness to the needs of the poor and the absence of a sense of connection with elected representatives and bureaucrats. Conventional forms of expertise and representation are being questioned. The rights and responsibilities of corporations and other global actors are being challenged, as global inequalities persist and deepen.

In response, this series argues, increased attention must be paid to re-examining contemporary understandings of rights and citizenship in different contexts, and their implications for related issues of participation and accountability. Challenging liberal understandings in which citizenship is understood as a set of rights and responsibilities bestowed by the state, the series looks at how citizenship is claimed and rights are realised through the agency and actions of people themselves.

Growing out of the work of an international network of researchers and practitioners from both South and North, the volumes in this series explore a variety of themes, including locally rooted struggles for more inclusive forms of citizenship, the links between citizenship, science and globalisation, the politics and dynamics of participation in new democratic arenas, and the relationships between claiming rights and ensuring accountability. Drawing from concrete case studies which focus on how people understand their citizenship and claim their rights, the volumes contribute new, empirically grounded perspectives to current debates related to deepening democracy, realising rights-based development, and making institutions more responsive to the needs and voices of poor people.

Titles in the series

Volume I: *Inclusive Citizenship: Meanings and Expressions*
Edited by Naila Kabeer

Volume 2: *Science and Citizens: Globalization and the Challenge of Engagement*
Edited by Melissa Leach, Ian Scoones and Brian Wynne

Volume 3: *Rights, Resources and the Politics of Accountability*
Edited by Peter Newell and Joanna Wheeler

Volume 4: *Spaces for Change? The Politics of Citizen Participation in New Democratic Arenas*
Edited by Andrea Cornwall and Vera Schatten Coelho (forthcoming Autumn 2006)

Volume 5: *Claiming Citizenship: Rethinking Democratic Participation*
John Gaventa (forthco~   ~~~

About this book

Many conflicts in development can be understood as struggles by the poor to hold the powerful to account. Contests over the rights and responsibilities of actors in development are increasing in intensity amid conflicts between the promotion of rights-based approaches to development and market-based notions of access and entitlement to resources. How these conflicts are played out has enormous implications for efforts to tackle poverty and achieve the Millennium Development Goals. Understanding how the poor claim their rights and demand accountability for the realisation of those rights becomes critical.

This book contributes to such an understanding by exploring the conditions in which poorer groups mobilise around rights in a diversity of settings and employing a broad range of strategies to do so. *Rights, Resources and the Politics of Accountability* looks at a range of exciting and imaginative ways in which poorer groups organise to claim their rights and construct mechanisms of accountability with the state, the private sector, international institutions and within civil society itself.

Amid the diversity of regions covered and the breadth of strategies examined, a series of overarching themes emerges. These address key questions about how and when the poor are able to improve the accountability of powerful actors in development for their actions and inactions. *Rights, Resources and the Politics of Accountability* will therefore be essential reading for development practitioners, activists and academics alike.

Praise for this book

'Development is a process, Amartya Sen famously noted, of "expanding the real freedoms that people enjoy". But freedoms depend on political and civil rights, or more properly a corpus of rights capable of removing such unfreedoms as tyranny, exclusion and neglect. This book is the first study to explore seriously how the poor claim, contest and secure rights and how the rights of the powerful are deployed to defend their privileges, and to control resources and access to power. Here is a provocative new agenda that lays out the competing forms and mechanisms of accountability by which the poor can improve their well-being ... a state-of-the-art book: theoretically rich, empirically compelling and irresistibly forward-looking.' – Michael Watts, Director of African Studies, UC Berkeley

'This book is fascinating not only because it puts accountability at the centre of the debate between rights and access to resources and questions some inherently flawed assumptions about accountability oft repeated by today's development pundits, it is fascinating because it tells stories about how the poor and marginalised come together to negotiate and claim their rights to resources from the rich and the powerful.' – Chandra Bhushan, Head, Industry & Environment Centre and Associate Director of Centre for Science and Environment, New Delhi.

Claiming Citizenship SERIES
Rights, Participation and
Accountability

Series editor
John Gaventa

Volume 3

Rights, Resources and
the Politics of Accountability

EDITED BY
Peter Newell and Joanna Wheeler

Zed Books
LONDON AND NEW YORK

Rights, Resources and the Politics of Accountability was first published by Zed Books Ltd,
7 Cynthia Street, London N1 9JF, UK and Room 400, 175 Fifth Avenue,
New York, NY 10010, USA in 2006
www.zedbooks.co.uk

Cover designed by Andrew Corbett
Set in 10.5/12.5 pt Goudy by Long House, Cumbria, UK
Printed and bound in Malta by Gutenberg Press Ltd

Distributed in the USA exclusively by Palgrave Macmillan, a division of
St Martin's Press, LLC, 175 Fifth Avenue, New York, NY 10010

A catalogue record for this book is available from the British Library

US Cataloging-in-Publication Data
is available from the Library of Congress

ISBN 1 84277 554 5 (hb)   ISBN 978 1 84277 554 7 (hb)
ISBN 1 84277 555 3 (pb)   ISBN 978 1 84277 555 4 (pb)

No Power without Accountability (p.viii) composed by
Bragg/Barker/McLagan/Mandelson/Edmonds/Edwards
Published by Union Productions Ltd/BMG Music Publishing Ltd
Used by permission. All rights reserved.

Contents

The contributors

Oga Steve Abah is Professor of Theatre for Development at Ahmadu Bello University, Zaria, Nigeria. One of Abah's main interests is the exploration of different methodologies, especially Theatre for Development (TfD) and Participatory Learning and Action (PLA) in doing citizenship research. He is the Nigeria Country Coordinator for the Citizenship Development Research Centre.

Vaijanyanta Anand is a Social Worker and a Scholar at the Department of Sociology, University of Mumbai. She is a Senior Faculty Member at the College of Social Work, Nirmala Niketan, University of Mumbai. She is also Honorary Director of Nirman, an NGO working with unorganised labour. Her interests are issues of corporate accountability, environment and labour.

Hasrat Arjjumend is a freelance researcher on development issues. He is based in India.

Andrea Cornwall is a Fellow at the Institute of Development Studies at the University of Sussex, UK. A Social Anthropologist by training, her current research focuses on the history and politics of participation in development. Her publications include *Realizing Rights: Transforming Approaches to Sexual and Reproductive Wellbeing* (edited, with Alice Welbourn, Zed Books, 2002) and *Gender in Africa* (James Currey, 2004).

Silvia Cordeiro is a feminist, a doctor, and general coordinator of the Women's Centre of Cabo de Santo Agostinho, Municipality of Sao Paulo, Brazil. She was President of the Municipal Health Council of the Cabo de Santo Agostinho for two terms, representing users of health services.

Carlos Cortéz, Doctor in Anthropology, is a Postgraduate Professor of Rural Development at the Autonomous Metropolitan University (Universidad Autónoma Metropolitana) in Mexico. He coordinates an interdisciplinary research programme on human development. He has undertaken research and published on social strategies for development, on governmental policies and on action-research oriented methodologies.

Nelson Giordano Delgado is a Professor of the Graduate Programme on Development, Agriculture and Society (CPDA) of the Federal Rural University of Rio de Janeiro in Brazil. He has published articles and essays on agriculture and macroeconomic policies, public policies for rural development, international trade regimes, the World Social Forum, and democracy and public spaces for participation. He has been a consultant for several public agencies in Brazil, and has worked with numerous international agencies, NGOs and grassroots movements.

Harsh Jaitli holds an MPhil in American Studies from Jawaharlal Nehru University, New Delhi, and has 16 years of extensive experience in capacity building, socio-economic research, impact assessment, policy analysis and advocacy, conflict resolution, project management and evaluation. He is currently working at PRIA as Programme Director of PRIA Consultants. His research has focused on occupational and environmental health and safety and sustainable industrial development. He has been actively developing methodologies for participation and corporate accountability.

Naila Kabeer is Professorial Fellow at IDS and a member of the Poverty and Social Policy Team. Her research interests include gender, livelihoods and labour market issues. Recent books include *The Power to Choose: Bangladeshi Women and Labour Market Decisions in London and Dhaka* (Verso, 2000) and *Gender Mainstreaming in Poverty Eradication and the Millennium Development Goals* (Commonwealth Secretariat/IDRC, 2003).

R. D. Sampath Kumar is an Associate Professor at the Department of Social Work, Andhra University, India. His field of expertise is social research methodology and his areas of work are child abuse, child labour, human resource management, labour welfare and unorganised labour.

Rohit Lekhi is Head of Research at Research Republic, a public policy research consultancy, and Honorary Research Fellow at the Ahmed Iqbal Ullah Race Relations Resource Centre, University of Manchester.

Stephanie Luce is an Assistant Professor at the Labor Center, University of Massachusetts-Amherst. She is the author of *Fighting for a Living Wage* (Cornell University Press, 2004), and co-author with Robert Pollin of *The Living Wage: Building a Fair Economy* (New Press, 2000). She researches and teaches labour economics, economic development, and low-wage labour markets. She received her PhD in Sociology from the University of Wisconsin-Madison.

Simeen Mahmud studied Statistics at the Dhaka University and Medical Demography at the London School of Hygiene and Tropical Medicine. She joined the Bangladesh Institute of Development Studies after completing her Masters and is currently Senior Research Fellow in the Population Studies Division. Her past research has been on demographic estimation methods; the relationship between women's work, status and fertility; micro credit and its impact on women; and group behaviour. Her current work on social policy focuses on health and education; citizenship and rights; demographic transition under poverty; and globalisation and its implications for women workers in the export sector.

Lyla Mehta is a sociologist and has worked as Research Fellow at IDS since 1998. She has conducted research on the dynamics of water scarcity, forced displacement and resistance to large infrastructure projects, and conceptual issues around the 'public' and 'private' nature of water. She has extensive field experience in India and more recently has begun research in South Africa. She uses the case of water to explore questions around knowledge/power linkages, social differentiation in natural resource management, rights to resources, and how competing forms of governance shape people's rights and access to resources. She is the author of *The Politics and Poetics of Water: Naturalising Scarcity in Western India* (Orient Longman, 2005).

Peter Newell is Senior Research Fellow at the Centre for the Study of Globalisation and Regionalisation, University of Warwick. Prior to this he has held posts as Fellow at IDS, Visiting Researcher at FLACSO, Argentina, Lecturer in International Studies at the University of Warwick and Researcher and Lobbyist for Climate Network Europe in Brussels. He is the author of *Climate for Change: Non-State Actors and the Global Politics of the Greenhouse* (CUP, 2000), co-author of *The Effectiveness of EU Environmental Policy* (MacMillan, 2000) and co-editor of *Development and the Challenge of Globalisation* (ITDG, 2002) and *The Business of Global Environmental Governance* (MIT Press, 2005). His main research interests are the political economy of environmental governance and the politics of corporate accountability and regulation.

Celestine Nyamu-Musembi is a Kenyan Lawyer with a background in legal anthropology who is currently a Fellow at IDS. She researches and writes on land relations and gender equity in resource control, the functioning of formal and informal justice institutions at the local level, implementation of international human rights standards, rights-based approaches to development, and integrating participatory approaches to rights advocacy. Her geographical focus is Eastern Africa.

Jenks Zakari Okwori is a lecturer in Drama at Ahmadu Bello University, Zaria. As one of the lead researchers at the Citizenship Development Research Centre in Nigeria, he has focused on exploring questions of identity in Nigeria, as well as developing new communication strategies.

Luisa Paré is an anthropologist, and works as a full-time Researcher at the Instituto de Investigaciones Sociales, Universidad Nacional Autónoma de México. She currently works on environment, natural resources management and local development issues.

A. B. S. V. Ranga Rao is on the faculty at the department of Social Work, Andhra University, Visakhapatnam, Andhra Pradesh, India.

Carlos Robles is an economist specialising in rural development. He has worked in urban and rural participatory planning, transfers of technology for sustainable production, and the creation of spaces for grassroots territorial management organisations, emphasising the relationship between quality of life, environmental quality and informed social participation.

Joanna Wheeler is the Research Manager of the Development Research Centre on Citizenship, Participation and Accountability (Citizenship DRC), a collaborative initiative working on how rights and citizenship matter. She has worked for ten years with NGOs and research initiatives in Brazil, Argentina and the US on issues of citizenship, gender and exclusion. Prior to joining IDS, she conducted postgraduate research on gender and citizenship in Rio de Janeiro as a Fulbright scholar. Her recent publications include *Developing Rights?* (*IDS Bulletin*, 36, 1), co-edited with Jethro Pettit in 2005, and 'New Forms of Citizenship: Democracy, Family, and Community in Rio de Janeiro, Brazil' in *Gender, Development and Citizenship* (Oxfam, 2004).

Abbreviations

AFL–CIO	American Federation of Labour – Congress of Industrial Organisations
ANDM	Alfred Nzo District Municipality
APEN	Asian Pacific Environmental Network
ASK	Ain O Salish Kendra
BGMEA	Bangladesh Garment Manufacturing and Exporters Association
BIGUF	Bangladesh Independent Garment Workers Union Federation
CNA	Comision Nacional de Agua (National Water Commission)
COHRE	Centre on Housing Rights and Evictions
COMPITCH	Indigenous Medical Organisations of Chiapas State
CONANP	National Commission for Protected National Areas (Mexico)
CSR	corporate social responsibility
DC	District Commissioner
DDT	Dichloro-diphenyl-trichloroethane
DfID	Department for International Development
DRC	Development Research Centre
DWAF	Department for Water Affairs and Forestry
EJ	environmental justice
EPA	Environmental Protection Agency
EPZ	export processing zone
FBW	Free Basic Water
GATS	General Agreement on Trade in Services
GDP	gross domestic products
GEAR	Growth, Employment and Redistribution
GNA	good neighbourhood agreement
HSRC	Human Sciences Research Council
ICESCR	International Covenant on Economic, Social and Cultural Rights
IEN	Indigenous Environmental Network
IFC	International Finance Corporation
ILO	International Labour Organisation
IMF	International Monetary Fund

INGO	international non-governmental organisation
INTRAC	International NGO Training and Research Centre
JV	joint venture
MFA	Multi-fibre Arrangement
NGO	non-governmental organisation
NHP	National Hydraulic Programme
NNPC	Nigerian National Petroleum Corporation
NRM	natural resource management
NTPC	National Thermal Power Corporation
ODC	Ogulaha Development Council
PCB	polychlorinated biphenyl
PDP	People's Democratic Party
PFL	Partido da Frente Liberal
PLA	participatory learning and action
PMDB	Partido do Movimento Democrático Brasileiro
PNA	protected natural area
PPP	Plan Puebla Panama
PROCEDE	Programa de Cesión de Derechos Ejidales (Programme for Cession of Ejido Rights)
PRODERS	Regional Development Programmes
PROFEPA	Procuraduría Federal de Protección al Ambiente
RDP	Reconstruction and Development Programme
RMG	ready-made garments
SEMARNAT	Secretaría de Recursos Naturales y Medio Ambiente (Ministry of Environment and Natural Resources)
SINAP	System for Protected Natural Areas (Mexico)
SNEEJ	Southern Network for Economic and Environmental Justice
SPDC	Shell Petroleum Development Company
SSC	Solidarity Sponsoring Committee
STPP	Simhadri Thermal Power Project
SUS	Sistema Único de Saúde
TFDC	Theatre for Development Centre
TNC	transnational corporations
TRIPs	Trade-Related Intellectual Property Rights
UCC	United Church of Christ
UNDP	United Nations Development Programme
UNICEF	United Nations Children's Fund
US	United States
USAID	United States Agency for International Development
USAS	United Students Against Sweatshops
WSSA	Water and Sanitation Services Africa
WTO	World Trade Organisation

Acknowledgements

We would like to acknowledge the support and contributions of a number of people to this volume. We are hugely grateful to John Gaventa as director of the Centre and as an enthusiastic and supportive colleague. He has tirelessly encouraged us throughout the production of this book and during the research programme which preceded and underpins it. Rohit Lekhi and Stephanie Luce deserve thanks for getting involved in the work of the programme in its latter stages, contributing invaluable 'Northern' insights and experience which helped to broaden, challenge and enrich our understanding of the accountability politics we were exploring in the global South. Mike Kirkwood and Lucila Garcia Lahitou provided invaluable copy-editing, administrative and editorial support in the final stages of producing the book. Reviewers of individual chapters, as well as the overall manuscript, helped to improve the coherence of the volume significantly, for which we are hugely thankful. We hope we have all been able to do justice to their comments. We are grateful to Robert Molteno as commissioning editor and to Anne Rodford for seeing the book through the final stages of publication.

We owe an enormous debt to the team of researchers that made up the 'Rights and Accountabilities' programme of the Development Research Centre on Citizenship, Participation and Accountability, whose work made this volume possible. We would like to thank them for their commitment to, and engagement in, an ever-evolving research programme over a number of years and in a number of countries, requiring attendance at numerous meetings and patience with the endless stream of editorial demands!

We would like to dedicate this book to Lucila Garcia Lahitou and Rob Worthington for their patience and love, without which our right to produce ambitious volumes such as this would not be realised and whose role in holding us to account for our duties as responsible partners, as well as active researchers, was critical to the maintenance of sanity.

Peter Newell and Joanna Wheeler
Brighton, February 2006

Foreword

JOHN GAVENTA

'Accountability' is one of the latest buzz words in development. It may be used variously to refer to the relationship of states to their citizens, NGOs to their members, elected representatives to their voters, corporations to their stockholders, and government departments to one another. In the development context, the argument is that through greater accountability aid will be channelled to those for whom it is intended, governments will move from clientelistic to more inclusive and transparent practices, corporations will become more responsible to social, environmental and ethical concerns, and large NGOs will become answerable to the publics they claim to represent. Achieving accountability is essential if the Millennium Development Goals are to be met or if the core planks of the Make Poverty History and Global Campaign Against Poverty for more aid, less debt and fairer trade are really to make a difference to the lives of poor people.

In many of its more conventional uses, accountability is often reduced to a somewhat technical process of 'accountancy', to be achieved through clear procedures, transparency of information, and compliance with legal processes and regulations. Strategies for accountability may also involve a focus on systems of auditing and monitoring through 'counting', be it of indicators and performance targets, funds and expenditures, or legal offences and violations.

This book, the third in the series on Claiming Citizenship, challenges the conventional, technocratic view. While good management, disclosure of information and legal process are important, they are not enough. Like other aspects of citizenship, accountability is not only created from above through institutional procedures or mandate, but also must be constantly claimed through strategies of mobilization, pressure and vigilance from below. Ultimately, the book argues, accountability is about power. In a context of globalisation and neoliberalism where configurations of power are rapidly changing, so too the sites and strategies for realising accountability are in flux. Where once we might have expected the state to regulate markets and to ensure accountability for its citizens, increasingly citizens themselves play an important role in monitoring state activities, regulating the behaviour of corporations, and claiming responsiveness from local, national and international institutions.

While accountability is seen as an important strategy for overcoming poverty and social injustice, it cannot be separated, the book also argues, from contests over the realisation of rights and the distribution of resources. Rights must be understood in practice as well as in the law. Through case studies of grassroots struggles to claim diverse sets of rights – be they to water in South Africa or Mexico, to shelter in Kenya, to a safe environment in Nigeria, to health in Brazil, to a 'living wage' for low-income workers in the United States, or to 'dignity and daily bread' for garment workers in Bangladesh – the book shows the enormous gap that can exist between internationally proclaimed rights discourses and every-day life, and between global standards and local circumstances. At the same time, in each of these areas, the case studies reveal a range of exciting and imaginative ways in which poorer groups mobilise to claim their rights and to construct mechanisms of accountability with the state, the private sector and international institutions, and within civil society itself.

For poor and marginalised groups, struggles for accountability gain traction when they involve access to the basic resources and services that are necessary for survival and for sustainable livelihoods. We see in this volume multiple examples of the ways in which resources and livelihoods are being destroyed by unchecked practices of corporate actors, be they chemical companies in minority communities in the United States or the tribal regions of India, oil companies in the heart of the Niger Delta, bioprospecting companies in Chiapas, or land speculators in Kenya. Yet we also see the myriad formal and informal ways in which citizens mobilise to hold corporations and global investors accountable, including the use of peoples' hearings as well as the courts in India, popular theatre and direct action in Nigeria, participation in government fora and mass protest in Mexico, and appeals to international legal frameworks and mobilisation of the media in Kenya. Each of these cases suggests that while corporate responsibility and accountability are critical in an era of growing privatisation, they are unlikely to be attained through voluntary compliance of the corporate sector or through regulation by increasingly weakened governments alone. Rather, citizen mobilisation and action form a necessary and important part of any corporate accountability strategy.

Like the previous volumes in this series, this volume has been supported by the Development Research Centre (DRC) on Citizenship,

Participation and Accountability, an international research network based at the Institute of Development Studies in the UK, with partner institutions in Brazil, Bangladesh, India, Mexico, Nigeria and South Africa. Founded in 2000, the Citizenship DRC is funded by the research division of the UK Department for International Development (DFID), with additional funding from the Rockefeller Foundation, which has enabled the inclusion of Northern case studies in its work. (See www.drc-citizenship.org for more information about the Citizenship DRC and for other publications.)

Also, as in the previous volumes, the chapters in this volume aim to bring understanding and insight to international debates on rights, participation and accountability through concrete, empirically grounded case studies from both South and North. The cases in this book were not produced in a one-off commissioned fashion, based on pre-set hypotheses or concepts, as is often the case with international research projects. Rather, the questions that the book addresses evolved over time, as researchers and activists associated with the Rights and Accountability Working Group of the Citizenship DRC came together to discuss their contexts, concerns and experiences, often in one another's countries, where they could also observe firsthand some of the realities about which they were writing. The research process was an iterative one, in which concepts and questions were developed, applied to local settings, and then re-discussed and refined. From an initial focus on accountability, the programme of work expanded to explore the multiple ways in which poorer groups could use rights-based claims to hold more powerful groups to account across a range of settings and resources.

The research process also has been enriched by bringing together a mix of academics and activists from eight countries and from a range of disciplines and backgrounds. Many of the cases featured in the book – especially those from Mexico, Nigeria and India – have involved action research approaches, in which the authors and the organisations they represent have engaged over time with the cases being studied, and therefore also have a stake in the accountability struggles they recount. For almost all of the cases, the chapters in this book represent only one of the products of the research. Other more popular means – such as videos, theatre, posters, newsletters, newspaper interviews, policy briefings and workshops – have also been used to communicate the results of the research to those with whom it was conducted.

The volume is also the result of a highly collaborative process amongst the contributors, which evolved its own forms of feedback and critique, learning and solidarity in places as diverse as Abuja, Oaxaca, Delhi, Cape

Town, Barra do Sahy (Brazil) and Brighton. Over time, the relationships that grew among the participants were not only important in themselves, but allowed a coming together of perspectives and disciplines, across contexts and institutions, that rarely can be achieved through individual research projects alone.

As the editor of the Claiming Citizenship series, I want to thank the editors of this volume and each of the chapter contributors for the effort which they invested in this project. It represents a degree of commitment far beyond the resources that were received. Thanks also to all those who assisted in the process, including research assistants Lucila Lahitou and Alex Hughes and, of course, our colleagues and editors at Zed Books, whose support for this series is greatly appreciated.

John Gaventa
Director, Development Research Centre on Citizenship,
Participation and Accountability
Institute of Development Studies
December 2005

No Power without Accountability

Lost my job, my car and my house
when 10,000 miles away
Some guy clicked on a mouse
He didn't know me, we never spoke
He didn't ask my opinion
Or canvass my vote.
Gotto find a way to hold them to account
Before they find a way to snuff our voices out.

The ballot box is no guarantee
That we achieve democracy
Our leaders claim their victory
When only half the people have spoken
We have no job security in this global economy
Our borders closed to refugees
But our markets forced wide open

Can you hear us?
Are you listening?
No power without accountability

Billy Bragg

CHAPTER 1

Rights, resources and the politics of accountability: an introduction

PETER NEWELL AND JOANNA WHEELER

Many conflicts in development can be understood as struggles by the poor to hold the powerful to account. Contests over the rights and responsibilities of actors in development are increasing in intensity amid clashes between the promotion of a rights-based approach to development and market-based notions of access and entitlement to resources. How these conflicts are played out has enormous implications for efforts to tackle poverty and achieve the Millennium Development Goals. Understanding how the poor claim their rights and demand accountability for the realisation of those rights becomes critical.

This book contributes to such an understanding by exploring how poorer groups mobilise around rights to resources in a diversity of settings, employing a broad range of strategies to achieve accountability. It places accountability at the intersection between rights and resources, asking: what is the relationship between greater accountability and people's ability to realise their rights to resources? Struggles over key livelihood resources such as health, housing and labour, as well as natural resources such as water and oil, provide the backdrop to an enquiry into the ways in which poorer groups hold powerful state, corporate and civil society actors to account. The process of claiming rights provides one (but certainly not the only) way in which they do this.

Accountability has come to assume a central place in contemporary development discourse over the last ten years in the context of increasing donor attention to the idea of good governance. Its association with this agenda has meant that the politics of accountability has been reduced to questions of state reform. Whilst of course state reform is crucial, this book shows that accountability cannot be achieved through institutional reform alone, and it is often the case that state institutions act as rights violators as well as rights enforcers. The conventional focus on the state has created an over-reliance on the law as a mechanism to generate positive social change, without looking at the ways in which social mobilisation also changes the law.

Accountability is not an apolitical project. The leading global actors promoting accountability initiatives, despite claims to the contrary, have a political stake in advancing some forms of accountability and some groups' rights over others. For example, a narrow focus on questions of financial reporting and accountancy fails to address the political processes by which the powerful insulate themselves from accountability to the poor and efforts to promote the private provision of state services without addressing accountability to the poor often serve to create accountability deficits. The global reach of actors such as the World Bank and other leading donors, however, means that accountability models have often been transplanted from one setting to another with little regard for local context.

An explicitly political framing of accountability in development, on the other hand, requires a different approach. Where earlier work on accountability emphasised change through legal reform and tech-nocratic notions of governance, here we advance an understanding of accountability that is more directly relevant to the lives of the poor, where power assumes a central place. Despite the current fashion for the term accountability in development debates, the term and the relationships it seeks to describe have a much longer history. Contexts of globalisation and neoliberal reform have, nevertheless, fundamentally changed the division of rights and responsibilities between states, market actors and civil society in ways that directly affect the liveli-hoods of the poor. As the roles and power of key actors in development change so, therefore, do the processes by which people seek to hold them to account. This book documents the strategies they employ to do this: formal and informal, legal and non-legal, collaborative and confrontational.

Capturing this new landscape of accountability politics requires us to look at a range of state and non-state actors, going beyond traditional preoccupations with state reform. Here we look at struggles for corporate accountability in the absence of state protection of marginalised groups, and we explore mobilisations around rights that are conferred by the state but unevenly realised in practice. We explore the role of community-based organisations and the accountability strategies they adopt to challenge the state and civil society organisations claiming to act on their behalf. Rarely is the state absent in such conflicts, even if its presence is often felt as a failure to act. This being so, it is unsurprising that marginalised groups often claim accountability from below, rather than relying on the state to provide it from above. The challenge is to map the web of accountabilities that flow between these actors in specific contexts in order to understand the directions from which opportunities for change are most likely to come.

Reflecting these new political dynamics also means emphasising accountability processes. These are the strategies, tactics and repertoires of mobilisation by which movements and communities seek to realise rights to livelihood or to express their citizenship. While often hoping to trigger changes within the state or other actors, such strategies can also be an end in themselves, aimed for example at raising awareness about rights or articulating citizenship through accountability claims. Abah and Okwori (Chapter 10) explore the role of theatre as a tool enabling people to express the barriers they face to realising accountability in their day-to-day lives, while Newell et al. (Chapter 8) show how NGOs in rural India are creating new platforms and arenas for the articulation of accountability claims through informal public hearings and the construction of 'Peoples' Development Plans'. These are a few of the many different methods for demanding accountability that this book will explore.

Understanding the nature of accountability struggles means appreciating the historical, material and cultural contexts in which they take place. By looking at cases in the global North and South and across a range of livelihood resources, we build up an eclectic view of the diverse ways in which disenfranchised groups pursue accountability claims and the context-specific circumstances that enable or frustrate their ability to do this. The cases here also cover a range of institutional contexts which are politically, socially and culturally diverse. We have situations in which a strong state is present (India, the United States, Brazil); in which litigious legal cultures exist (South Africa, the United States); and where inequalities are being challenged through social movement mobilisation (Mexico, Brazil, India). In other contexts, corporations have become the dominant actors, with direct implications for accountability (Nigeria, Bangladesh).

A grounded empirical assessment of which accountability strategies work, when, and for whom provides an important antidote to the inappropriate export of accountability models from one setting to another without sufficient regard for key political, social and cultural differences. Each chapter seeks to reflect on those elements that were important to the outcome of the accountability struggle they describe. The chapters are framed around the following key questions:

- Does the strategy used achieve greater accountability in relation to access to resources?
- When does it work? Under what conditions? (Historically, institutionally, economically, culturally?)
- For whom does it work? Who benefits?
- What are the implications for contemporary debates about accountability in development?

The book includes examples of mobilisations around a range of resources from more narrowly defined notions of natural resources to broader notions of livelihood resources such as housing and health, for example. We are able to compare struggles around resources such as oil and water with campaigns for better working conditions, access to health services, and housing provision in order to draw conclusions about how different types of resources influence the nature of accountability.

Rather than viewing the lack of accountability as a problem that only afflicts developing countries, we explore 'global' experiences of accountability struggles from North and South. Despite differences of context, there are many interesting parallels, for example, between the experience of mobilising for worker rights in the United States and in Bangladesh, as well between struggles for corporate accountability in the United States and India. Lessons can be learned about accountability strategies in ways that transgress geographical and sectoral distinctions. In so far as they seek to address patterns of inequality and marginalisation that are globally present, but manifest themselves in distinct ways in local settings, accountability strategies aimed at challenging power resonate with poor peoples' experiences the world over.

The next section maps out the relationships between rights, resources and accountability that emerge from the cases in this book.

Rights, resources and the politics of accountability

There is a complex and overlapping relationship between rights, resources and the politics of accountability. Figure 1.1 shows how each is intimately related to the other in a dynamic way. In many ways, the nature of a resource, and who has access to it, defines possibilities for justice, redistribution and change. In this book, resource struggles and efforts to realise key developmental rights, such as the right to housing and water, provide the anchor for an exploration of the relationship between rights and accountability. The centrality of resources to the livelihoods of the poor means questions of access and entitlement are imbued with relations of power and conflict. Hence, while the deprivation of a resource may be predominantly economic in character, gaining the right to access resources and the right to claim accountability is a political project, with citizenship at its core.

The chapters in this book show how resources are not a politically neutral variable in the relationship between rights and accountability. Beyond a deterministic, single-dimensional understanding of the relationship between resources and politics, we focus on the impact of the dynamics of institutional practices and cultural values upon the realisation of resource rights. Questions of access, management and distribution vary, depending on whether we are talking about water, oil or health. Each implies a different infrastructure, brings different actors into conflict, implies different sensitivities and is symbolically and culturally understood in a distinct way. Themes we pick up throughout the book on the materiality of resources, the importance of law and institutions and competing cultures of accountability help us to explore these themes.

Mobilisations to claim rights can produce new forms of accountability, just as the ability to claim rights and have them realised assumes relations of accountability between the state and citizens. For example, the trajectories of mobilisation around rights in India, Brazil and South Africa have informed and shaped the meaning of rights within those

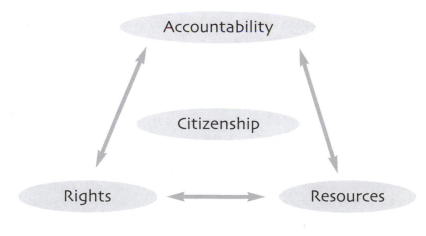

FIGURE 1.1 THE RELATIONSHIP BETWEEN RIGHTS, RESOURCES AND ACCOUNTABILITY

countries, from the way rights are used in practice to the encoding of specific rights in national constitutions (Pettit and Wheeler 2005). The relationship between rights and resources hinges on issues of access in terms of who controls and benefits from particular resources. The relationship between resources and accountability is informed by power, as more powerful groups monopolise control over resources and undermine accountability. This book focuses, then, on rights as a tool of accountability, where disenfranchised and marginalised groups use rights claims around key resources in order to demand greater accountability from state, private sector and civil society actors.

Cutting across processes of demanding accountability and claiming rights over resources, and at the centre of the triangle that we use (Figure 1.1) to describe the relationships between rights, resources and accountability, is the notion of citizenship. Citizenship relates to the claims that people believe they should be able to make of institutions, as well as their entitlements to access to material resources. We return to this theme in the conclusion to this chapter. Given the broad nature of this overview of the triangular relationship between rights, resources and accountability, the next section explores each of the dimensions of this relationship in more detail.

Rights and accountability

It is perhaps the case that more people are now claiming more rights than ever before (Jones 1994). The proliferation of types of rights claims is occurring in parallel with the increasingly salient discourse of rights in development (Cornwall and Nyamu-Musembi 2005). Though rights-based approaches have gained in popularity among some in the development community, their value, application and reach remain contested (Piron 2005). On the one hand, rights claims can provide a greater degree of access to justice. The long history of mobilisations around rights shows that they have the potential to provide a measure of access to justice that regulation does not, to support claims that other legal procedures do not recognise, and to ignite a level of activism that claims grounded in other discourses often fail to achieve. Framing a claim in the language of human rights gives it a certain status, legitimacy and moral weight; it constitutes a title which, at least in theory, others must recognise and respect (Dworkin 1978). On the other hand, 'rights talk' has increasingly been adopted in development debates in ways that render it vacuous and abstract. 'Rights talk is both pervasive and exciting ... rights talk is also frequently confused and inconclusive' (Merills 1996: 25). This has serious implications for those whose rights have been denied or who are seeking to have their rights protected and respected (Pettit and Wheeler 2005).

Like accountability, rights and rights-based approaches, therefore, have a complex role within development. They have the potential to oppose technocratic top-down interpretations of accountability discussed earlier, but, as some of the chapters in this book show, powerful groups have also used rights discourse to advance their own agendas. Nonetheless, a conception of rights is at the heart of many mobilisations for accountability, a fact that becomes particularly clear in relation to struggles for resources. Our interest in rights here is guided by the ways in which poorer groups employ them to secure accountability from key actors, claiming basic development rights and rights to resources in order to enhance their livelihoods. We suggest that the right to claim accountability is fundamental to making other social and economic rights real, an idea we explore further in the final section of the chapter on citizenship. Hence, in considering rights in relationship to accountability, it is important to ask:

- How do marginalised or excluded groups use rights as part of a strategy for improving accountability?
- Under what conditions do rights enhance accountability to the poor?
- What is the relationship between the right to demand accountability and the protection of a broader set of economic and social rights?

Many rights, in and of themselves, are not *de facto* accountability tools; they have to be fashioned as such through processes of claiming, mobilisation and struggle. This becomes clear in Mexico, where obstacles to accountability are derived from the highly politicised disputes about different meanings and interpretations of rights (Paré and Robles, Chapter 4; Cortéz and Paré, Chapter 5). Similarly, in Brazil and South Africa, it was through sustained social protest that formal legal recognition for rights was achieved (Mehta, Chapter 3; Cornwall *et al.*, Chapter 7).

Since accountability is not just about promoting answerability but also about delivering enforceability, the process of how these rights can be realised is important. It is in this context that we encounter the limits of an (over-)reliance on rights. Many of the accountability strategies and tools that we explore in this book take as their starting point the lack of recognition or implementation of rights of particular groups, such as the right to water in South Africa, to adequate housing in Kenya and to a living wage in the United States. There is a difference, therefore, between *rights in theory* and *rights in practice*. Our concern is more with the latter and the ways in which poorer groups secure rights through a multitude of formal and informal creative strategies of accountability. The diverse forms of mobilisation that we explore in this book are reflective of this dynamic. In so far as the law is the medium through which rights-based claims are traditionally expressed, our work helps to explain the limitations of legally based constructions of rights and the ways in poorer groups often employ 'living' notions of rights that reflect more adequately the material deprivation or social exclusion they experience (Clark, O'Reilly and Wheeler 2005). The lack of protection provided by the law to poorer communities of colour in the US – despite civil rights claims – has given rise to notions of environmental justice that better embody people's experience of environmental harm (Lekhi and Newell, Chapter 9).

Nevertheless, claiming a right is not a short-cut to avoiding, pre-empting or reducing conflict over resources. Rights claims compete; they have to be balanced or reconciled, as the cases from Chiapas and Veracruz clearly show (chapters 4 and 5). There is also a political risk that attaches to efforts to politicise claims by invoking rights claims; the attention of rights violators, whether they be states or private actors, is drawn to vulnerable groups who may suffer the recriminations of high-lighting the negligence of powerful actors, as the cases from India demonstrate (Chapter 8). The value of a resource subject to conflict may mean that political freedoms are often denied and strategies of intimidation and violence invoked as the chapters from Mexico, India, and Nigeria show (chapters 4–5, 8 and 10). Particularly when confrontations with powerful actors are implied by an accountability struggle, the merits of action over silence or acquiescence need to be carefully evaluated. Accountability claims, therefore, are not easily made. Neither are they free of the costs and trade-offs that characterise other forms of mobilisation and claim making.

Rights are just one, albeit very important, means by which the poor seek accountability from those that exercise power over them. Social actors have to be clear about what is to be gained by framing a question in terms of rights and whether the same result could not be achieved equally well by other means. The choice of which strategy to pursue is a critical one for community-based organisations such as the tenants' association in Mombasa, Kenya with very limited resources and ambitious goals (Nyamu-Musembi, Chapter 6). The appeal of global reach should not mislead us into believing that the process of realising those rights demonstrates uniformity across the world. The limits of attempts to secure workers' rights through supplier-imposed labour standards in Bangladesh are a case in point (Mahmud and Kabeer, Chapter 11).

This is not just a book about how the poor claim, contest and secure rights, however. It is also a book about the rights of the powerful, used to defend their privileges, control of resources and access to power. At issue here is not just the rights of the state to claim land in the public interest for industrial development, as we see in the India case, or the right to admit investors to locate in economically impoverished but resource-rich areas of a country (Chapter 10). It is also the rights that have been conferred upon corporations, or in some cases assumed by them, to relocate their operations without offering compensation to communities that host them, to invest where they choose and to socialise costs while privatising profit. The struggles we explore in this book about campaigns to secure a living wage (Chapter 12) or to contest the social, economic and environmental effects of capital mobility and the economic blackmail that is used to suffocate communities' rights claims (chapters 8 and 9), provide evidence of attempts to challenge the privileging of rights to profit over rights to welfare and social justice.

Rights and resources

Contests over rights of access to resources and to the benefits that derive from their exploitation define many contemporary and historical struggles in development. They affect the interests of the powerful and the poor simultaneously, often bringing them into conflict with one another. The political and economic histories of resources and commodities as diverse as oil, sugar and coffee offer, in microcosm, a history of colonialism, capitalism and the origins of the modern order (Mintz 1986; Wild 2005; Evans, Goodman and Lansbury 2002). We see in the Nigeria case, for example, how contemporary accountability problems have been exacerbated by the country's experience of colonialism. Contests over how resources are to be used, for what, and by whom assume fundamental relations of social power. The chapters in this book suggest that it is this social power, related as it is to political and material power, that defines the context determining who is in a position to hold who to account and the means by which they are able to do so.

What emerges, then, is a *political economy of rights* in which questions of access to and distribution and production of resources are paramount. A focus on resources changes the way we think about the relationship between rights and accountability. The challenge is not to over-emphasise the material dimensions of this relationship and to acknowledge instead that economic rights are in many ways indivisible from social, political and cultural rights. Realising the former is in many ways contingent on having access to the latter rights. Though it is often a felt

deprivation of resources that drives accountability demand making, the right to claim accountability presupposes all other claim making.

Indeed, it is often the absence of responsiveness from states, corporations or even community-based organisations that fuels situations of conflict around resources. For example, in Nigeria, the juxtaposition between the extreme poverty in the Niger Delta and the large amounts of wealth generated by oil extracted from the region is the starting point for many of the struggles over accountability. When people are denied shelter as in the case from Kenya, unable to get access to water or fail to receive compensation for land taken from them as in the cases from Mexico and India, they seek redress by locating responsibility for upholding that right or providing that service.

Increasingly this process takes place across different arenas and levels of decision making. In the case of the Tuxtlas Reserve in Mexico, there are multiple and overlapping institutions involved and establishing lines of accountability becomes very difficult. Even those conflicts which appear to be local in scale and orientation are often implicated in, and affected by, broader regional and global dynamics. For example, in Bangladesh, global standards set by powerful international buyers and trade unions can undermine the ability of groups of garment workers to define and claim labour rights they judge important. Efforts to conserve biospheres in Mexico illustrate how regional and global agendas make themselves felt at the local level, changing the balance of accountability relations.

Our concern here is less with key civil and political rights, though these often form the bedrock of future activism: the givens and prior enabling conditions of a broader social struggle. For example, the right to equal treatment and non-discrimination in the United States is the premise for mobilisations around environmental racism (see Chapter 9). We look instead at material struggles for subsistence and survival focused on resources such as water and oil, and rights such as those to health, housing and a living wage. Clearly this constitutes a broad spectrum of rights and ensuing chapters will show that there are important differences between these rights in terms of how claimants articulate and mobilise around them, and how *justiciable* and *realisable* they are.

The limitations of a notion of legal indivisibility of rights should not be confused with the interrelatedness of particular rights in practice and the struggles around them. In Kenya, for example, attempts by the tenants' association to uphold the right to shelter are difficult to separate from political rights to organisation and information, as well as citizenship defined by having access to a legitimate residence. Resource rights, therefore, are often indivisible from other forms of rights claims. In a close parallel to the India case, Zarsky (2002: 45) notes that 'Worker exposure to hazardous chemicals, for example, is at once a labour rights and an environmental concern. The expropriation of indigenous peoples from ancestral lands to make way for a mining operation has implications for both human rights and environmental protection.' These inter-relations help us to understand the coalitions that activists form, recognising and consolidating these links.

Resources and accountability

This book takes a broad approach to resources, where cultural under-standings of resources, the political economy of who has rights to resources, and the varied institutional configurations that mediate societal relations make for very different forms of accountability politics. Though much of our work explores accountability struggles around key resources such as oil and water, we are anxious not to draw conclusions about the possibilities of pro-poor action that are unduly determined by the nature of a resource, as in debates on the resource curse reviewed in Chapter 10. Our emphasis, instead, is on the ways in which institutions and the relations of social power that underpin them mediate the relationships between rights, resources and accountability.

Accountability challenges do, nevertheless, differ according to the resource in question. There are important differences between the politics of access, process and redress, depending on whether the struggle is for resource rights, rights to environmental protection or rights to welfare in the form of health and housing. Factors such as the centrality of a resource to a country's economy or, in turn, the location of that country in the global marketplace can have a strong bearing on which accountability mechanisms can be utilised and by whom. The seasonality of the garment industry in terms of fashion cycles and corresponding orders gives some advantages to workers demanding their rights, as they can use pressures from buyers on delivery deadlines to extract gains from factory owners (Chapter 11). The high value attached to oil, and its location in often remote and disputed territories, places it at the centre of many conflicting rights claims around land, livelihood and compensation (Chapter 10). Oil production both reflects and reproduces divided communities and petro-states complicit in rights violations, inevitably constructing a particular type of accountability politics in its wake where violence and intimidation are the tools of enforceability. Sometimes, it is not merely the material value attached to a resource, but competing perceptions of its worth and cultural significance that generate account-ability conflicts. Radically different understandings of the environment and nature as a resource, when combined with institutional complexity in Mexico, create a context where accountability is very difficult to achieve through institutional design.

Just as people clearly attempt to demand accountability from different starting points, so too institutions and the élites that manage them feel different degrees of responsiveness to those they claim to represent. While in Mexico and Brazil, for example, there are legal provisions for citizen participation in major sectors of public policy such as health, in contrast, the state structures of Bangladesh and Nigeria are not orien-tated towards a significant level of accountability towards their citizens. While accountability towards poor and marginalised groups is imperfect in every case, the scope for particular states to respond to accountability demands varies enormously. It is when rights claims come into conflict over specific resources that we are able to see which accountability ties pull strongest, and power reveals itself.

Beyond issues of materiality or the nature of a particular resource and the institutional structures that mediate access to resources, there is also a cultural politics of resources: processes of constructing and attributing meaning to resources, which generate expectations about rights, duties and, therefore, accountabilities (Baviskar 2003; Mehta 2003). These can be derived from societal givens, religious and spiritual beliefs in ways which fundamentally alter the practice of accountability politics. They derive from the 'complex material and symbolic dimensions of how "natural resources" come to be imagined' (Baviskar 2003: 5051). For example, indigenous perceptions of water and the sacred meanings associated with water in Veracruz have informed the nature of account-ability politics there. Hence there are symbolic as well as material dimensions to conflict, partly derived from the fact that 'Each resource has distinctive use values that emerge in relation to particular modes of production' (Baviskar 2003: 5052). In this sense, culture itself becomes a site of struggle where inequalities and exclusions around resources get challenged and reproduced.

Earlier work on the role of environmental movements in broader struggles over democracy and development (Garcia-Guadilla and Blauert 1994) and studies of the democratising potential of social movements in redefining notions of development (Peet and Watts 1996; Escobar and Alvarez 1992) have drawn attention to the politics of these struggles. As the chapters in this book on Mexico, South Africa and Brazil show, such campaigns are often focused on specific resources, mobilised around certain rights or targeted at specific institutions. There is increasing attention, however, to the global political dynamics of such mobilisations[1], reflecting the increasing implication of globalised actors in local resource struggles – as shown by the chapters on the living wage in the United States, the garment industry in Bangladesh, and disputes over knowledge rights in Mexico. This book reinforces the idea that people's experiences of and struggles over social and environmental rights are globally lived but locally felt (Eckstein and Crowley 2003: xiii).

The next section develops the links between these themes further through reference to cross-cutting themes that are developed in the book, summarising what we learn about accountability from the case studies and setting us up to explore the implications of this for contemporary debates about accountability and development in the final section of the chapter.

Key themes

Accountability aims and outcomes

Existing work on accountability suggests there are two key dimensions to effective accountability mechanisms: answerability (the right to make claims and demand a response) and enforceability (mechanisms for delivering accountability, for sanctioning non-responsiveness) (see Chapter 2). Accountability, in many of the cases in this book, is not an end in itself. It is a means to achieving a wider set of goals such as broader forms of social and political change, including greater justice, equity and the redistribution of resources. This is an important point, given the often-technocratic and target-driven approaches to accountability, and the often-apolitical approaches to rights in development (see Pettit and Wheeler 2005).

We see in this book how accountability is not only an outcome, but also a process, where both answerability and enforceability are achieved through ongoing engagement between citizens and institutions. This is a crucial point in cases where the formal or legal mechanisms are in place for accountability, but the enforcement of these rights and standards is weak. Mehta explores how, in South Africa, the constitutional provision of 20 litres of free basic water for all is unevenly translated in practice – and has led to a series of court cases to establish lines of accountability between different levels of government in fulfilling this right. As Luce shows in her contribution, the victories of the US labour movement in the first half of the twentieth century have been eroded: campaigns for a living wage have had to struggle for new labour rights legislation to be adopted, and then use leverage over the municipal governments to enforce living wage standards. The chapters in this book explore the complexities of both accountability processes and accountability outcomes, and the ways in which processes inform outcomes.

Struggles for accountability driven by different aims and processes inevitably lead to the construction of distinct forms of accountability politics. If the aim of the struggle is to expose state corruption, gaining media attention – as the tenants' associations seek to do in Mombasa – is an appropriate strategy. If, on the other hand, legal recognition of the right to housing is also an aim, then drawing on international legal agreements to secure that right is the preferred choice. This point is further illustrated in Luce's chapter, which looks at the difference between standards and rights in terms of the living wage campaign in the United States. The standard of the minimum wage in the United States has been drastically eroded. As a result, living wage campaigns have organised around the right to a living wage, which is contextually determined. Standards provided important gains in labour rights, but have not been sufficient to guarantee substantive rights to a living wage.

Several of the chapters in this book show how the presence of multiple actors involved in any accountability struggle serves to blur lines of accountability. Cortéz and Paré explore how, in the biosphere reserves in Southern Mexico, a tangled web of actors including indigenous groups, international conservation NGOs, pharmaceutical companies, and state and federal government agencies all have competing interests in relation to the environment, inhibiting the development of clear accountability mechanisms between them. Local accountability conflicts are increasingly embedded in global politics in a context in which relations between public/state and private/market actors are undergoing change. The commodification and commercialisation of resources (water, indigenous knowledge, oil, labour) is accelerating these changes – and catalysing conflict over rights to resources. This produces gaps and deficits, creating accountability challenges across multiple levels from community organisation up to global institutions as global market penetration creates more opportunities for actors to encounter one another in new ways.

Another crucial theme is the way in which many of the actors and stakeholders involved in accountability politics often perform contradictory roles. The cases of India, Kenya, Mexico, Nigeria and the United States illustrate how the state can act as both the guarantor and the violator of rights. Caught at the competing intersection of rights-based and market-based approaches to the provision of water, the South African government engages in 'sins of omission and commission', as Mehta puts it, enabling some rights while denying others. Newell *et al.* show how the government in India, far from being a buttress against corporate irresponsibility, is implicated in acts of negligence resulting in serious environmental degradation that disproportionately affects tribal and lower-caste groups. Similarly, in cases where the state apparatus is weak or being eroded (such as Bangladesh and Nigeria), the increasing influence and power of corporate actors diminishes the ability of the state to act as the enforcer of accountability.

Contradictory and competing obligations are not just issues faced by states and corporations. Within particular communities, the very people who are demanding accountability can themselves undermine it, as in Nigeria where internal divisions between traditional authorities and youth groups have led to increasing cycles of violence. The chapters in this book explore the many dimensions of accountability – from different meanings and goals, to the variety of actors involved. Overall, this points to the importance of context in understanding how accountability can lead to real gains in social, economic and political equity.

How does context matter?
It is clear that context matters in understanding struggles for accountability and rights, but certain elements of context have greater salience in explaining the conditions and prospects for improving accountability. First, the institutional complexity described above is an important contextual factor. We see throughout the book how a wide range of institutional actors with responsibilities for accountability can generate confusion and disable action. These actors often represent a diverse and shifting set of interests cutting across private and public spheres, so the strategies for achieving accountability and the types of accountability relationships that can be established are also shifting. In her chapter on the Mombasa tenants' association struggle, Nyamu-Musembi suggests that one of the most difficult challenges for grassroots organisations is to gauge the appropriate strategy given their goals and the rapidly changing map of actors and political interests. As Paré and Robles emphasise in the Veracruz case, changes in government administrations can easily undermine years of careful work to build stable relations of accountability between different institutions and actors.

Legal settings and traditions also have important implications for increasing accountability to the poor. This book challenges assumptions that law generates social change by looking at ways in which the reverse is equally true. Approaches to accountability that rely solely on legal reform are unlikely to appreciate the limits of the law, in terms of access and reach, for the majority of the world's poor. For example, constitutionally guaranteed rights (as with the right to water in South Africa and the right to health in Brazil) can create new possibilities for demanding accountability. Yet the difference in how these rights fit into legal traditions is critical. In Brazil, social mobilisation around constitutional provisions has provided an entry point for political struggles over accountability because the judiciary does not fill that space, while in South Africa court cases such as *Grootboom v Republic of South Africa* have had a more central role. In the United States, where there is a strong tradition of litigation, environmental justice groups have employed 'judicial activism', invoking civil rights and environmental legislation to hold polluters to account. By contrast, in India, despite the fact there is a strong tradition of using public interest litigation, there has also been resort to mock legal processes such as citizen hearings. And in Mexico, where there is little possibility of resolving accountability struggles through legal structures perceived to be convoluted and corrupt, social mobilisation around political objectives is key to increasing accountability. While law often allows for equity of treatment, it can also reinforce social inequities. In Bangladesh, the laws covering workers' rights date from the colonial period and heavily favour educated men. Women, who work almost entirely in the informal sector, do not fall under the auspices of these laws in practice. In Kenya and India the colonial Land Acquisition Act has been invoked to remove people from their land, often without compensation or redress.

An apolitical view of promoting accountability through law reform, capacity building, training judges and the like is unlikely to yield improved access for the poor unless structural barriers and social hierarchies that inhibit meaningful use of the law by the poor are also addressed. The high degree of attention given to law reform by key actors such as the World Bank needs to respond to other reports from the same institution emphasising that legal initiatives alone are not enough to tackle corruption and improve access to redress (Soopramien *et al.* 1999). If building accountability stops at the level of reforms to institutional procedures, it is unlikely to generate the sort of change that only comes through building coalitions to oversee and contest the translation of legal obligations into lived realities. We see from the chapters in this book the importance of this process of translation, of giving meaning to legal commitments.

More broadly, the chapters in this book also emphasise the different cultures of accountability that characterise specific contexts. In Bangladesh, a culture of accountability is slowly beginning to emerge that goes beyond the current culture of compliance, which is more concerned with meeting the short-term demands of contractors for observable enforcement of workplace conditions than in changing the relations of power that create abuses of workers rights in the first place. Paré and Robles also explore the meanings of accountability within rural indigenous communities in Southern Mexico, where, although the word 'accountability' does not exist in local languages, the meaning of accountability is encoded in certain traditions and practices. In this case, demands for accountability have become combined with prior notions of fairness and community obligation to produce a new definition of accountability based on co-responsibility. In Brazil, dissonant cultures of participation and a history of clientelism within the health care system make it difficult for clear lines of accountability to be drawn. In sum, there are different cultures of accountability grounded in different histories of conflict, trust and corruption.

Which strategies, when?

This book surveys a bewildering array of strategies for demanding accountability and realising rights, some of which are summarised in Table 1.1 below. Amid this diversity, however, some important trends emerge. In each case the factors that have inhibited or encouraged increased accountability are explored. The strategies are not static, however; there is often an evolution in strategy as accountability struggles change over time. This can involve a transition from resistance to dialogue and solution finding, as the case of the management of the watershed in Mexico shows, indicating ongoing processes of reflection within movements about which accountability strategies work, when, why and for whom.

Advances in accountability and rights claims are not linear, nor are they irreversible. In several of the studies in this book, setbacks in struggles for accountability have been as important as gains. A common feature across several of the cases, including Nigeria, Mexico and India, are the cycles of negotiation and conflict that have emerged as part of struggles for accountability. In Nigeria, as Abah and Okwori demonstrate, short-term demands for concessions by communities to oil companies have resulted in tangible results. But, at the same time, oil companies have reinforced and exacerbated internal divisions and conflicts within communities by granting concessions and financial

TABLE 1.1 SOCIAL ACTORS, STRATEGIES, RIGHTS AND RESOURCES

Who?	Types of strategies used		Rights involved	Resources involved
	Formal	Informal		
Indigenous groups in Chiapas and Veracruz, Mexico	Environmental round tables with government	Armed conflict Protests Re-settlement in reserve areas	Land rights knowledge rights	Environmental resources in general
Rural poor in South Africa	Court cases		Right to water	Water
Tenants' association in Mombasa, Kenya	Using international legal frameworks	Blocking illegal construction Gaining media attention Mobilising residents	Right to housing Right to information	Adequate housing
Community-based organisations in Cabo, Brazil	Participation in government-mandated health councils		Right to health	Adequate health care
Indigenous groups in Veracruz, Mexico	Negotiations with reserve management, municipal government Construction of alternative plans	Blockading dam to cut off water supply Citizen Water Management Council Participatory environmental audit	Right to water	Water

Who?	Types of strategies used		Rights involved	Resources involved
	Formal	Informal		
Landless groups in India	Court cases Complaints to government officials	Public hearings People's Development Plans Gaining media attention Citizen health and environmental monitoring	Land rights Right to work Right to a clean environment	Minerals Energy Water
Environmental justice movement, US	Civil rights legislation Court cases Legal clinics Public hearings	Protest Citizen health monitoring	Right to a clean environment	Water Air
Poor communities in the Niger Delta		Theatre Youth groups Womens' groups Protest Sabotage	Right to work Right to compensation Right to a clean environment	Oil
Municipal workers, US	Court cases State labour laws	Boycotts Gaining media attention	Right to a living wage	Labour
Garment workers, Bangladesh	Supplier-led standards State labour laws	Strikes/walkouts Forming workers' associations	Right to fair working conditions	Labour

windfalls to particular groups. Hence these concessions are only ameliora-
tive and tend to fuel conflict rather than addressing the fundamental
rights violations occurring in the Niger Delta. A similar though less
violent situation has emerged in Mexico, where municipal governments
appease rural indigenous communities by conceding certain rights and
benefits without addressing the underlying causes of the lack of accountability.

Many of the chapters focus on the interface between formal and
informal strategies for accountability, and the potential for important
advances towards outcomes positive to the poor when these strategies
combine, as in the tenants' struggle in Mombasa and the living wage
movement in the United States. Though much of the current debate
about accountability focuses on formal mechanisms of accountability
aimed at transparency and redress, for example, the chapters in this book
show that informal approaches and strategies are often equally important. Struggles around accountability do not just take place through
institutions, but between actors in civil society and the market and
among communities. These groups also employ both 'inside' and 'outside'
strategies, strategies that work within existing institutional channels as
well as those that seek to contest and broaden formal spaces of
engagement (see Chapter 12).

Several of the chapters also show how non-engagement in formal
processes can also be an accountability strategy by contesting the
boundaries of engagement and by opposing particular practices. In
Chiapas, as discussed by Cortéz and Paré, the position of resistance of
the Zapatista movement is predicated on non-engagement with the
state. This position has forced the government to address the Zapatistas'
demands in different ways to those it adopts when it deals with claims
from other indigenous groups in Mexico. Given the limitations of technocratic approaches to accountability, social movements are investing
their efforts in new spaces for accountability such as creating new
institutions; constructing economic and livelihood alternatives to exit
exploitative relationships; and disengaging from interactions with the
state when they are perceived to compromise the strength of the social
movement.

In all cases where demanding rights is a strategy for achieving
accountability, the key questions are: when, how, and for whom do rights
make a difference? In many of the cases formal legal rights are an important first step (as in South Africa), but the implementation of rights
becomes the central site of struggle. International legal rights can have a
similar role. In the absence of national legislation granting the right to

shelter, the tenants' association in Mombasa has drawn on international conventions on human rights, to which Kenya is a signatory, that protect this right. But appealing to national or international law and formal rights encoded in those laws can only take the attempts to establish accountability so far. Formal rights (whether derived from national or international legal frameworks) are insufficient on their own to guarantee substantive changes for poorer people. We also need to consider the fact that law and rights are as likely to work for powerful interests as for those without the power to advance rights claims, as we see in the cases of India and Kenya regarding legal provisions concerning land and property.

Implications

What are the implications of the key themes that we have identified above as emerging from the case studies in this book? In particular, what are the implications of what we have learned for predominant contemporary framings of accountability agendas in development debates?

We noted in the introduction a number of assumptions in contemporary debates about accountability in development: (1) that models of accountability can be transferred from one setting to another, and that what works in one place can be expected to work elsewhere; (2) that accountability is about accountancy; (3) that accountability is provided by states to citizens; (4) that the law is the primary vehicle for clarifying the respective duties and obligations of states and citizens; (5) that accountability can be created through institutional reforms; and (6) that promoting accountability is an apolitical project. Here we show how the contributions of this work challenge these assumptions and suggest the bases of a broader and more explicitly political understanding of accountability.

Cultures of accountability

There are many issues that arise from the framing of accountability as a problem of institutional engineering, legal reform and better accounting. One is denial of the political and historical context of accountabilities by which people make sense of rights, duties and obligations. Because they emerge from rooted experiences, defined by different cultural expectations of accountability, rights and duties are shaped by material conditions, which generate or subdue expectations of what is possible and affordable. Generic models of accountability reform necessarily encounter local realities, which will more often than not be at odds with how institutions are 'meant' to operate. Proscriptions of how to tackle accountability problems based on the experience of a limited number of countries tend to overlook the context-specific ways in which problems are understood and need to be confronted. This is true of World Bank 'model contracts' aimed at helping policy makers and bank executives 'discipline troubled banks' (Roulier 1995) as well as efforts by the same institution to 'transplant' institutions to Africa (Dia 1996).

The extent to which rights can be meaningfully exercised and enforced rests on institutional configurations and cultures of account-ability that take distinct forms in different parts of the world. These cultures of accountability impose different rights, duties and obligations on 'accountability seekers' and 'accountability providers' (Goetz and Jenkins 2004). They assume reciprocal ties and social contracts between key elements within the state, civil society and the market. They derive from distinct historically constructed experiences of exclusion and expectations regarding the performance of institutions. Globally led efforts to promote accountability are often frustrated by such local realities.

This helps us to understand the process we observe in many of the chapters in the book, when accountability cultures imposed from the outside often conflict with more indigenous or traditional understandings of accountability. It is expressed, for example, in the difference between 'cultures of compliance' and 'cultures of accountability' discussed here in relation to Bangladesh. Universally proscribed protection only goes so far and there remains a key role for mobilisation around implementation. This book explores the difference between US labour movement strategies aimed at securing a living wage through an international standard and other struggles for that right in diverse settings. By looking at these forms of accountability politics in practice, we hope the insights contained in this book will contribute to an enhanced understanding of the embeddedness of strategies and institutions in particular social, cultural and political frameworks, which are important for making sense of those institutions.

Beyond accountancy

Technocratic framings of accountability generate a kind of naivety that reform processes can generate pro-poor change without challenging power inequities. This illusion arises through a focus on interventions that are easy to implement, monitor and evaluate (DfiD 2005). By constructing the problem as one of corruption and better service provision, for example (World Bank 2000; 2004), the systemic and institutional biases that permit conscious anti-poor decision making are left unchallenged.

Likewise, with debates about corporate accountability, emphasis is placed on improved systems of auditing, reporting and monitoring, often without questioning the indicators by which performance is measured or, more broadly, whether the activities of a firm are contributing to the achievement of wider societal and developmental goals. Again, the point is not to question the importance of greater transparency in political and financial affairs. Indeed a key theme throughout the book is the importance of rights to information as a precondition for effective mobilisation. Rather, the plea is not to reduce the concept of accountability to the pursuit of improved accountancy. The shift towards defining indicators and measuring accountability is problematic in this sense, with UNDP describing indicators for human rights advocacy as a 'cutting-edge area of advocacy' (UNDP 2000) and Narayan, writing for the World Bank, arguing that 'if empowerment cannot be measured, it will not be taken seriously in development policy making and programming' (Narayan 2005). For Shah, too, 'the power of accountability is significantly reduced if citizens are unable to measure their governments' performance in a meaningful way.... The abstract concept of government performance can only be an effective tool in public debate when there are concrete statistics measuring performance and benchmarks against which asset indicators can be compared' (Shah 2005). Accountability can and should be much more this, especially when viewed from the perspective of tackling those accountability deficits that serve to entrench poverty and frustrate attempts to combat it.

Multiple and embedded accountabilities

We lose a sense of the importance of prior processes of mobilisation and coalition building that generate demands for reform and sustain reform efforts when we assume that institutional change can occur in a social and political vacuum. In other words, without engaging broader processes of social change, institutional innovations, however far-reaching, are unlikely to deliver the sort of reform that is desired. Whether it is anti-corruption strategies that can be reduced to 'six steps' or emphasis on accountability through performance-related rewards for bureaucrats aimed at promoting civil service reform (Dia 1993), the assumption that intra-state institutional change should be the sole focus of policy attention seems increasingly at odds with the momentum for change generated above, beyond and below the state. This implies a wider focus on the diverse accountability strategies adopted by the poor to bring about change on their own terms. Hence the contribution of this book is to encourage the shift from an exclusive focus upon intra-state mechanisms of horizontal accountability to exploring more seriously the potential of society-centred models of vertical accountability discussed in Chapter 2. The state-centredness of prevailing approaches to accountability (DfiD 2001), noted above, is problematic, then, in the sense that it runs the risk of reinforcing the reliance of the poor on the very state institutions that have shown themselves to be singularly ineffective in responding to the needs of the poor.

In defence of the primacy of public accountability, Paul, writing about India, argues that 'government and its agencies are the key players in the poverty reduction arena, judged by their own public policy pronouncements and commitments' (2002: 1). By claiming that international institutions and NGOs are of 'marginal significance' in India, and that the commitment of business to poverty reduction is 'indirect and limited at best', Paul focuses on actors who identify themselves as key accountability brokers through their pronouncements and official mandates. In contrast, our approach is to examine critically the roles and performance of the broader range of actors who wield power over the lives of the poor in practice and in increasingly direct ways, rather than to read accountability politics from the formally proscribed accountability roles of actors.

This is clearly not a case for abandoning the state on the basis of its unreformability or structural inability to respond to the needs of the poor. Rather, it is a plea to recognise the many levels at which reform takes place; how informal strategies outside the immediate sphere of the state can serve to generate state reforms; but how also, on occasion, pro-poor accountability strategies emerge in ways and through arenas where the state is not, perhaps should not, be present. Cases in this book from India and Nigeria, for example, illustrate that it is often distrust of the state or an appreciation of the state's complicity in accountability abuses, experienced through resource conflicts, that drives people to construct alternative accountability mechanisms that do not rely on state endorsement or enforcement. The civil accountability that results (see Newell, Chapter 2) raises other significant issues for democratic politics, but failing to recognise its importance as an alternative site of accountability in the face of state negligence would be a mistake.

The importance of deepening accountability within civil society, particularly when representative functions are performed on behalf of the poor, is a theme that runs through the book. Power shifts resulting in part, but certainly not exclusively, from myriad processes of globalisation have altered profoundly the balance of rights and responsibilities and hence accountabilities between state, market and civil society actors (Newell *et al.* 2002). The ways in which this has occurred and its consequences are discussed at greater length in Chapter 2. Here the point is that we need to challenge the bias towards the state as the most appropriate and significant site of accountability reform. By looking in depth at struggles around corporate and civil society accountability, we hope this book takes forward thinking about the ways in which accountability can be deepened in new ways amongst a broader range of actors operating in multiple arenas. Increasing emphasis on 'citizen democracy' (UNDP 2004), 'citizen-centred governance' and 'global accountability' (Kovach *et al.* 2003) can be seen as evidence of the increasing acceptance, in some quarters at least, of a less state-centred approach to accountability. As Shah and Matthews note, 'technocratic approaches to public sector reform are unlikely to succeed…. Instead citizen empowerment through a rights-based approach to demand accountability from their governments and a rights-based culture of governance holds significant potential for success' (2005).

The politics of accountability

There is a tendency to assume that those actors supporting, funding and overseeing institutional reform for accountability do not have a stake in the reform process themselves. They do. And far from being neutral advocates of pro-poor accountability reforms, the way in which they intervene has an impact on rights that are respected or denied and accountabilities that are created or overlooked. The World Bank is an increasingly important actor in this area, but can hardly be said to be a neutral player in conflicts between competing rights claims, especially when revenues from natural resources are at stake. This book shows how the World Bank's association with the Plan Puebla Panama and the Global Environment Facility's role in local conservation projects in Mexcio have generated suspicion about the intentions of these actors regarding the control of environmental resources. The 2003 World Development Report on *Sustainable Development in a Dynamic Economy* advances the idea that the spectacular failure to tackle poverty and environmental degradation over the last decade is due to a failure of governance, 'poor implementation and not poor vision' (Foster 2002). As the report notes, 'Those [poverty and environmental] problems that can be coordinated through markets have typically done well; those that have not fared well include many for which the market could be made to work as a coordinator.' The challenge for governments is therefore to be more welcoming of private actors through, among other things, 'a smooth evolution of property rights from communal to private' (World Bank 2003). By pushing strongly for the protection of property rights as a solution to many conflicts over resources (Primo Braga *et al.* 2000), the rights of capital are automatically privileged over many communities with whom those rights may be in conflict.

Similarly, the neoliberal biases of many development institutions lead them to assume that clients and consumers are more effective accountability seekers and demanders than 'passive recipients' (or non-recipients) of state services. The World Development Report of 2004, for example, emphasises the importance of 'enabling the poor to monitor and discipline service providers' (World Bank 2004). Fiszbein, also writing for the World Bank, argues that the key issue in this regard is 'whether those responsible for designing and delivering services are accountable to the citizens who are demanding the services and also paying the taxes and fees that finance services' (2005). Power exercised through consumer choice in the market is said to improve basic services as firms compete to attract new customers. Corrupt, unresponsive firms will quickly lose customers in this model. The problem with such *marketised* notions of accountability is that they tend to overlook prior issues of exclusion and lack of access to key services. The very poorest, those most in need of services responsive to their needs, are of least interest to private utilities seeking to make a profit. For example, we shall see how in South Africa private contractors have cut off access to water when people are unable to pay, despite their constitutional right to water. Hence reducing accountability relationships to purchasing power invites an anti-poor bias (Whitfield 2001; Goetz and Gaventa 2001).

Placing power centrally, it becomes easier to discern why some forms of accountability politics are privileged over others, why some actors face more scrutiny than others, why some accountability deficits are addressed and others neglected. As we see in Chapter 2, this has to be understood in relation to the power wielded by key actors in development and their ability to project preferred discourses of accountability. For now, it is sufficient to note that, despite claims to the contrary, the politics of accountability are not value-neutral and key actors advancing the contemporary agenda in development are neither neutral bystanders nor indifferent to the outcomes.

Accountability and social justice

By framing the issue of accountability in narrow institutional terms we run the risk of failing to ask, let alone answer, the question of accountability *for what* and *for whom*? Who benefits, for example, from efforts to reform the state in ways prescribed by global economic institutions? If improved access for the poor is the aim, it is questionable that shifting service provision to private hands in the name of efficiency and combating corruption will achieve that, for some of the reasons stated above. On the other hand, promoting the accountability of corporations to the communities in which they invest through more effective use of public hearings or efforts to screen investment proposals – measures aimed at enhancing the exercise of social control over economic actors – may bring about a shift in the power imbalances that currently protect the powerful from scrutiny. A key theme emerging from the work presented in this book is that accountability struggles are invariably struggles for a broader social or economic good. They provide the means to an end which has to be specified in order to understand the utility and likely effectiveness of the strategy adopted.

Central to instances where these strategies lead to improved accountability are a set of methods that rely on the participation of poor and marginalised people. This book touches on a range of these methods, including citizen health monitoring and participatory development reports in India, community-based environmental audits in Mexico, local-level health councils in Brazil, and environmental justice clinics in the United States. Many of the chapters in this book are based on 'action research' engagements, where participatory methods for demanding accountability are part of the research process. Some important questions arise from these examples: how do these methods affect wider political structures and power relations; and what is their potential for contributing to the democratic processes that could contribute to wider social change? The potential of such strategies to contribute towards civil accountability is explored in Chapter 2, as well as more fully in the context of the case studies that describe the settings from which they are derived.

In sum, the project of accountability is not a politically neutral philanthropic exercise aimed at removing the obstacles that prevent the poor from realising rights and accessing justice. It can also seek to fulfil those aims, but it does not necessarily do so. Depending on the actor and the goal in mind, it may even be considered unlikely to do so. Misguided reforms can serve to further consolidate power if extra checks and balances are not introduced simultaneously – and not just within the formal institutions of governance but across society, creating new opportunities for democratic engagement about who performs which roles in society, on behalf of whom, and for what.

Neither is accountability a new concept. Rather it has been a narrative, albeit sometimes silent or subdued, running through the course of history, that describes the relations of power between those with more and less power. In this sense, the studies contained in this book suggest the need to reclaim the concept of accountability from the bureaucrats, the institutionalists and the development industry in general. It is a potentially powerful and emancipatory concept given that, at its core, it seeks to describe the appropriate relationship between state, market and civil society. Within the good governance agenda, this has been predominantly understood as a legal relationship, devoid of the social contracts that underpin it. This is a mistake, because it negates the politics and practice of accountability as it is experienced and lived by the world's poor on a daily basis. A conversation about accountability should be a conversation about democracy and rights, and how these can be constructed to reinforce one another. Acknowledging this allows us to engage in a more fundamental debate about what type of democracy we want. Struggles over resources provide one site for this conversation to begin, because access to resources is fundamental to substantive rights and the exercise of citizenship.

Conclusion: the citizenship dimension

Because rights frame the possibilities for making claims, and accountability frames the relationships between actors and institutions that are necessary for these rights to be realised, important implications for citizenship emerge.

Understanding the politics of the relationships between rights, resources and the politics of accountability draws attention to both the risks of greater exclusion and fragmentation, as powerful interests marshal control over important resources, and the potential for an increase in awareness and implementation of rights that can construct substantive citizenship. What is at issue here is the right to have rights, particularly where resources are at stake. Accountability struggles and strategies, through seeking to challenge the power relations that shield state and other actors from answerability, are an important element in making citizenship real.

Though we have argued that accountability, in the first instance, should be about the relationship between the powerful and those with less power, we have noted that state accountability is privileged over all other forms of accountability, not least within the good governance agenda. The assumption is that democracy will be achieved once the institutional mechanisms that allow citizens to hold states accountable are in place. Yet the strategies for demanding accountability explored in this book demonstrate a variety of actor-orientated forms of citizenship, where the boundaries between state and society are blurred, and citizen participation in accountability struggles is an essential element of how citizenship is constituted (see Leach, Scoones and Wynne 2005).

By shedding new light on diverse strategies and approaches to accountability, a more nuanced picture of citizenship emerges. Kabeer argues in *Inclusive Citizenship*, an earlier book in this series, that substantive citizenship from the perspectives of marginalised and excluded groups is based on justice, recognition, self-determination and solidarity. She goes on to make a case for recasting 'vertical' citizenship, based on the narrow relationship between people and states, into 'horizontal' citizenship, which recognises the multiple and overlapping connections and relationships that actually emerge from daily experiences. As many of the chapters in that volume show, collective action has been crucial in addressing 'situations where the state has proved consistently unresponsive to the needs of its citizens' (Kabeer 2005: 23).

Citizenship, then, is also understood in relation to processes of demanding accountability from powerful actors and institutions. Possibilities for accountability are, therefore, strongly shaped by how citizenship is exercised, enforced and denied. If making accountability demands (on the state, or even the private sector and civil society actors) is a way of expressing citizenship, then there are important linkages between accountability struggles and the character of citizenship. In order to be able to make accountability claims, there must be an implicit assumption about the roles and responsibilities of the state, as well as the rights and entitlements of citizens.

Several chapters in this book also point to how involvement in struggles for accountability can change people's perceptions of their rights, responsibilities and, indeed, their role as citizens. Because demands for rights are linked to accountability, these struggles can change the way people understand citizenship. In Bangladesh, the right of women to work in the garment industry has had important implications for citizenship. Despite the accountability problems in the garment sector, the right to work has challenged certain elements of patriarchy by giving a new sense of entitlement and citizenship to many women. Through increased financial independence, women have gained an awareness about rights and citizenship that might not have been possible otherwise.

In so far as citizenship confers material and political (process) rights, it also implies access to resources and channels of representation in decision-making processes that govern their use. Even with an increased awareness of rights, marginalised and excluded groups are unlikely to consider themselves true citizens if they are unable to access resources and entitlements such as adequate housing, health care, clean water and unpolluted living areas (see Wheeler 2003). When we use a resource lens to understand struggles for rights and accountability, the importance of daily struggles against material deprivations comes to the fore. This highlights the role that the lack of access to resources can play in denying substantive citizenship and unravelling shared imaginings of political community. Watts (2003: 5097) notes the importance of oil to the nation-building process and the creation of an 'oil nation'. He argues that it 'is a national resource on which citizenship claims can be constructed. As much as the state uses oil to build a nation and to develop, so communities use oil wealth to activate community claims.' The lack of access to resources and the politics of gaining that access are bound up not only in individual perceptions of citizenship, but also in the overall sense of belonging and recognition that underlies national citizenship.

Though we have sought to locate this book in relation to existing literatures and debates, and to summarise some of their insights for a broader audience, we hope that one of the greatest contributions of these studies will be to illuminate experiences of struggles for rights and accountability from around the world as *lived* experiences. As Eckstein and Wickham-Crowley note: 'A full understanding of rights begs for empirically grounded analyses, not philosophical "what ifs"' (2003: 1). 'Ordinary people ... respond to their lived experiences and their understanding of those experiences, not to the intellectual frames the scholarly community imposes to make sense of those experiences' (2003: 51). The studies that form the basis of this book attempt to engage people's own terms of reference for making sense of accountability and rights struggles. This helps to capture the diverse value systems people have and the cultural repertoires they employ to understand the politics of accountability. We hope that this book offers some insights into the prospects for substantive improvements in accountability, where poor and marginalised groups have a central role in achieving change.

Structure of the book

Chapter 2 provides a critical overview of debates about accountability in development, exploring competing notions of political, social, financial and civil accountability in relation to the key themes of the book.

The remainder of the book is divided into two sections. The first focuses on cases where the entry point for accountability struggles is formal and informal rights that are directly related to particular resources. The second brings together cases where accountability claims are broader than a specific right to a resource, framed around concerns with land, working conditions or access to resource revenues. This section includes examples where accountability struggles engage more specifically with corporate actors.

The first section of the book includes chapters where rights to a particular resource are at the heart of attempts to claim accountability. In Chapter 3 Lyla Mehta explores the case of South Africa, where there is a constitutional right to water, in order to understand issues of accountability where the state nevertheless fails to implement the right to water. It looks at how the right to water is implemented in practice – and at the contradictions between a rights-based approach to water and a market-driven approach. This chapter shows both the difficulties of operationalising formal rights, and how the right to water has had mixed effects on the lives of the poor in South Africa.

In Chapter 4 Luisa Paré and Carlos Robles focus on struggles for accountability by rural indigenous groups engaged in the sustainable management of a rapidly declining watershed in Veracruz, Mexico. There are many different actors and overlapping institutions involved, with often competing interests, including traditional/communal structures such as *ejidos*[2] and urban and rural municipal governments. Paré and Robles, on the basis of their long engagement as action researchers in the region, discuss how, together with the indigenous communities, they have been able to implement mechanisms to increase accountability, where the meanings of accountability are deeply rooted in local experiences and culture.

In Chapter 5 Carlos Cortéz and Luisa Paré, presenting another case from Mexico, compare the accountability issues emerging from two protected natural areas (PNAs) or reserves designed to conserve rainforest. As these PNAs are established, conflicts over the meaning of land rights and knowledge rights (especially traditional medicinal knowledge) emerge. These conflicts are in part a result of the overlapping web of actors and institutions involved in the PNAs. Within a context of conflict, where there are fundamental and underlying disagreements about what the environment and 'nature' mean, the prospects for accountability lie in political mobilisation.

In Chapter 6 Celestine Nyamu-Musembi documents the story of a tenants' association in Mombasa, Kenya, which is seeking to claim the right to housing and demand accountability from the local government. In the process, the association calls upon international legal frameworks that guarantee the right to adequate shelter. But when the local government proves unresponsive, residents use direct action to challenge the lack of accountability. This chapter help expose dilemmas facing community-based groups who use rights as an accountability strategy.

Finally, Chapter 7 by Andrea Cornwall, Silvia Cordeiro and Nelson Delgado focuses on the right to health in North-eastern Brazil. The main mechanism for accountability in this case is a local health council, mandated by the Brazilian constitution, that acts to oversee health care provision in a particular municipality. This chapter explores how the complex political dynamics involved in the council undermine the prospects for accountability.

The second part of the book explores questions of corporate accountability. Chapter 8 – by Peter Newell with Vaijanyanta Anand, Hasrat Arjjumend, Harsh Jaitli, Sampath Kumar, and A.B.S.V. Ranga Rao – uses three case studies from India to expose the frontline of corporate accountability where communities confront corporations in situations of huge power disparity. The case studies include the controversy surrounding the National Thermal Power Corporation power plant in Andhra Pradesh; the struggles around the development of the Lote Industrial area in Maharastra; and conflicts around tribal rights and mining in Jharkhand. Newell et al. catalogue some of the community-based strategies that have been used to challenge corporate power at a local level, reflecting on their effectiveness and the implications for corporate accountability.

In a similar vein, Chapter 9 by Rohit Lehki and Peter Newell also analyses community-based strategies for corporate accountability. It does so by bringing experiences from the global North into the book, focusing on the environmental justice movement in the United States. The chapter documents some of the strategies used by activists from communities of colour to demand greater accountability from state and corporate actors for the location of sites of hazardous and toxic waste in their neighbourhoods. Reflecting on the role of law in particular, this chapter shows both the importance of judicial activism and the ways in which the law can work against the poor.

Amidst the extensive literature on oil and the resource curse in Nigeria, Chapter 10 by Oga Steve Abah and Jenks Okwori explores community-level perspectives on accountability through drama and participatory research. The focus of this chapter is on the meanings and dynamics of accountability at the community level in a context of resource abundance where corporations exert significant influence. Perceived collusion between government and the oil companies operating in the Niger Delta has led to the creation of youth groups and womens' organisations, working with and at times claiming to represent communities in ways that themselves create new accountability challenges. Their activities are understood as a response to the failures of the state to guarantee accountability.

Chapter 11, by Naila Kabeer and Simeen Mahmud, considers the challenge of creating a culture of accountability around labour rights in the context of the garment industry in Bangladesh. They contrast a culture of compliance, deriving from buyer pressure for the adoption of international standards, with a culture of accountability that challenges more fundamental relations of power in the workplace. The competitive and globalised nature of the garment industry, and the poor track record of the state and labour unions in protecting labour rights, mean that garment workers are confronted with difficult choices in demanding accountability from their employers and articulating the rights that matter to them most.

Finally, also on the theme of worker rights, Stephanie Luce documents the experiences of the living wage movement in the United States. She shows how the movement has had to use strategies both within existing power structures (in direct negotiations with municipal government) and outside them (through public protest) in order to achieve greater accountability and the implementation of the living wage. Facing the difficulty of setting an acceptable and applicable living wage standard, workers' organisations have fought instead for the right to a living wage that can be tailored to the context in which it is to be realised.

NOTES

1 See, for example, Edwards and Gaventa 2001; Keck and Sikkink 1998; Cohen and Rai 2000.

2 *Ejidos* are traditionally communally-held plots of land, where the right of use is passed through inheritance.

REFERENCES

ADB (2005) 'ADB's accountability mechanism', Asian Development Bank, www.abd.org/ Accountability-mechanism/default.asp, 13 April, accessed 6 July 2005.

Anderson, M. (1996) 'Human Rights Approaches to Environmental Protection: an Overview', in A. Boyle and M. Anderson (eds), *Human Rights Approaches to Environmental Protection*, Oxford: Clarendon Press, pp. 1–25.

Bannon, I. and Collier, P. (2003) *Natural Resources and Violent Conflict: Options and Actions*, Washington, DC: World Bank, August.

Baviskar, Amita (2003) 'For a cultural politics of natural resources' in *Economic and Political Weekly* Vol. XXXVIII No.48, pp. 5051-5056.

Boyle, A. (1996) 'The Role of International Human Rights Law in the Protection of the Environment', in A. Boyle and M. Anderson (eds), *Human Rights Approaches to Environmental Protection*, Oxford: Clarendon Press, pp. 43–71.

Boyle, A. and Anderson, M. (eds) (1996) *Human Rights Approaches to Environmental Protection*, Oxford: Clarendon Press.

Cohen, R. and Rai, S. (2000) *Global Social Movements*, London: Athlone.

Cornwall, A. and Nyamu-Musembi, C. (2005) 'Why Rights, Why Now? Reflections on the Rise of Rights in International Development Discourse,' in Pettit, J. and Wheeler, J. (eds), *Developing Rights?* IDS Bulletin 36: 1, Brighton: Institute of Development Studies.

DfiD (2001) *Making Government Work for Poor People*, Governance Target Strategy, London: Department for International Development.

—— (2005) 'Public Financial Management and Accountability', Department for International Development, www.dfid.gov.uk/aboutdfid/organisation/pfma/pfma-pets.pdf, accessed 6 July 2005.

—— (2005a) *Promoting Institutional and Organisational Development*, London: Department for International Development.

Dia, M. (1993) *A Governance Approach to Civil Service Reform in Sub-Saharan Africa*, Washington: World Bank.

—— (1996) *Africa's Management in the 1990s and Beyond: Reconciling Indigenous and Transplanted Institutions*, Washington, DC: World Bank.

Dworkin, R. (1978) *Taking Rights Seriously*, London: Duckworth.

Eckstein, S. E. and Wickham-Crowley, T. (2003) *Struggles for Social Rights in Latin America* London: Routledge

Edwards, M. and Gaventa, J. (eds), (2001) *Global Citizen Action*, Boulder: Lynne Riènner Press.

Edwards, S. (1996) *Dismantling the Populist State: the Unfinished Revolution in Latin America and the Caribbean*, Washington, DC: World Bank, July.

Escobar, A. and Alvarez, S. (eds) (1992) *The Making of Social Movements in Latin America: Identity, Strategy and Democracy*, Boulder, Colorado and Oxford: Westview Press.

Evans, G., Goodman, J. and Lansbury, N. (eds) (2002) *Moving Mountains: Communities Confront Mining and Globalisation*, London: Zed Books.

Fabra, A. (1996) 'Indigeous Peoples, Environmental Degradation and Human Rights: a Case Study' in A. Boyle and M. Anderson (eds), *Human Rights Approaches to Environmental Protection*, Oxford: Clarendon Press, pp. 245–65.

Fiszbein, A. (2005) *Citizens, Politicians and Providers: the Latin American Experience with Service Delivery Reform*, Washington, DC: World Bank.

Foster, P. (2002) 'The WDR 2003: Greenwashing Globalization' in *Managing Sustainability World Bank Style: an Evaluation of the World Development Report*, Washington, DC and

London: Heinrich Boll Foundation and Bretton Woods Project, pp. 48–53.

Frynas, G. (1998) 'Political Instability and Business: Focus on Shell in Nigeria', *Third World Quarterly*, Vol. 19, No. 3, pp. 457–79.

Garcia-Guadilla and Blauert, J. (eds) (1994) *Retos para la desarallo y la democracia: Movimentos ambientales en America Latina y Europa* Mexico: Fundacion Fredrich Ebert de Mexico y Venezuela: Nueva Sociedad.

Goetz, A. M. and Gaventa, J. *et al.* (2001) 'Bringing Citizen Voice and Client Focus into Service Delivery', IDS Working Paper 138, Brighton: Institute of Development Studies.

Goetz, A. M. and Jenkins, R. (2004) *Reinventing Accountability: Making Democracy Work for Human Development*, Basingstoke: Palgrave.

Goldman, M. (1998) *Privatizing Nature: Political Struggles for the Global Commons*, London: Pluto Press.

Jones, P. (1994) *Rights*, Issues in Political Theory series, Basingstoke: MacMillan.

Keck, M. E. and Sikkink, K. (1998) *Activists Beyond Borders: Advocacy Networks in International Politics* Itacha and London: Cornell University Press.

Kovach, H., Negan, C. and Burrall, S. (2003) *Power without Accountability? The Global Accountability Report*, London: One World Trust.

Leach, M., Scoones, I. and Wynne, B. (eds) (2005) *Citizens and Science: Globalisation and the Challenge of Engagement*, London: Zed Books.

MacKay, F. (2002) 'The Rights of Indigenous People in International Law', in L. Zarsky (ed.), *Human Rights and the Environment: Conflicts and Norms in a Globalizing World*, London: Earthscan, pp. 9–31.

Mehta, L. (2003) 'Contexts and constructions of water scarcity' in *Economic and Political Weekly* Vol. 38, No. 48 pp. 5066–72.

Merills, J. G. (1996) 'Environmental Protection and Human Rights: Conceptual Aspects', in A. Boyle and M. Anderson (eds), *Human Rights Approaches to Environmental Protection*, Oxford: Clarendon Press, pp. 25–43.

Mintz, S. W. (1986) *Sweetness and Power: the Place of Sugar in Modern History*, New York: Penguin.

Narayan, D. (ed.) (2005) *Measuring Empowerment: Cross-disciplinary Perspectives*, Washington, DC: World Bank, April.

Newell, P., Rai, S. and Scott, A. (eds) (2000) *Development and the Challenge of Globalization*, London: Intermediate Technology Development Group (ITDG) Press.

Paul, S. (2002) 'New Mechanisms of Public Accountability: the Indian Experience', United Nations Development Programme (UNDP), www.undp.org/governance/discount/ new-mechanisms-accountability.pdf, accessed 6 July 2005.

Peet, R. and Watts, M. (1996) (eds) *Liberation Ecologies: Environment, development, social movements* London: Routledge

Pettit, J. and Wheeler, J. (eds) (2005) *Developing Rights?* IDS Bulletin 36:1 Brighton: Institute of Development Studies.

Piron, L-H. (2005) 'Rights-based Approaches and Bilateral Aid Agencies: More Than a Metaphor?' in Pettit, J. and Wheeler, J. (eds), *Developing Rights?* IDS Bulletin 36: 1, Brighton: Institute of Development Studies.

Primo Braga, C., Fink, C. and Paz Sepulveda, C. (2000) *Intellectual Property Rights and Economic Development*, Washington, DC: World Bank.

Puymbroeck, R. van (2001) (ed.) *Comprehensive Legal and Judicial Development: Towards an Agenda for a Just and Equitable Society in the Twenty-first Century*, Washington: World Bank.

Roulier, R. P. (1995) 'Bank Governance Contracts: Establishing Goals and Accountability in Bank Restructuring', World Bank Discussion Paper No. 308, Washington, DC: World Bank, November.

Sanchez Rubio, D., Solorzano Alfaro, N. J. and Lucena Cid, I. V. (eds) (2004) *Nuevos Colonialismos del Capital: Propriedad Intelectual, Biodiversidad y Derechos de los Pueblos*, Barcelona: Icaria y FIADH (Fundacion Iberoamericano de Derechos Humanos).

Shah, A. (2005) *Public Services Delivery*, Washington, DC: World Bank, June.

Shah, A. and Andrews, M. (2005) *Citizen-Centred Governance*, Washington, DC: World Bank.

Soopramien, R., Ofosu-Amaah, W. P. and Uprety, K. (1999) *Combating Corruption: a Comparative Review of Selected Aspects of State Practice and International Initiatives*, Washington, DC: World Bank, July.

Stephens, C., Bullock, S. and Scott, A. (2001) 'Environmental Justice: Rights and Means for a Healthy Environment for All', Special Briefing No. 7 (November), Swindon: Economic and Social Research Council.

Watts, M. (2003) 'Economies of violence: More oil, more blood' *Economic and Political Weekly* Vol. 38, No. 48, pp. 5089–99.

Wheeler, J. S., (2003) 'New Forms of Citizenship: democracy, family, and community in Rio de Janeiro, Brazil'. *Gender and Development*, Vol 11: No 3.

Whitfield, D. (2001) *Public Services or Corporate Welfare: Rethinking the Nation State in the Global Economy*, London: Pluto Press.

Wild, A. (2005) *Black Gold: a Dark History of Coffee*, London: Harper Collins.

UNDP (2000) 'Using Indicators for Human Rights Accountability', Chapter 5, *Human Development Report*, New York: Oxford University Press and United Nations Development Programme.

—— (2004) *Democracy in Latin America: Towards a Citizen's Democracy*, New York: United Nations Development Programme.

—— (2005) United Nations Development Programme website, (www.undp.org.fi/gold/accountability.ftm)

World Bank (1992) *Governance and Development*, Washington, DC: World Bank, May.

—— (1994) *Governance: the World Bank's Experience*, Washington, DC: World Bank.

—— (1998) *Beyond the Washington Consensus: Institutions Matter*, Washington, DC: World Bank.

—— (2000) *Anti-Corruption in Transition: a Contribution to the Policy Debate*, Washington, DC: World Bank.

—— (2003) *Sustainable Development in a Dynamic World: Transforming Institutions, Growth and Quality of Life*, World Development Report, New York: Oxford University Press.

—— (2004) *Making Services Work for Poor People*, World Development Report, New York: Oxford University Press and World Bank.

Zarsky, L. (2002) 'Global Reach: Human Rights and Environment in the Framework of Corporate Accountability', in L. Zarsky (ed.), *Human Rights and the Environment: Conflicts and Norms in a Globalizing World*, London: Earthscan, pp. 31–57.

CHAPTER 2

Taking accountability into account: the debate so far

PETER NEWELL

> Accountability is a perpetual struggle when power is delegated by the many to the few in the interests of governability.... To these perennial problems, globalisation and political liberalisation have added new ones. Powerful non-state actors capable of influencing the lives of ordinary people have multiplied, often act with impunity across borders and can evade the reach of conventional state-based accountability systems. (Goetz and Jenkins 2004: 1)

The idea that accountability is central to ensuring that political and market institutions respond to the needs of the poor has acquired the status of a 'given' in mainstream development orthodoxy. However, the popularity of the term in contemporary development debates, devoid of an analysis of the power relations that it assumes, will do little to help us understand the ways in which institutional and market failure and abuses of power impact upon the lives of the poor. Though it has some potential to identify and challenge the circuits of power that maintain and validate social exclusion and inequity, the way accountability is currently understood and promoted in development debates is as likely to reinforce hierarchy and marginalisation and miss important opportunities to generate change. Politicising the term, on the other hand, provides for a more fundamental set of conversations about power in development, for whom it is exercised, how and with what consequences. Such a shift brings to our attention how the webs of accountability that flow between dispersed and disaggregated decision makers and decision takers graft on to the changing relations between state, market and society. It allows us to ask:

- *what* is accountability for? (what broader political ends does it serve);
- *who* is it for? (who benefits, who articulates those claims, who bears rights to accountability);

- *how* is it practised? (through what means and processes);
- *where* is it practised? (in which sites and across what levels of political decision making).

Each of these questions is intimately connected to the others and implies a different set of strategies and claim making, as the discussion below reveals. At the same time, each allows us to explore different and volatile dimensions of the accountability debate. Goetz and Jenkins (2004: 4) argue, for example, that it is the dimension of the debate around '*for what*' the powerful are being held to account that is being most dramatically reinvented, as expectations proliferate about the functions of *governance* and the standards by which performance of these obligations should be judged. As we see in the section of the book on corporate accountability, this is as true of corporate actors (amid claims about their broader responsibilities to society) as it is of the state. Impact upon a community's human development, rather than compliance with narrowly defined financial and technical rules, is increasingly relevant as a standard of accountability for judging the private sector. Posing these critical questions provides a starting point for reclaiming the transformative potential of ideas about accountability to change structures and relations of power, and not merely to consolidate the power of the already powerful through better systems of reporting and auditing that validate their actions and omissions.

The argument developed in this chapter is, first, that the ability to demand and exercise accountability implies power. The right to demand and the capacity and willingness to respond to calls for accountability assume relations of power. This seemingly obvious observation is at odds with much of the contemporary debate, which seeks to render accountability claims manageable by reducing them to improved systems of management and auditing. Second, these power relations are in a state of flux, reflecting the contested basis of relations between the state, civil society and market actors. These relations both create and restrict the possibilities of new forms of accountability by generating novel dynamics of power through material change and changes in the organisation of political authority.

Beyond these material and political shifts, at a discursive level we find that exercises of power are justified and advanced by prevailing constructions of accountability and the entitlements they presume. These narratives, which are the product of a particular set of historical and material circumstances, validate some forms of power and delegitimise others. The interaction between political action, material change and discursive practices is what helps us to understand the distinct expressions of accountability politics explored in this book – in diverse settings and issue arenas, and as they are applied to different actors. These interactions also provide the basis for understanding the place of accountability in broader constructions of citizenship and discourses around rights, who gets to define these, and the implications of this for the poor. Challenging prevailing conceptions of accountability means engaging with change at the material, organisational and discursive levels that define the possibilities of alternative accountabilities.

Conceptualising accountability

In so far as an enquiry into the practice of accountability in development is an enquiry into how to control the exercise of power, we can view contemporary debates as a continuation of concerns that have driven political philosophy for several hundred years. Beginning with the ancient philosophers, political thinkers have been concerned to prevent abuses by restraining power within established rules. In contemporary usage, the notion of accountability continues to express this concern, attempting to apply checks, oversight and institutional constraints on the exercise of power. It implies both a measure of *answerability* (providing an account of actions undertaken) and *enforceability* (punishment or sanctions for poor or illegal performance) (Schedler *et al.* 1999). In its broadest sense, then, accountability is about the construction of a grammar of conduct and performance and the standards used to assess them (Day and Klein 1987).

During the last decade, the language of accountability has gained increasing prominence in development debates (Newell and Bellour 2002). Appropriated by a myriad of international donor and academic discourses, accountability has become a malleable and often nebulous concept, with connotations that change with the context and agenda. The widespread use of the term means that 'its field of application is as broad as its potential for consensus' (Schedler 1999: 13). It represents, nevertheless, 'an under-explored concept whose meaning remains evasive, whose boundaries are fuzzy and whose internal structure is confusing' (*ibid.*). For Brinkerhoff, the worrying implication of the lack of conceptual and analytical clarity is that 'Accountability risks becoming another buzzword in a long line of ineffectual quick fixes' (2004: 372). Its prevalent use in recent years can be explained by shifts in the strategic thinking of key development agencies with regard to the state, in particular, and the importance of creating mechanisms of accountability to citizens of the state (Goetz and Gaventa 2001). Though the term accountability generally refers to holding actors responsible for their actions, questions such as accountability for what, by whom, and to whom immediately arise (Cornwall, Lucas and Pasteur 2000). This, indeed, has been the entry point of the contributors to this book, who pose questions about accountability in exactly these terms.

Rather than attempting to formulate another definition of accountability or to refine one of the many existing formulations, in this book we have sought to interpret the conflicts of power through multiple lenses of accountability which derive from the contexts in which they are situated. There is no global grammar of accountability that makes sense across settings. The diversity of struggles explored in this book demonstrates the different expectations, histories and values that people bring to bear upon understandings of the respective rights, duties and responsibilities of social actors. Even agreeing a common working understanding of the term among the contributors to this book was a difficult task: for example, the very term accountability does not exist in Spanish. It is clearly a malleable and evolving concept that has to be understood in relation to the conflicts and struggles it is being used to describe. The following section explores some of the macro manifestations of shifting understandings of accountability politics.

Shifting accountabilities

In so far as accountability implies practices of power, it is unsurprising that its ideas and ideologies are promoted, sustained and contested by competing political actors. These discourses generate expectations, duties and conduct that change the practice of accountability politics. The historical and material context in which they are produced ensures that they relate strongly to the structures and actors that generate them. In this sense the construction of accountabilities, the definition of the rights and duties that flow from relations of accountability, is fundamentally a political process driven by broader economic and political agendas. For example, the predominant focus on state accountability can be understood in the light of prevailing notions about the appropriate relationship between states and markets, and assumptions within neoliberal ideology about the inefficiency and lack of responsiveness of states to the needs of citizens, defined as consumers.

From states…
From being the traditional subjects for the application of political and fiscal accountability measures, states are also becoming the principal

targets for improving the responsiveness of services to the poor. In the case of health sector reform, Brinkerhoff notes that concern with accountability derives from 'dissatisfaction with health system performance ... costs, quality assurance, service availability ... financial mismanagement and corruption and lack of responsiveness' (2004: 371). This market rationale for accountability is apparent in the way state functions are often equated with 'service delivery', a move which makes it easier for market advocates to argue that private actors may be able to provide the same services more cost-effectively and efficiently. As state service delivery systems have become more complex and as providers' roles have changed, it has become more difficult to assign responsibility, however. With service provision being increasingly shared with other actors, the boundaries of state accountability are blurring, as we see in Chapter 3 on water provision in South Africa.

Since initial conceptualisations of accountability have been derived from ways to improve state mechanisms, policies and processes, it is unsurprising that current debates should reflect and focus upon state-based notions of accountability. Indeed states remain the predominant reference point in debates about accountability and development despite the fact that accountability demands are increasingly made of non-state actors. The rhetoric of public accountability has grown with the increasing popularity of new public management approaches and renewed attention to state bureaucracy and administration associated with the 'good governance' agenda pursued by donors (Considine 2002). According to the United Nations Development Programme (UNDP), the concepts of responsiveness, accountability and transparency are among the core characteristics of good governance (UNDP 1997: 4). The turn back towards viewing the state as a key actor in development was in many ways led by the World Bank in its 1997 *World Development Report*, on 'The State in a Changing World' (World Bank 1997). Since then there has been repeated emphasis on enhancing accountability through increased state responsiveness.

Contemporary discourses of democracy have also highlighted the importance of state accountability to wider processes of democratisation (Luckham and White 1996). By promoting free and fair elections and mechanisms to hold governments accountable to their publics, international donors have emphasised themes of democratic governance (UNDP 1997: 3). While concepts of public accountability have long been associated with democratic theory and practice, the contemporary wave of transitions from authoritarian rule to democratic governance has highlighted the importance of answerability and enforcement mechanisms in new democracies (Oxhorn and Ducatenzeiler 1998). These trends have shown that without systems providing 'credible restraints' on power, many democratic regimes remain 'low-quality'. If deficiencies in accountability structures are often more visible in new democracies, demands for public accountability in old and new democratic states share a core assumption that elections are, by themselves, no guarantee of good governance. The experience of many new democracies provides evidence of this, as many continue to be haunted by human rights violations, corruption, clientelism and abuses of power, despite universal suffrage and multi-party elections (Schedler *et al.* 1999: 2).

There has also been increasing attention to the potential of decentralisation to deepen democracy through democratic local governance (Blair 2000; Posner 2003). The rationale is that decision making is more likely to be responsive to local needs the more it involves those directly affected by decisions, and that embedding decision making within strong webs of accountability that flow in all directions increases the probability of governance that benefits the poor, making such a regime both 'more responsive to citizen desires and more effective in service delivery' (Blair 2000: 21). Manor reports, however, that despite the assumption that decentralising decision making serves to enhance state responsiveness to the needs of the poor and popular control over decision making, he has 'yet to discover evidence of any case where local élites were more benevolent than those at higher levels' (Manor 1999: 91). Where enforcement mechanisms complement processes for creating answerability, the situation may be different. In Bolivia, for example, vigilance committees are entitled to monitor local budgets and can wield a legal instrument called a *denuncia* against local councils. This means that there is a process by which central funds to the local council that has been denounced can be suspended. As with other strategies aimed at enhancing the accountability of public and private actors, the combinations of tactics that will make an impact depend, amongst other things, on the responsiveness of the state, the sensitivity of the issue in question and the prevailing political culture.

... To markets ...

Recent global trends, however, are bringing into question the appropriateness of this focus on holding governments to account for decisions and actions that increasingly result from bargains with, and the actions of, non-state and private actors. The rapid growth in cross-border economic transactions in trade, production and finance has brought about changes in political authority at national and international levels and, as a result, transformed many traditional arenas of accountability. In the wake of globalisation and associated patterns of deregulation and liberalisation, global corporate power has gained increasing sway, leading to greater corporate influence over activities that traditionally have been the prerogative of states. With revenues that often dwarf the gross domestic products (GDPs) of many developing countries, transnational corporations (TNCs) are often more powerful than governments, and the mobility that allows them to locate their business in the most favourable regulatory environment gives them sufficient leverage to play one government off against another. We see from the chapters in this book on the pursuit of labour rights in the United States and Bangladesh that capital mobility also strongly and negatively impacts upon the ability of trade unions to hold corporations to account over the recognition of labour rights. As a result, it often seems that TNCs wield power without responsibility: they are as powerful as states, yet less accountable. As Vidal notes, 'Corporations have never been more powerful, yet less regulated; never more pampered by government, yet never less questioned; never more needed to take social responsibility yet never more secretive.... To whom will these fabulously self-motivated, self-interested supranational bodies be accountable?' (Vidal 1996: 263).

The imbalance between the rights and responsibilities of firms is also increasingly manifested at the global level where there is an imbalance between *regulation for* business rather than *regulation of* business (Newell 2001a). The entitlements and rights of corporations are enshrined in international agreements aimed at freeing up restrictions on investment. The attempt to negotiate a Multilateral Agreement on Investment, the conclusion by the World Trade Organisation (WTO) of the Trade-Related Intellectual Property Rights (TRIPs) accord and the General Agreement on Trade in Services (GATS) all provide evidence of this. Gill (1995) refers to this as the 'new constitutionalism', in which the rights of capital are affirmed, legally protected and upheld above those of states. Each of these agreements affords new rights to companies while circumscribing the powers of national and local authority over investors.

Not only has this brought about a renegotiation of relations between state and market, but there is also some evidence of a transformation of relations between actors such as TNCs, non-governmental organisations (NGOs), and international organisations. This has resulted in a more complex and dense set of obligations and responsibilities between different actors in development, creating both opportunities for the construction of new accountabilities and new *accountability gaps*. Accountability gaps can emerge where shifts of political authority take place, between state and market for example, without the creation of new accountability mechanisms. The way in which both the private sector and NGOs have become involved in the delivery of services that were traditionally the preserve of the state, such as health and education, has raised concerns about whether these new service providers have the same incentives, or channels of access, to respond to public demands and complaints in the way expected of states. When private actors perform public functions in this way, the issue of responsiveness to the poor is heightened, because they are working to a different mandate: profit maximisation and not service delivery for all (Whitfield 2001).

... to civil society

Just as the private sector plays an increasingly privileged role in service delivery, so civil society organisations are increasingly used by development agencies as aid deliverers because they are thought to provide more accountable, effective and equitable services, in many areas, than public or private agencies. As a result, large amounts of aid are channelled through NGOs. The very popularity of NGOs among donors and publics, which helps to explain their exponential rise, creates its own accountability gaps, however. Where NGOs have formed global alliances in order to enhance their effectiveness, questions arise about the identity of the constituency – if any – to which they are answerable. There are concerns, too, over the potential of NGO activity to become disembedded once groups become less dependent on a traditional support base and work instead to global donor or campaign agendas, set and negotiated with other partners.

Hence there has been a reappraisal of the role of NGOs, once the darlings of the development world, as service delivers and agents of democratisation (Najam 1996; Edwards and Hulme 1995). While NGOs do not necessarily perform less effectively than other public or private organisations, they often perform less well than the popular image suggests (Edwards and Hulme 1995: 6). NGOs can be as susceptible as other institutions to the problems of corruption, cooptation, opportunism and political manoeuvring. The issue here is not only accountability gaps, but also the potential for inconsistent standards and expectations regarding the conduct and degree of answerability of public and private actors. On these grounds, the World Bank has been criticised for demanding far higher standards of accountability from governments than from the NGO and private actors that increasingly also provide 'state' services.

The challenge of ensuring accountability is multiplied when political authority is shared, as it increasingly is, across a number of levels from the local to the national, the regional and the global. The term *multi-level governance* describes the layers of overlapping authority that characterise decision making in the current global system. The spectacular growth of supranational authorities and regionalism, with international regimes governing an increasingly broad spectrum of areas of social and economic life, add to this institutional complexity and potentially create further democratic deficits. The challenge, from a development point of view, is how to ensure that decisions that affect the lives of the poor, but are taken in arenas remote from those lives, remain responsive to local needs.

It is clear from this discussion that traditional definitions of accountability are being expanded to adjust to new realities. Indeed, many of the political and economic changes described in Chapter 1 have rendered increasingly permeable the categorisations of accountability described below. Blurred lines of authority, competing jurisdictions and shifting social expectations have produced messier and denser webs of accountability between states, market actors and civil society. The following sections explore *accountability types*: whether political, financial, social or civil, all are principally associated with a particular type of actor but also describe distinct approaches to, and practices of, accountability. For example, we see how financial accountability is increasingly demanded of private and civil society as well as state actors; how political accountability is no longer provided within the state but increasingly also by civil society actors acting as watchdogs of state action; and how civil accountability, traditionally pursued by pressure groups, is increasingly being sought by community-based groups in defence of their livelihood rights. Notions of accountability *to whom* and *for what* are continually evolving – a product of the coincidence of proliferating accountability gaps and an increasing sense in which, even if accountability is not a right, people have a right to claim it.

Political accountability

Traditional notions of political accountability are derived from the responsibilities of delegated individuals in public office to carry out specific tasks on behalf of citizens. It is this sense of accountability, in which rulers explain and justify actions to the ruled, that traditionally distinguished a democratic society from a tyrannical one. In the Athenian state, this meant holding officials accountable for their actions; more modern notions of political accountability have focused on ministerial accountability and the ability of parliament to call the executive powers to account. Thus democratic accountability is characterised not only by elections to determine who runs the affairs of society, but also by the continuing obligation of these officials to explain and justify their conduct in public. Though accountability is traditionally seen as a retrospective account of past actions (*ex post*), more radical constructions involve actors making public their intended actions before they are taken, promoting public engagement through consultation and deliberation (*ex ante*) (Day and Klein 1987).

In the modern state, with the growth of bureaucracies, the lines of political accountability have become more blurred, making traditional concepts more difficult to apply. Contemporary discussions of accountability have broadened to include both *horizontal* and *vertical* mechanisms of political accountability. Horizontal mechanisms amount to self-imposed accountability within the state machinery. Vertical accountability, on the other hand, is that which is demanded from below by citizens and civil society groups (Schacter 2000: 1). In this sense, horizontal accountability refers to the capacity of state institutions to counter abuses by other public agencies and branches of government through checks and balances on the powers of the judiciary, executive and legislature. In reality it may also be exercised by anti-corruption bodies, auditors general, electoral and human rights commissions and other ombudsmen. To be effective, horizontal accountability needs to be buttressed by strong vertical accountability, in which citizens, mass media and civil associations are in a position to scrutinise public officials and government practice in the ways suggested by approaches to social accountability discussed below.

We noted above the centrality of mechanisms of enforceability to practicable notions of accountability. Different forms of accountability rely on different enforcement mechanisms, but accountability is only as effective as the mechanisms it employs, and 'inconsequential accountability is not accountability at all' (Schedler *et al.* 1999: 17). To deliver answerability effectively, sanctions are key. Sanctions can be both 'soft' and 'hard'. Soft sanctions refer to tools aimed at bringing about change without the use of coercion. Moral appeals, expectations, exposure and embarrassment, and appeals to pride and responsibility are among these tools. Civil society scrutiny can play a key role here in exposing wrongdoing and non-compliance with commitments made by governments or industries. Without the ties to diplomatic routine and without having to face the costs of political fallout that prohibit public institutions from speaking out, NGOs can create and police accountability mechanisms that go far beyond what is conceivable in the realm of formal politics. As with all aspects of accountability, therefore, protest and exposure are key tools in enforcing compliance.

A great deal of importance is also attached to the law as a mechanism for enforcing political accountability. The law can be seen as a political mechanism for defining rights, allocating responsibilities and thereby helping to construct prevailing notions of citizenship. This form of accountability seeks answerability and enforceability through the courts, a process that we examine in relation to South Africa (Chapter 3), India (Chapter 8) and the United States (Chapter 12), where rights have been violated and/or compensation sought. Where the law governs access to key resources, determines economic entitlements and shapes the rules of participation in public life, it can be applied positively to create an enabling environment in which poorer groups can secure their rights.

Yet the law is not a neutral vessel and legal processes are not insulated from political pressures. Law creation is always for someone, for some purpose, responsive to state needs or the concerns of well-organised and well-resourced political groups. Attempts to use the law to hold corporations to account for their social and environmental responsibilities have often failed because of state support for the corporations that are the subject of the suit or discrimination against the communities trying to bring the case, as we see in Chapter 9. As an accountability tool of the poor, the law has limitations and opportunities depending on the system in question. Countries such as India have a strong tradition of public interest litigation, for example. It should be noted, however, that basic resource constraints, lack of legal literacy and distrust of legal processes often conspire to dissuade poorer groups from using the legal system to seek redress (Newell 2001b). The perceived limits of these and other strategies by which the state is meant to hold itself to account have resulted in increasing interest in broader forms of social and civil accountability.

Social accountability

Related in many ways to political accountability is the notion of social accountability (Smulovitz and Peruzzotti 2000; Peruzzotti and Smulovitz 2002). Lent legitimacy by emerging rights-oriented discourses, social accountability explores the way in which citizen action, aimed at overseeing political authorities, is redefining the traditional concept of the relationship between citizens and their elected representatives. Social mobilisations, press reports and legal cases are the repertoires of protest that produce such forms of accountability. The targets are often election processes, government restrictions imposed on access to information and instances of police violence (Stanley 2005). The aims are variously to tackle issues of citizen security, judicial autonomy and access to justice, electoral fraud and government corruption (Peruzzotti and Smulovitz 2002; Dodson and Jackson 2004). The strategies provide, in effect, extra sets of checks and balances on the proper conduct of government in the public interest, exposing instances of corruption, negligence and oversight that vertical forms of accountability are unlikely or unable to address. Social forms of political control intend to go beyond the limitations of relying upon traditional mechanisms of accountability: elections; the separation of powers; and the checks and balances that exist, in theory, between state agencies.

More radical notions of accountability might question the state-centred nature of such approaches, which (re)produce a reliance on the state as an agent of change. The emphasis is explicitly to explore the ways in which civil society 'adds to the classic repertoire of electoral and constitutional institutions for controlling government' (Smulovitz and Peruzzotti 2000: 149). To work, however, such strategies require a responsive state that demonstrates a level of concern for what citizens or voters think and is willing to implement reforms aimed at pacifying those concerns. Social accountability mechanisms often explicitly aim at activating or reinforcing the operations of other agencies of horizontal accountability, again assuming their existence, effectiveness and willingness to pursue public interest agendas. Their aim, for example, is to 'trigger procedures in courts or oversight agencies that eventually lead to legal sanctions' (Smulovitz and Peruzzotti 2000: 151), to catalyse state-based mechanisms of enforceability. Rather than being effective in their own right, therefore, societal mechanisms need to pull other levers of change through the law or media.

A problematic assumption in this regard relates not just to the limits of the law or of the critical capacity of the media to work in these ways, but to issues of the capacity of actors promoting social accountability to perform these watchdog functions on an ongoing and sustained basis. Besides issues of resourcing, there is an implied assumption that societal mechanisms provide a viable system for tracking and addressing instances of misconduct or acts of negligence. But what if the problems are systemic, deep-rooted, ingrained in the everyday administration of the state? The problem is then not one of temporary institutional failure, nor one of institutional failure at all, but of institutions working very well for those that benefit from prevailing concentrations of power, distributions of resources and institutional indifference or blindness towards the needs of poorer groups.

If the problem is more fundamental in nature, we can expect less to be achieved by single-issue campaigns targeted at particular abuses of power, well-intentioned as those may be, and in spite of their potential to draw attention to broader patterns of neglect. We see this in Chapter 9 of this volume, where environmental justice advocates claim that acts of environmental racism are not evidence of a breakdown in a decision-making process. Rather, they manifest a deliberate, state-endorsed strategy, one that works well for those who profit from the social and environmental externalities passed on to poorer groups. As Goetz and Jenkins claim more generally:

> Many of the initiatives that profess to promote accountability target only very 'soft' aspects of accountability ... treating the structural difficulties of democratic systems as temporary glitches requiring the application of technical expertise. Such initiatives side-step institutionalised anti-poor biases that prevent accountability institutions from recognising and responding to injustices that disproportionately, or even exclusively, affect marginalised groups. (Goetz and Jenkins 2004: 7)

A further limitation of approaches to social accountability is their applicability to contexts in which the state tolerates and accommodates such forms of protest and criticism; where a free media exists, willing and prepared to engage in critical exposé journalism; and an accessible and functioning legal system operates, able to back citizen claims against the state with financial support and expertise. Such conditions could be said to apply to an increasing number of developed and developing countries, but in many settings they remain a distant prospect. Even in contexts where these basic conditions are met in theory, in practice barriers to accessing the media and the justice system continue to frustrate change. Hence, although Peruzzotti and Smulovitz claim that 'The politics of social accountability has taken place under authoritarian contexts', they do acknowledge that

> Under authoritarianism, the struggle for access to information becomes a precondition for any initiative oriented at controlling government behaviour. Authoritarianism also weakens the politics of social accountability in so far as it reduces the repertoire of institutional tools available to the citizenry for the exercise of control. (Peruzzotti and Smulovitz 2002: 226)

Exploring the limitations of strategies of social accountability is not to undermine their importance in generating significant and much-needed checks and balances on the often arbitrary exercise of state power. Work on law and development, in particular, explores the conditions in which poorer and marginalised groups have been able to secure change through legal systems (Crook and Houtzager 2001; McClymont and Golub 2000) and this book cites a number of cases in which legal challenges have yielded important pro-poor outcomes. Similarly, the fact that social accountability is stronger on answerability than enforceability does not render it insignificant. As Peruzzotti and Smulovitz argue, 'the fact that most societal mechanisms do not have mandatory effects does not mean that they cannot have important "material consequences"' (2002: 227).

Rather, raising such concerns about the possibilities of social accountability forms part of a generic concern articulated throughout this book to look at accountability in terms not defined exclusively by state power. Many of the chapters in this book explore the crucial roles of community-based and civil society groups that plug accountability deficits in public institutions or address their lack of responsiveness to the needs of the poor by taking action directly, albeit sometimes in ways which invoke rights or entitlements in theory conferred by the state. The state is rarely absent in accountability struggles, therefore. The question is whether it always makes strategic sense for it to be the primary focus of campaign energies. Again, the answer has to depend on the goal of an accountability struggle and the extent to which change is contingent on reform in state practice.

Financial accountability

Managerial and financial approaches to accountability describe specific practices of accountability, traditionally applied to states but increasingly also to the private sector and civil society. Managerial accountability generally refers to the answerability of those with delegated authority for carrying out tasks according to agreed performance criteria. This less explicitly political form of accountability is concerned with inputs, outputs and outcomes; monitoring expenditure as agreed and according to the rules; and making sure that the processes and courses of action are carried out efficiently to achieve intended results (Day and Klein 1987: 27). If political accountability focuses on questions of institutional engineering, financial accountability focuses on accountancy. Broader accountability challenges in such conceptualisations run the risk of being reduced to performative functions: institutional planning and the assembling of incentives to motivate rational actors. Hence, for health, standards, benchmarks, practice guidelines and compliance mechanisms are key to improving 'service utilisation and client satisfaction' (Brinkerhoff 2004: 372). In a simple logical sequence between incentives and outcomes, 'accountability is achieved through the application of the laws, standards and procedures these frameworks put in place, which shape the incentives for various actors to comply' (*ibid.*: 372).

In its origins, financial accountability can be distinguished from political accountability by virtue of its proclaimed status as a neutral, technical exercise essentially concerned with keeping accurate accounts, with using the tools of auditing, budgeting and accounting to track and report on the allocation, disbursement and utilisation of financial resources. Current notions of financial accountability have expanded beyond the balancing of public books to the management of resources, shifting from economy to efficiency. Fiscal accountability mechanisms and auditing practices are continuing to evolve and expand, moving away from being strictly accounts-based to incorporating new indicators of financial integrity and performance. The recent emergence of social and environmental auditing practices, discussed below, represents this shift.

Managerial accountability has also expanded to include notions of *administrative accountability*. In the arena of public service delivery, new management approaches aimed at enhancing financial accountability can generate competing accountability demands and conflicting trade-offs. Efficient performance of services, demonstrated through ever more elaborate and transparent systems of accounting, may be at odds with the need to widen the access and availability of services to poorer groups. Such conflicts are most visible in those public services of greatest impor-tance to the poor, such as health, education or the supply of water (Paul 1992). In this sense, while the purposes of accountability can overlap, they can also yield tensions. Brinkerhoff notes that 'accountability for control, with its focus on uncovering malfeasance and allocating "blame", can conflict with accountability for improvement, which emphasises managerial discretion and embracing error as a source of learning' (2003: xii).

It is in the corporate sector, perhaps, that we see the clearest evidence of an audit culture taking root, combining elements of managerial and financial accountability. The range of indicators of corporate perfor-mance has been broadened, in some cases to include social and environ-mental factors. Clear performance indicators are difficult to quantify, however, stretching conventional auditing techniques that rest on the assumption that 'what can't be counted doesn't count', but their increased emphasis does indicate how auditing processes are responsive to evolving demands for the accountability of actors.

Increasing numbers of social and environmental reports and externally verified statements provide evidence of the attempt by corporate managers to demonstrate a commitment to the public at large (Beloe 1999), though it remains the case that in global terms very few companies make such data publicly available. Similarly, though the indicators of social and environmental reporting are becoming more numerous and sophisticated, there are as yet few standard formats for the type of information companies report, or how that information is collected, analysed and presented. Because of this, a variety of organisations and initiatives are attempting to standardise social and environmental reporting procedures to enable stakeholders to compare companies more easily across sectors and regions. Standards such as SA8000 (established in 1997 by Social Accountability International), and AA1000 (developed by the Institute of Social and Ethical Accountability in 1999) incorporate frameworks to improve performance and the quality of assessments.

Heightened public interest in questions of corporate accountability and responsibility has forced (some) companies to go beyond declarations of good intent and the self-enforcement of codes of conduct and to involve third-party consultants and accreditation agencies in the verification of their commitments. There has been a role for consultancy firms such as Ernst and Young and KMPG, verifying company claims once site inspections and interviews with employees have taken place. But crosschecking of these assessments rarely takes place and questions have been asked about their thoroughness and effectiveness. When there is pressure for a speedy audit, companies are given notice of inspections and interviews with workers take place in the work environment, where they may be less free to speak out (O'Rourke 1997).

The involvement of private auditors in verifying compliance also raises the question of who audits the auditors. Questions have been asked about the independence and commitment of consultancy firms, such as KPMG, since they perform these roles for profit and are paid by the companies whose activities they are meant to be monitoring (Simms 2002). The recent corporate governance scandals in the US involving corporations such as Enron and WorldCom have served to focus attention on the unhealthy degree of collusion between companies and those they employ to oversee their accounts. In this context, second-order accountability is an important issue: 'how can we hold institutions of accountability accountable themselves?' (Schedler et al. 1999: 25).

Unsurprisingly, this emphasis on accountancy has extended to civil society groups in development, given their heightened role in aid delivery. With regard to development projects, often the simplest mechanism by which an NGO can be held to account is accounting for expenditure. To demonstrate this, measures and indicators are needed, yet few agreed performance standards are available. Indicators of quality of organisational performance are rare, with most assessments favouring short-term visible results and evaluations that emphasise control and fiscal responsibility. The types of appraisal procedures insisted on by donors favour 'accountancy rather than accountability', audit rather than learning (Edwards and Hulme 1995: 13). Given tendencies towards loose oversight by a board, periodic elections of officers, minimalist reports of activities and summary financial records, Scholte suggests such 'pro forma accountability mainly addresses the bureaucratic requirements of governments and donors.... Thus in civil society, just as much as in governance and market circles, formal accountability may well fall short of effective accountability' (2005: 107).

Towards civil accountability?

The conceptualisations above fail to capture an increasingly important type of accountability; civil accountability. Strategies of civil accountability are non-state, often informal and distinct in form from political, social and financial accountability (see Table 1.1, page 18). They most closely resemble strategies of social accountability, but are less focused on achieving change in the state as an end itself and towards this end adopt different activist repertoires. Sometimes citizen action takes the form of problem solving as a self-help strategy, often in the absence of, or because of, a prior state intervention. Efforts to engage citizens in the management of water resources, explored in Chapter 4, are an example of this. At other times, the aim is raising awareness or improving consciousness about the ways in which accountability deficits frustrate the development prospects of the poor – as in the case of consciousmess raising through theatre in Nigeria, discussed in Chapter 10. Innovative participatory methodologies bring new citizen knowledge to the fore to challenge existing approaches to regulation. Participatory health assessments or pollution monitoring by citizens in India, discussed in Chapter 8, provide examples of these types of strategy in practice.

Building on the argument of the previous chapter that accountability is often a means to an end, by specifying the aim of a struggle it becomes easier to comprehend the strategies groups adopt to secure those ends. The strategic use of accountability tools shifts with time, so that it is unsurprising to find groups employing simultaneously a diverse range of tactics. In Mexico we find evidence of groups moving from registering dissent through cutting off water supplies to more proactive engagement in water management alternatives (Chapter 4). In practice then, multiple and hybrid forms of accountability are sought and practised by social actors working within available spaces and beyond them to construct new arenas of engagement, fusing strategies in combinations that make sense in the pursuit of diverse and shifting goals. This partly reflects a reading of existing political opportunity structures. As Eckstein and Wickham-Crowley note (2003: 4): 'State institutional arrangements ... can influence whether people turn to collective or individual, and formal or informal strategies to secure or protect social rights and to redress violations thereof.'

When such formal channels fail to operate or perform poorly, aggrieved citizens often resort to alternative mechanisms of redress. Arenas for the contestation of rights and duties can be created by movements and citizen groups where new spaces for accountability can be constituted. Indeed, as Goetz and Jenkins note, in many cases it is

> shortcomings in conventional accountability systems – secrecy in auditing, ineffective policy reviews in legislatures, the electorate's difficulty in sending strong signals to decision makers between elections, excessive delays in courts and inadequate sanctions for failure to apply administrative rules or respect standards [that] have created pressure for better channels for vertical information flows and stronger accountability mechanisms between state agents and citizens. (Goetz and Jenkins 2001: 2–3)

Sometimes activists imitate official accountability procedures in order to raise issues and highlight the limitations of existing mechanisms. The public hearings described in Chapter 8 of the book are an example in this regard, where formal hearings are called for, but often not undertaken, and communities and activists have sought to construct their own hearings for dealing with accountability claims. While to some extent mocking state procedures by staging them in informal ways, such experiments can yield institutional change. Often accountability mechanisms are fashioned in ways that seek to engage state actors without mimicking state-based accountability tools. Strategies of citizen water management in Mexico described in Chapter 4 aim to secure water supply in a context of acute conflict without resort to state mechanisms of redress.

Such experiments in accountability politics are often aimed at challenging prevailing political cultures of secrecy, official arrogance and institutional unresponsiveness. In so doing, they often contest the very purposes for which accountability tools are invoked. The 'new accountability agenda' includes the use of such experiments, whereby disenfranchised groups are provided with 'opportunities to operationalise rights and to shift the terrain of governance from technical solutions to a more immediate concern with social justice' (Goetz and Jenkins 2004: 3). The challenge is to move from *accountability as spectacle*, as it is practised in these events, useful as they are, to *accountability as norm*, a routine and mundane feature of everyday decision making.

There is clearly a difference between accountability that can be created *passively* and that which is produced *actively*. Passive accountability implies that the authority to act on behalf of others is conferred on leaders of communities, heads of NGOs, and, of course, governments. A mandate is given such that continual approval is not required for each and every decision that is made on behalf of a broader political community. This is the minimalist notion of democracy described by the term 'delegative democracy' (O'Donnell 1994). It is best represented in notions of political and managerial accountability, described above, which emphasise the self-regulating ability of state, private and civil society actors. Active accountability, on the other hand, is that which is continually (re) negotiated, where demands have to be vocalised and where closure is not reached on how accountability should be exercised and on whose behalf. This assumes both a right and a capacity to articulate accountability demands. It resonates more strongly with the notions of social and civil accountability where the focus is respectively on monitoring the state's ability to self-regulate or attempting to reproduce, compensate for or mimic state action in its absence. There is an important balance to strike, therefore, between building citizens' capacities to articulate rights *and* the capabilities of political-economic institutions to respond and be held to account (Gaventa and Jones 2002).

Conclusion

This chapter has shown that while accountability is an increasingly crucial reference point in development debates, its use in diverse discourses remains loose and under-specific as a result of the essentially contested nature of the term and the broad range of political claims it can be used to advance. This, indeed, is the whole point of our enquiry into the relationship between rights, resources and accountability. In understanding these processes, we have placed power centrally: power to define accountability, and power to create and enforce the mechanisms of accountability. We have seen throughout the discussion how power operates at different levels, reinforcing itself through discourse, process and the actions of actors. We noted a complex interplay between the way narratives of accountability construct rights and obligations (and notions of citizenship in so doing) and the way strategies of accountability generate new expectations about the appropriate conduct of others, contesting or reinforcing prevailing notions of accountability. In understanding predominant applications of accountability, we emphasised the importance of historical and material circumstances to the construction of rights and entitlements to accountability. It is to be expected, therefore, that future struggles for accountability will both reflect and help to redefine prevailing historical processes and material changes.

Inevitably, such a broad overview has raised as many questions as it has provided adequate answers to the key accountability questions we set out at the start of the chapter. Hard questions remain about whether accountability makes a difference, how much difference it makes, and for whom. As Chapter 10 on struggles over labour rights makes clear, there are social costs associated with accountability struggles. Despite claims to the contrary, they are neither win-win for all concerned, nor cost-free. In many of the contexts explored in this book, indeed, we have seen how people risk their lives in the face of violence and intimidation to protest abuses of power and advance accountability claims. More accountability may ultimately contribute both to the effectiveness and legitimacy of political institutions, but that hope must be demonstrated, not assumed. The question for many of the actors engaged in the accountability struggles described in this book is not what accountability does for those institutions that already wield power, but what it can do for the victims of institutional inaction, political oversight, economic marginalisation and overt repression.

REFERENCES

Beloe, S. (1999) 'The Greening of Business?' *IDS Bulletin*, Vol. 3 No. 3.

Blair, H. (2000) 'Participation and Accountability at the Periphery: Democratic Local Governance in Six Countries', *World Development*, Vol. 28, No. 1 (January).

Brinkerhoff, D. (2003) 'Accountability and Health Systems: Overview, Framework and Strategies', Technical Report No. 018 (January), Bethesda, Maryland: Partners for Health Reform*plus* project, Abt Associates Inc.

—— (2004) 'Accountability and Health Systems: Towards Conceptual Clarity and Policy Relevance', *Health Policy and Planning*, Vol. 19, No. 6, pp. 371–9.

Cornwall, A., Lucas, H. and Pasteur, K. (2000) 'Introduction: Accountability Through Participation: Developing Workable Partnership Models in the Health Sector', *IDS Bulletin*, Vol. 31, No. 1.

Considine, M. (2002) 'The End of the Line? Accountable Governance in the Age of Networks, Partnerships and Joined-up Services', *Governance*, Vol. 15 No. 1 (January).

Crook, R. C. and Houtzager, P. P. (2001) *Making Law Matter: Rules, Rights and Security in the Lives of the Poor*, *IDS Bulletin*, Vol. 32, No. 1, Brighton: IDS.

Day, P. and Klein, R. (1987) *Accountabilities: Five Public Services*, London and New York: Tavistock.

Dodson, M. and Jackson, D. (2004) 'Strengthening Horizontal Accountability in Transitional Democracies: the Human Rights Ombudsman in Central America', *Latin American Politics and Society*, Vol. 46, No. 4 (Winter).

Eckstein, S. E. and Wickham-Crowley, T. (2003) *Struggles for Social Rights in Latin America*, London: Routledge.

Edwards, M. and Hulme, D. (eds) (1995) *Beyond the Magic Bullet: NGO Performance and Accountability in the Post-Cold War World*, London: Save the Children Fund.

Gaventa, J. and Jones, E. (2002) 'Concepts of Citizenship: a Review', IDS Development Bibliography No. 19, Brighton: Institute of Development Studies.

Gill, S. (1995) 'Theorising the Interregnum: the Double Movement and Global Politics in the 1990s', in Hettne, B. (ed.), *International Political Economy: Understanding Global Disorder*, London: Zed Books.

Goetz, A. M. and Gaventa, J. *et al.* (2001) 'Bringing Citizen Voice and Client Focus into Service Delivery', IDS Working Paper 138, Brighton: Institute of Development Studies.

Goetz, A. M. and Jenkins, R. (2001) 'Hybrid Forms of Accountability: Citizen Engagement in Institutions of Public Sector Oversight in India', *Public Management Review*, Vol. 3, No. 3 (September).

—— (2004) *Reinventing Accountability: Making Democracy Work for Human Development*, Basingstoke: Palgrave.

Luckham, R. and White, G. (eds) (1996) *Democratization in the South: The Jagged Wave*, Manchester: Manchester University Press.

Manor, J. (1999) *The Political Economy of Democratic Decentralisation*, Washington, DC: World Bank.

McClymont, M. and Golub, S. (2000) *Many Roads to Justice: the Law-related Work of Ford Foundation Grantees around the World*, New York: Ford Foundation.

Najam, A. (1996) 'NGO Accountability: a Conceptual Framework', *Development Policy Review*, Vol. 14.

Newell, P. (2001a) 'Managing Multinationals: the Governance of Investment for the Environment' *Journal of International Development*, Vol. 13.

—— (2001b) 'Access to Environmental Justice? Litigation against TNCs in the South', *IDS Bulletin*, Vol. 32, No. 1.

Newell, P. and Bellour, S. (2002) 'Mapping Accountability: Origins, Contexts and Implications for Development', IDS Working Paper 168 (October), Brighton: Institute of Development Studies.

O'Donnell, G. (1994) 'Delegative Democracy', *Journal of Democracy*, Vol. 5 (January).

O'Rourke, D. (1997) 'Smoke from a Hired Gun: a Critique of Nike's Labour and Environmental Auditing in Vietnam as Performed by Ernst and Young', unpublished MS, available at http://www.corpwatch.org/trac/nike/ernst/.

Oxhorn, P. and Ducantenzeiler, G. (1998) *What Kind of Democracy? What Kind of Market? Latin America in an Age of Neoliberalism*, Pennsylvania: Pennsylvania State University Press.

Paul, S. (1992) 'Accountability in Public Services: Exit, Voice and Control', *World Development*, Vol. 20, No. 7, pp. 1047–60.

Peruzzotti, E. and Smulovitz, C. (2002) 'Held to Account: Experiences of Social Accountability in Latin America', *Journal of Human Development*, Vol. 3, No. 2, pp. 209–30.

Picciotto, S. and Mayne, R. (eds) (1999) *Regulating International Business: Beyond*

Liberalisation, London: Macmillan Press.

Posner, P. W. (2003) 'Local Democracy and Popular Participation: Chile and Brazil in Comparative Perspective', *Democratization*, Vol. 10, No. 3 (Autumn), pp. 39–68.

Schacter, M. (2000) 'When Accountability Fails: a Framework for Diagnosis and Action', Institute on Governance, Policy Brief No. 9.

Schedler, A., Diamond, L. and Plattner, M. (1999) *The Self-restraining State: Power and Accountability in New Democracies*, Boulder and London: Lynne Rienner Publishers.

Scholte, J. A. (2005) 'Civil Society and Democratically Accountable Global Governance', in Held, D. and Koenig-Archibugi, M. (eds), *Global Governance and Public Accountability*, Oxford: Blackwell, pp. 87–110.

Simms, A. (2002) *Five Brothers: the Rise and Nemesis of the Big Bean Counters*, London: New Economics Foundation.

Smulovitz, C. and Peruzzotti, E. (2000) 'Societal Accountability in Latin America', *Journal of Democracy*, Vol. 11, No. 4 (October), pp.147–58.

Stanley, R. (2005) 'Controlling the Police in Buenos Aires: a Case Study of Horizontal and Social Accountability', *Bulletin of Latin American Research*, Vol. 24, No. 1 (January), pp. 71–92.

UNDP (1997) 'Corruption and Good Governance', MDG (Millennium Development Goal) Discussion Paper 3.

Vidal, J. (1996) *McLibel: Burger Culture on Trial,* Basingstoke: MacMillan.

Whitfield, D. (2001) *Public Services or Corporate Welfare: Rethinking the Nation State in the Global Economy*, London: Pluto Press.

World Bank (1997) *The State in a Changing World*, World Bank Development Report, Washington, DC: World Bank.

Overview The political economy of resources and the cultural politics of rights: challenges for accountability

PETER NEWELL AND JOANNA WHEELER

The current focus on good governance in development debates implies some assumptions about accountability, in particular that increased accountability will lead to greater social, economic and political equity. By the same token, an inherent assumption in much of the current enthusiasm for rights-based approaches in development is that implementing rights will help create predictability for poor and marginalised groups by establishing clear relationships of responsibility between powerful actors and these groups. This section of the book will challenge both of these assumptions by examining, in rich empirical detail, the relationship between rights and resources in terms of accountability.

These chapters consider how marginalised groups contest access to a range of resources, including adequate housing, health care and water. These 'resources' are not defined in the narrow sense of extractable natural materials like oil and minerals, which are the focus of the literature on the 'resource curse', referred to in Chapter 10. Instead, these chapters take a wider view, exploring the interaction between the material features of resources and the social and political struggles over the control of their use. The starting point for understanding rights and accountability in relation to these resources is the deprivation of, or lack of access to, the resources in question. And while there is, in most cases, an important and pressing material deprivation (lack of adequate housing, lack of clean water, lack of appropriate health care), these chapters will focus on the political contestations to gain access to these resources. This section explores both the political economy of gaining rights to resources and the cultural politics of how resources are constituted and contested.

Within these processes of political contestation over resources, some key themes have emerged that shed some light on the relationship between rights and resources, and speak to the assumptions about accountability outlined above. In particular, these chapters focus on a variety of formal and informal strategies adopted by different groups to contest access to specific resources (see Table 1.1 in the Introduction). The rights claims in these cases can be categorised into two types. Some are claims of entitlement to a particular resource, as in the case of water in South Africa, housing in Kenya, and the health care system in Brazil. Others are claims of access to a resource, as in the case of the watersheds and natural reserves in Mexico. What is important is how these different rights claims are interrelated, and the intertwining of different types of rights (political, social and economic) in practice. While the claims to entitlement may spring from the immediate and pressing material deprivations people experience, the struggles over gaining access and control over these resources bring a whole range of other rights and accountability relationships into play. For example, the struggle of the Mombasa tenants' association to secure access to adequate housing has had to address the significant political corruption and lack of transparency in the council authorities, bringing political rights, such as the right to information, to the fore. For these tenants, securing access to housing is important for reasons beyond their physical needs – it is also about their sense of belonging and citizenship, which is tied to having a legitimate claim to their homes.

As we noted in the introduction, the cases in this book show not only how different types of rights are indivisible, but also how there can be conflicts between and among different rights. We see in the next section on corporate accountability how the rights of corporate actors can conflict with those of poorer communities, but there can also be conflicts between rights that emerge through the mobilisation strategies of communities. For example, in Mexico, the direct action of rural indigenous groups in cutting off a dam deprived downstream urban groups of their right to water. Yet this direct action was part of the informal strategies the rural indigenous groups used to demand accountability from municipal governments. These conflicts between rights have important implications for the extent to which they can be used as a strategy for demanding accountability.

The chapters in this section offer some important lessons about the circumstances in which these mobilisations to demand accountability can be successful. There is a clear division between short-term and long-term strategies for gaining access to resources. The short-term strategies of indigenous municipalities in the watershed in Veracruz, Mexico have led to a tokenistic response by the government in order to forestall direct social action. When the indigenous people shut down the dam and the water supply to the cities below, the municipal government reacted with offers of paved roads, funds towards clinics and schools for the indigenous communities. But these concessions, while couched in the language of fulfilling the rights of the indigenous communities, actually served as a palliative for defusing the social mobilisation without addressing the real issue of the responsibility for managing the watershed that is the essential basis of the right to water for both rural and urban communities. On the other hand, there is also the possibility that even short-term strategies, which result in rapid victories over marginal issues, can eventually have more transformative effects.

Another challenge for informal strategies and mobilisations around rights over resources is scale. In many cases – including Mexico, Brazil, South Africa and Kenya – mobilisations have led to key victories. But the challenge, given the complexity of actors and institutional relationships, is how to scale up (or down) these advances in a way that leads to substantive changes to government institutions. In South Africa, the right to water exists in the constitution, but in practice the right is not evenly upheld. In Kenya, gains at the local level by the tenants' association are difficult to sustain and scale up to council authority level because of political and financial pressure on the groups demanding accountability.

In Chapter 1, we discussed the limits of the law and the role of the state in the politics of how rights are defined. In addition, these chapters show how national and international legal frameworks have a central role in determining how rights over resources are realised and accountability relationships are established. But far from being a neutral enforcer of these obligations, the state plays a political role in terms of how resources are defined and allocated, so that the limits of the law and of legal frameworks become apparent. In the case of protected natural areas (PNAs) in Mexico, conflict continues over how natural resources are defined – indigenous groups are claiming knowledge rights in these areas, while international NGOs and others are constructing the rainforest as the object of conservation, and the government is attempting to enforce bans on using the rainforest for conservationist and geopolitical reasons. The chapters in this section reinforce the focus in the existing literature on ecological democracy (Watts 2003) and feminist political ecology (Rochelau *et al.* 1995) on 'how local communities resisted the incursions of the state, and how the state in turn attempted to "criminalise" local customary rights' over access to and control over resources (Watts 2003). These cases demonstrate how the state can act as a guarantor of accountability and also perpetuate a lack of accountability.

This section will explore the complex relationships between rights and resources in terms of accountability both by broadening the definition of resources and by focusing on the multiple strategies, informal as well as formal, for making rights claims in relationship to those resources. In so doing, these chapters raise some important challenges to dominant assumptions about the transformative effects of technocratic approaches to accountability and top-down versions of rights. By taking deprivation and the lack of access to resources as a starting point, these chapters investigate the political economy of gaining access to these resources, and the cultural politics of making rights claims. Within this complex landscape of actors, interests and discourses, it becomes clear that accountabilities must be claimed and negotiated by poor and less privileged people themselves if the fundamental issue of access to society's wealth and resources is to be addressed.

REFERENCES

Rocheleau, D., Thomas-Slayter, B. and Wangari, E. (eds) (1995) *Feminist Political Ecology*, London: Routledge.

Watts, M. (2003) 'Economies of Violence: More Oil, More Blood' *Economic and Political Weekly*, Vol. 38, No. 48, pp. 5089–99.

CHAPTER 3

Do human rights make a difference to poor and vulnerable people? Accountability for the right to water in South Africa[1]

LYLA MEHTA

To what extent is accountability key to realising rights? In struggles over access to water, conflicts between market- and rights-based frameworks imply distinct strategies of accountability. The former implies consumers holding service providers to account. In this understanding, citizens are consumers and accountability is exercised through the implied contract, mediated by the market, between customer and water utility, even if the state remains responsible for regulating private service providers to ensure they meet the needs of the poor. Rights-based frameworks, on the other hand, assume that accountability claims will be pursued through and mediated by the state. This confers upon the state the power to both respect and deny rights, the consequences of which are explored below.

In the past decade, the rights discourse has gained currency in international development. A human rights approach to development is seen as moving away from looking at charity or handouts to empowerment and securing firm rights to 'the requirements, freedoms and choices necessary for life and development in dignity' (Hausermann 1998). Despite the fact that support for the human rights movement has been growing considerably and a human rights approach to development is now fairly mainstream, there is a growing acknowledgement that many of the world's poor and marginalised have yet to enjoy the benefits of these rights. There are many possible reasons for this.

First, *sins of omission* may deny citizens access to social and economic rights. It is well known that poor states may not prioritise the provision of education, water and housing for all. Also, many developing countries lack the resources to make good the rights that allow all citizens to live a life of dignity, or the institutional capacity to establish these rights. Conversely, citizens may not be aware of their rights and may not have the capacity to mobilise around them. Second, *sins of commission* may deprive people of rights. The rights of vulnerable people may knowingly be put at risk or even violated for a variety of reasons. For example, freedom of speech and the right to protest are severely restricted under dictatorships. Moreover, as this chapter demonstrates, states and global players may introduce macroeconomic policies that violate basic rights in the name of development or growth. It is, however, the lack of mechanisms of accountability and poor regulation on the part of states that allow both sins of omission and commission to flourish, preventing economic and social rights from becoming real.

Accountability is usually seen as the means through which the less powerful can hold more powerful actors to account (Goetz and Jenkins 2004). Traditionally, it is governments that are mainly responsible for protecting people's rights, but there is an increasing need to hold private sector and global actors to account for policies and programmes that have a far-reaching impact on the rights and well-being of poor and vulnerable people. Diffuse and unclear rules of accountability for global players and non-state players are problematic when most human rights declarations focus on states as the primary deliverers and protectors of rights.

Rights claiming is a way to demand accountability from powerful players. But, as this chapter demonstrates, accountability is an issue that is still missing from many human rights debates. For the Millennium Development Goals and other processes to be successful, attention must be paid to several contradictions and questions. Do paradoxical outcomes arise from a dual commitment to markets and rights, compromising people's basic rights while making it difficult to enforce accountability mechanisms? Can poor institutional capacity and low resource allocation impede the realisation of economic and social rights? Do the necessary accountability mechanisms exist to hold the powerful to account? Is there an ambiguity about responsibilities and duty bearers when economic and social rights are violated?

This chapter focuses on these issues and questions by examining the right to water in South Africa.[2] In 2002, the UN Economic, Social and Cultural Council gave a lot of prominence to the right to water through its General Comment No. 15, which applies an authoritative interpretation of the International Covenant on Economic, Social and Cultural Rights (ICESCR, 1966), ratified by 148 states. The Comment, not a legally binding document, stated explicitly that the right to water is a human right and that responsibility for the provision of sufficient, safe, affordable water to everyone, without discrimination, rests with the state. States are thus clearly responsible for progressively realising the right to water.

Here I examine both the ideological currents underpinning the water debate in South Africa and its institutional, administrative and policy environment in order to understand the importance of accountability in realising the right to water. The chapter draws on empirical research conducted in 2002 and 2003. Interviews were conducted with NGO representatives, villagers, academics, policy makers and private sector representatives in Cape Town, Pretoria, Johannesburg and in the Eastern Cape province of South Africa.

Dancing to the two tunes of rights and markets?

South Africa is the only country that recognises the human right to water at both the constitutional and policy level. Moreover, its Free Basic Water (FBW) policy goes against the grain of conventional wisdom in the water sector, which stresses cost recovery mechanisms and shies away from endorsing the human right to water (Mehta 2003). Since early 2000, the Department for Water Affairs and Forestry has been investigating providing a basic level of water free to all citizens. In February 2001 the government announced that it was going to provide a basic supply of 6,000 litres of safe water per month to all households free of charge (based on an average household size of eight people). The Water Services Act 108 of 1997 states that a basic level of water should be provided to those who cannot pay, and the FBW policy emanates from the legal provisions of the Act. The main source of funding for this initiative is the Municipal Infrastructure Grant, a conditional capital grant for the provision of infrastructure, and the Equitable Share Grant, an unconditional grant from the central government to local authorities intended for operational expenditure. The latter amounts to about R7.5 billion a year (R1 = US$0.158) and is from national taxes for the provision of basic services.[3]

While the government of South Africa stands alone internationally in endorsing the constitutional right to water, its policies have been informed by several dominant water management frameworks, which include an emphasis on cost recovery as well as a shift in the role of the state from direct provider of water-related goods and services to a more regulatory function, with privatisation seen as the means to overcome the past failure of public systems to provide water to the poor. Government policies draw on a quasi-consensus amongst multilateral and bilateral agencies on issues such as cost recovery, user fees, and demand management, manifested in both poor countries and middle-income settings like South Africa. For example, several authors have demonstrated the extent to which the World Bank and the International Finance Corporation (IFC) have shifted South African government thinking away from its Reconstruction and Development Programme (RDP) commitments in infrastructure and service provision, based on entitlement and welfare, towards a cost-recovery approach that can deprive poor communities of their basic right to an adequate provision of water (Pauw 2003; Bond 2001; 2002). In 1996 total cost recovery became an official policy of the government when it adopted its fiscally conservative Growth, Employment and Redistribution macroeconomic policy (GEAR). The central features of the policy are a reduced role for the state, fiscal restraint and the promotion of privatisation.

Thus, alongside the remarkable commitments to providing free water, several policy changes were introduced under World Bank influence (Pauw 2003; Bond 2001). These include the 'credible threat of cutting service' to non-paying consumers, a move which has been linked by some to cholera and other gastrointestinal outbreaks (Pauw 2003; McDonald 2002). From 1997 municipalities began to witness widespread cut-offs of basic services to non-payers (ibid.). As the cost-recovery principle was applied, households that used more than the basic amount, and found themselves unable to pay, faced disconnections. In the case of Manquele v Durban Transitional Metropolitan Council 2001 JOL 8956 (D), the High Court found that the City Council had a right to disconnect the water supply of the applicant, Mrs Manquele, because she chose not to limit herself to the water supply provided to her free of charge. However, commentators argue that by completely disconnecting her water supply the municipality deprived Mrs Manquele even of the free basic amount; this was problematic, since the right to a basic level of water supply exists notwithstanding the ability to pay (Community Law Centre 2002). While cut-offs took place even during apartheid times (when non-payment for services was a form of political resistance),[4] the level of public indignation is undoubtedly higher today, not least because of the strong importance attached to economic and social rights in South Africa's constitution.

There are controversies over the number of people who have experienced cut-offs. According to the Municipal Services Project, using representative national survey data from the Human Sciences Research Council (HSRC), ten million people have experienced cut-offs in recent years (McDonald 2002). This figure is contested, however, and has been refuted by the Department for Water Affairs and Forestry (DWAF) (Kasrils 2003) and further revised by the HSRC to approximately 2 per cent of all connected households, or over 250,000 people. Despite

DWAF's admission that such numbers are a matter of serious concern, McDonald stands by the figure of ten million and has challenged DWAF and other agencies to research a more accurate figure (*Sunday Independent* 2003). DWAF maintains, nevertheless, that under certain conditions cut-offs are permissible on the legal basis of the Strategic Framework for Water Services.[5]

As part of GEAR, the South African government also reduced grants and subsidies to local municipalities and city councils. This forced cash-strapped local authorities to turn towards privatisation as well as to enter into partnerships in order to generate the revenue no longer provided by the national state (McKinley 2003). Since local government structures were incapable of dealing with past backlogs on their own, they began to privatise public water utilities by entering into service and management partnerships with external agencies. These ranged from multinational water corporations to South African firms. The role of consortia was also key. For example, Suez, which collaborated with the apartheid government in providing water largely to the white minority, formed Water and Sanitation Services Africa (WSSA). It subsequently won 'delegated management' contracts in Queenstown, Fort Beaufort and Stutterheim (all in the Eastern Cape) (Bond *et al.* 2001). Ruiters (in Pauw 2003), who researched water privatisation in these three towns, argues that water tariffs increased up to 300 per cent between 1994 and 1999. Pauw (2003) argues that by 1996 a typical township household was paying up to 30 per cent of its income for water, sewerage and electricity. Average income in the area at the time was less than US$60 per month, with more than 50 per cent unemployed. Those who could not pay their bills (the majority) were cut off and in Queenstown special debt collectors were appointed and a reinstatement fee was introduced that was almost twice the average township income.

Implementing FBW: experiences from the Eastern Cape

The Eastern Cape is the poorest of South Africa's nine provinces, with a predominantly rural population, high unemployment, and poor access to social services. Located on the south-eastern coast, the Eastern Cape province accounts for approximately 16 per cent of South Africa's population. Of all Equitable Share Grants to the nine provinces, the Eastern Cape receives 17–18 per cent (National Treasury 1999; 2004). Research was conducted in two district municipalities in the former Transkei.[6] The Alfred Nzo District Municipality (ANDM) is one of the poorest district municipalities in the Eastern Cape. It has 50 per cent unemployment and no manufacturing industry to curb the problem.[7] Across ANDM's large, poor rural population, 214 villages have a reliable water supply, whilst more than 400 villages do not have any water scheme whatsoever. ANDM is one of the poorest district municipalities in the Eastern Cape. The O. R. Tambo District Municipality is slightly larger, with a population of over 1.6 million and an unemployment rate of 51.8 per cent. Currently available statistics indicate that only 13.2 per cent have acceptable access to safe water (SSA 2002).

The FBW policy was conceived by DWAF at the national level, but its implementation rests with local authorities, including district and local municipalities, who are designated water services authorities (local municipalities, however, have to apply to be water services authorities). Although they are free to interpret it according to the resources and capacity available, operationalising the policy has been difficult. After all, the mere endorsement of the principle of social justice does not determine how resources are to be distributed. Instead, the distribution of resources and the implementation of rights-based approaches are usually at the discretion of professionals and bureaucrats in the public sector, who lack a clear directive on how to 'implement justice' (Plant 1992: 20). This certainly echoes the experiences of officials in South Africa's Eastern Cape. Many worked in bureaucracies of the former homelands and inherited a massive backlog in 1994. They also struggle to grapple with the many political and institutional changes arising through South Africa's decentralisation process.[8]

Many of the poorer district municipalities lack financial and institutional resources to implement the policy, despite Equitable Share Grants. Monitoring and rationing the quota of free water is also very difficult. Often, it can cost more to install a water meter than to provide the water free.[9] In some cases, the FBW policy has also made charging for water difficult. Many communities understood that they would now stop paying for water (Jackson 2002), making it increasingly difficult for cash-strapped district municipalities to raise the money required.

How do poor municipalities such as ANDM raise the money to ensure water delivery? The ANDM authorities believe that it is too costly to charge for water in rural areas. They have been down that road in the past and find it an administrative burden to try to collect tariffs. Moreover, many of the schemes were underutilised – Build–Operate– Train–Transfer (BOTT) schemes, for example, which relied on expensive technology and outside experts rather than local knowledge and expertise. Existing pre-paid schemes were highly underutilised and most people continued to use natural sources of water such as untreated streams. Those using the pre-paid scheme were only collecting an average of three litres of water per person per day, which meant that a million-rand investment could not yield the benefits intended and remained underutilised. Moreover, the scheme was not addressing the problems of health and the need to free women from long-distance water collection. It is for this reason that ANDM moved away from the policy of cost recovery and is now implementing the FBW policy. ANDM has not announced the policy to the entire district municipality, however, lest serious financial problems arise in implementing it. Thus many people in the Eastern Cape, especially in the remote rural areas, are not even aware of the policy of FBW.

Free water or basic water?
It has been argued that FBW is difficult to realise in rural areas dogged by a massive backlog with respect to water supply and sanitation. In ANDM in 2003, 132 villages (with a population of about 170,000 people) were being serviced with basic schemes. By 2010 the district municipality plans to serve 420 villages (a population of about 540,000 people), still only 63 per cent of the villages in the entire district.

Clearly a long road lies ahead in ensuring water for all. ANDM has to consider both the free basic water policy as well as basic water for all. In principle, basic water for all takes precedence in the work of ANDM, together with sanitation priorities. However, there is a trade-off in implementing free water for some and basic water for all. ANDM has contracted consultants to develop business plans for priority villages within the municipality. A village with a high population size, a clinic and/or a school is generally high on the list of priorities. However, if a priority village is next to a village with low priority, the consultants have to develop a business plan that encompasses both villages as one project, because people in the next village would fail to understand why they are being bypassed whilst the other village is earmarked to get a water scheme. Indeed, failure to recognise adjacent villages could result in pipes being destroyed and water theft.

In order to ensure that basic water is provided, ANDM has introduced play pumps as interim measures in villages unlikely to receive water in the near future.[10] The play pumps are also supposed to curb the problem of cholera, which in the beginning of 2003 was a problem in other district municipalities. Play pumps cost anything between R20,000 and R100,000 with a reservoir. Thus, despite good intentions, district municipalities such as ANDM and O. R. Tambo are finding it difficult to realise FBW for all. In part this delay is due to the legacy inherited in 1994, combined with both financial and institutional constraints. At the time of writing, 55.2 per cent of the country's poor population was being served by FBW (DWAF 2005). In 2003, two years after the policy had been announced, only 50 per cent of the communities had implemented FBW (COSATU 2003).

Livelihood and poverty reduction impacts

The FBW policy was not intended to address redistribution issues, and there are other provisions in the National Water Act (for example, compulsory licensing) that deal with these. Still, we need to ask how it contributes to poverty reduction and wider social justice concerns. For example, it is intended that the 25 litres of water will be used primarily for drinking and cooking purposes. However, the poor also need to be assured of water during scarcity periods for their farming activities based on subsistence. The 25 litres a day policy largely applies to domestic water supply, and not to wider concerns of livelihood security and how to restructure existing water-user practices.

While the Committee on Economic and Social Rights does not lay down particular standards on how much water should be provided, it states that water supply must be sufficient for personal and domestic use, correspondent to WHO standards stipulating a minimum of 50–100 litres per day with an absolute minimum of 20 litres per day (COHRE 2004: 8). Thus South Africa is providing close to the absolute minimum.[11] This is why trade union leaders and other advocates argue that the South African state should grant everybody at least 50 litres of water per day *per capita*. This, they argue, is the only way in which poor farmers can successfully maintain their livelihoods and thus escape the trap of poverty and dependence on pensions.

Do enforceable social and economic rights make a difference to people's lives and livelihoods? As demonstrated above, rights-based approaches may not necessarily radically redistribute resources in a society. But do they make a difference to poor people, and what are local-level village experiences of FBW? I draw on Zolile Ntshona's interviews in two villages in the Eastern Cape (see Mehta and Ntshona 2004) to show how the daily lives of three rural women, of which two are pensioners and one is unemployed, have been affected by FBW. Mabombo is 61 years old and is entitled to an old age pension. Before the implementation of the FBW policy, she used to collect water from the spring far from her house, and used a ten-litre container to make two or three trips to the spring before sunrise. Collection from the spring was difficult for her because she had to wait for the sediments to settle before pure water emerged. She now feels that life has improved. She does not have to wake up in the morning before the livestock make the spring water murky and can concentrate her energy on other work. She uses the FBW for washing, drinking and cooking, though she still visits the spring to wash blankets. Mathungu, 70 years old, also supports a large family with her old age pension grant. She could not afford the R10 to pay for water services in her village before the implementation of the FBW policy. She has also been relieved of the need to make arduous trips to the spring on a daily basis. Masakala is an unemployed member of the water committee. Her main complaints under the FBW regime are the rules for water use. She feels that when she paid R10 a month for water she used as much as she wanted, but since the FBW policy there are restrictions, and she occasionally needs to pay for additional water.

Clearly, FBW has made a significant difference to the everyday lives of people like Mathungu, Masakala and Mabombo. For one thing, it frees women from the time taken to collect water and the health benefits are clear, since they do not need to resort to unprotected streams. However, the issue of poverty alleviation raises questions because of the restrictions imposed by the FBW policy. For example, water cannot be used or is not enough for agricultural production, which could alleviate poverty in the area. The ANDM has stated categorically that it needs to prioritise basic water provision largely for drinking and washing for all the villages first, before upgrading schemes for agricultural production.

In Mdudwa village, a gravity-fed scheme was implemented in 2001. The scheme has seven standpipes, of which six were working when the scheme started operating. In 2003, only three taps were still in operation. There is a compulsory fee of R5 at Mdudwa, which every household is expected to contribute towards operation and maintenance. Most people in the village have refused to pay the fee because the standpipes closest to their households are not working, while others are not paying because they cannot afford to pay. Still others do not want to pay because they are unhappy with the conditions of the scheme. For instance, the communities require large amounts of water for cultural purposes, such as the practice of washing blankets for funerals and other ceremonies. The scheme does not provide enough water for these activities. Therefore, since the scheme has not improved people's livelihoods and has also imposed restrictions on water use for activities which are important to them, people generally perceive it as useless. Finally, there are also many people in Mdudwa who are not aware of the FBW policy.

Lessons from South Africa's Free Basic Water policy

The South African government stands alone in recognising the constitutional right to water. This is a great achievement. Yet, despite the existence of a constitutional right to water and related policies, millions in South Africa are either not aware of or not given access to this right. Thus, a right conceived at the national level is still to be realised on the ground in many parts of the country. The South African case highlights several lessons about rights as an accountability strategy in this regard.

Realising rights in practice
The FBW policy has not been implemented in a standardised way. Water service providers (who could be private companies, water boards, district municipalities or community-based organisations) interpret the policy in different ways. In some areas, the right to water has also been hindered by market processes such as cost recovery, leading to controversial cut-offs. This chapter has demonstrated that economic and social rights fail to be realised owing to sins of omission (the lack of funds and institutional capacity) and sins of commission (where rights are knowingly put at risk). The most persistent stumbling block to realising the right to water are sins of omission, as outlined in the section on the Eastern Cape. These include capacity problems on the part of local authorities and financial constraints. But one may also argue that cut-offs and high payments are sins of commission that put poor and vulnerable people's right to water at risk. The result is that some South African citizens still do not enjoy FBW and many are not even aware of their constitutional right to 25 free litres of water per day. Thus there is very uneven access to the right to water in South Africa.

The South African case highlights the difficulty in apportioning blame for rights violations and identifying who bears obligations and responsibilities to realise rights. This is a generic feature of the contemporary world, in which processes of economic globalisation have led to the proliferation of service provision by actors other than the state. As we saw in Chapter 2 of this book, this confuses lines of accountability, as channels of representation and redress central to accountability fail to keep pace with dispersed responsibilities.

Linking rights and poverty reduction
The FBW has certainly made a difference to the lives of poor people by addressing health issues and freeing women from time taken in collecting water. Still, the issue of poverty reduction seems to be lagging behind,

especially with regards to water required for agricultural production purposes. The contentious issues concerning water for subsistence agriculture and cultural activities need to be resolved. The General Comment provides that states are required to ensure each person has access to sufficient, safe, acceptable, accessible and affordable water for personal and domestic use, and this is what the 25 litres per day per person achieves. But the Committee also states that while priority must be given to water for personal and domestic use, it is also important to recognise the need for water to meet the most essential aspects of each of the other relevant human rights (rights to livelihood, food, etcetera), for which the 25 litres do not suffice.

One reason why rights often do not make a great difference to poor people is because there is a marked lack of political will on the part of powerful stakeholders to enforce them in practice. The South African case highlights problems that arise when adequate financial resources are not provided to realise rights to water and when contradictions arise from market-based approaches. However, promoting the human right to water can only be the result of a conscious socio-political choice on the part of decision makers and local people. Continued attempts to mobilise around this right by communities and activists may provide governments with the mandate to stand by that right – for which they can subsequently be held to account, and which they can be pressured to enforce in an equitable manner.

Market dynamics versus rights

The discussion has highlighted the difficulty of implementing the principles of free basic water and cost recovery in tandem. The Committee clearly states that water should be affordable and not reduce a person's capacity to access other essential goods such as food and housing. This normally means that water must be subsidised for poor communities and provided free where necessary. This is the spirit of the FBW policy. But, the chapter has also demonstrated how cost recovery and privatisation dominate South Africa's water domain. Thus water is often unaffordable and cut-offs have contradicted and violated people's basic right to water. In rural areas such as the Eastern Cape, both willingness and ability to pay for water services were not very high, cost recovery was limited and there were many defaulters on payment for water use. There is thus a massive policy trade-off between thinking about free basic water for some and basic water for all. It is thus both dangerous and unrealistic to assume that cost recovery can be achieved amongst poor communities. When cost was an issue, a number of people continued to use unprotected sources of water. Apart from health implications, the returns on investment for schemes where cost recovery applies could not be realised, since people did not always use them. It is compounded by the inherent tensions between rights-based and market-based frameworks, which assume and require different types of account-ability politics. At times, though, markets may compromise social and economic rights since they 'can systematically deprive some individuals in order to achieve the collective benefits of efficiency' (Donnelly 1999: 628). Thus cost recovery and macroeconomic policies can have a direct negative impact on the right to water.

The politics of claiming rights and demanding accountabilities

Finally, how people demand accountability when their economic and social rights are violated is linked to the larger question of how rights are interpreted and deployed by local people. In urban areas, famous cases such as Grootboom (named after Irene Grootboom) have highlighted how poor people can be agents of change as they appeal to the Constitutional Court to advance their constitutional rights to basic services. In 2000, residents of Wallacedene, a large shantytown in the Cape Town area, made legal history when the Constitutional Court ruled in favour of their housing rights. Today, four years on, the people behind the historic Wallacedene settlement are still waiting for proper housing facilities. In fact, as one commentator argues, the only concrete building that the residents have is a stinking ablution block with broken pipes and inadequate sanitation (Schoonakev 2004). Since the Constitutional Court failed to specify which manifestation of the state – national, provincial or local – should honour the rights of the residents, there is a lack of clarity on where the locus of responsibility lies with regard to the implementation of the Grootboom judgement. The Constitutional Court also did not play any role in supervising or overseeing the implementation of the various orders, and the South Africa Human Rights Commission is only playing a monitoring role. Residents are angry because they now do not know where to turn. This highlights the difficulty of specifying duty bearers and their responsibilities in implementing economic and social rights.

In remote rural areas such as the Eastern Cape, the capacity of citizens to claim their constitutional rights to basic services is far lower than in the cities. Many people are not aware of their constitutional right to water. Therefore, they are less likely to hold the government to account if their rights are violated. In part this is because of their ignorance of these rights, and in part it is because the mediators of justice (courts, lawyers, activists) are more likely to operate in metropolitan areas than in remote rural ones.

These problems should not detract from the fact that constitutional endorsements of social and economic rights are very important. In acknowledging the right to water, the South African government has gone against the grain of conventional wisdoms, both on questions of the rights and entitlements of citizens and as reflected in donor debates on water provision. In this respect, the FBW is a remarkable achievement. Defending the constitutional right to water, poor people have success-fully moved the courts to grant interim relief from disconnections. However, in order for rights to be more effective, attention needs to be paid to the caveats presented here: the lack of attention to poverty and livelihood questions; the problematic implementation of the policy; the lack of awareness; and the variable levels of accountability mechanisms to provide redress.

Implications for accountability

With the inclusion of new private actors, states are not merely enforcers of rights, but increasingly act as regulators and facilitators of rights (INTRAC 2003). Unfortunately, the General Comment and other such instruments do not explicitly identify private actors as accountable and responsible. Ironically, too, rights are denied at the 'behest of powers beyond the state itself' (INTRAC 2003: 3). For example, International Monetary Fund (IMF) and World Bank policies oblige states to curtail basic services and impose charges that exclude large numbers of vulnerable people. In this sense, global pressures have led to the state assuming a schizophrenic role as both the enforcer and violator of rights. Only the state can properly regulate the behaviour of markets and ensure that economic actors operate in a fair and transparent manner; only the state can provide adequate social protection to those who suffer insecurity and a loss of rights (ICHRP 2004: 60). But governments also become violators of rights by enforcing policies and programmes such as privatisation and structural adjustment that can erode people's rights. Protective provisions do exist. For example, under the Water Service Act no disconnections can take place on the grounds of inability to pay. But the onus of proving ability lies with the water user and will depend on the user's ability to access legal advice and representation – a minimal resource in many communities (COHRE 2004: 54). Thus links between ordinary citizens and their representatives in South Africa have become obscured through policy shifts towards GEAR and orthodox forms of neoliberal economic globalisation. This makes tracking processes of accountability difficult across these multiple scales.

This should not detract from the fact that rights do and should matter. The right to water is internationally recognised by both developing and industrialised countries as defined in General Comment 15. It includes clearly defined and realisable obligations, and thus forms the basis of concrete negotiations between the state, the communities concerned and civil society advocates. Moreover, the right to water in principle provides justiciable components to local claims and struggles around water and can also be used as a countervailing force against the commodification of water, which can impinge on poor people's rights. That few people in South Africa or around the world are demanding compliance and answerability on the right to water is another matter. But local struggles to realise the right to water are on the rise and the demand for accountability from water providers and those responsible for protecting this right will also therefore increase. If human rights are really to make a difference, we can only hope that more attention will be paid to the accountability mechanisms through which compliance and answerability become an indispensable aspect of the human rights regime.

NOTES

1 The empirical material in this chapter was generated through research conducted for the DfID-funded Sustainable Livelihoods in Southern African research programme and some sections of the chapter draw on Mehta and Ntshona (2004). I am very grateful to all my interview partners in South Africa for sharing their knowledge with me and to Zolile Ntshona for his insights and meticulous research. I thank Nurit Bodemann-Ostow and Paul Wright for their research assistance and competent internet searches. Comments by Carlos Cortez, the editors, Ian Scoones and Lisa Thompson helped strengthen the chapter. However, all responsibility for the errors that remain rests with me.

2 The Centre on Housing Rights and Evictions (COHRE) in Geneva, which has done extensive research on the right to water, clearly lays down the legal basis for the right to water (COHRE 2004). At the 1977 United National Water Conference, the Mar del Plata Declaration recognised that all peoples 'have the right to have access to drinking water in quantities and of a quality equal to their basic needs'. It has subsequently been recognised explicitly in several legally binding treaties, such as the Convention on the Elimination of all Forms of Discrimination Against Women (CEDAW, 1979), the Convention on the Rights of the Child (1989) and, more recently, in the General Comment 15.

3 DWAF official, personal communication by email, 16 May 2005.

4 Barry Jackson, personal communication, 23 December 2003.

5 DWAF official, personal communication by email, 16 May 2005.

6 See Mehta and Ntshona (2004) for more details.

7 Interview with the Deputy Director, Water and Sanitation, Alfred Nzo District Municipality, 10 December 2002.

8 Budget cuts have gone hand in hand with decentralisation in South Africa (Manor 2001). The function of water services provision is now performed by the municipality itself or by other public or private bodies. While this process devolves power to local authorities and gives more voice to ordinary citizens, it can also lead to shedding of functions and the dumping of 'unfunded mandates' on lower levels of government, which poor rural municipalities are not able to implement (Olver 1998).

9 Interview with DWAF official, Mount Ayliff, 23 April 2002.

10 Play pumps are designed in such a way that anyone can operate them. Children, who can get on and off the wheel as they play, can turn the horizontal wheel.

11 Of course what counts as 'sufficient water' is controversial. It is known that people can also survive on 10 litres of water a day (Mehta 2005).

REFERENCES

Bond, P. (2001) 'Privatisation, Participation and Protest in the Restructuring of Municipal Services: Grounds for Opposing World Bank Promotion of "Public–Private Partnerships"', The Water Page, www.thewaterpage.com/ppp_debate1.htm (accessed 16 November 2003).

—— (2002) 'Local Economic Development Debates in South Africa', Occasional Papers Series, No. 6, Municipal Services Project.

Bond, P., McDonald, D., Ruiters, G. and Greeff, L. (2001) Water Privatisation in Southern Africa: the State of the Debate, Cape Town: Environmental Monitoring Group.

COHRE (2004) 'Legal Resources for the Right to Water: International and National Standards', Geneva: Centre on Housing Rights and Evictions.

Community Law Centre, Socioeconomic Rights Project (2002) 'South African Cases: High Court Cases: Residents of Bon Vista Mansions v Southern Metropolitan Local Council 2002 (6) BCLR 625 (W)', http://www.communitylawcentre.org.za/ser/casereviews/2002_6_BCLR_625.php (accessed 18 March 2005).

COSATU (2003) 'Joint Submission by COSATU and SAMWU on the Draft White Paper on Water Services Presented to the DWAF', Congress of South African Trade Unions and South African Municipal Workers' Union, http://www.queensu.ca/msp/pages/Project_Publications/Reports/CosatuSamwu.pdf (accessed 18 March 2005).

Donnelly, J. (1999) 'Human rights, democracy and development', Human Rights Quarterly, No. 21, pp. 608–32.

DWAF (2005) 'Free Basic Water Project, Implementation Status', Department of Water, Agriculture and Forestry, http://www.dwaf.gov.za/FreeBasicWater/Defaulthome.asp (accessed 18 March 2005).

Goetz, A. and Jenkins, R. (2004) Reinventing Accountability: Making Democracy Work for Human Development, Basingstoke: Palgrave Macmillan.

Hausermann, J. (1998) A Human Rights Approach to Development, London: Department for International Development.

ICHRP (2004) Enhancing Access to Human Rights, Versoix, Switzerland: International Council on Human Rights Policy.

INTRAC (2003) 'Viewpoint: Rights or Values?', Newsletter of the International NGO Training and Research Centre, Oxford.

Jackson, B. (2002) 'Free Water – What Are the Chances of Serving the Poor', mimeo, Johannesburg: Municipal Infrastructure Investment Unit.

Kasrils, R. (2003) 'Minister Kasrils Responds to False Claim of 10 Million Cut-offs', www.dwaf.gov.za/Communications/Articles/Minister/2003/Cutoffs%20article%20WE BSITE.doc (accessed 4 May 2004).

McDonald, D. (2002) 'The Bell Tolls for Thee: Cost Recovery, Cut-offs and the Affordability of Municipal Services in South Africa', Municipal Services Project, http://qsilver.queensu.ca/~mspadmin/pages/Project_Publications/Reports/bell.htm (accessed 12 December 2003).

McKinley, D. (2003) 'Water is Life: the Anti-Privatisation Forum and the Struggle against Water Privatisation', Public Citizen, http://www.citizen.org/cmep/Water/cmep_Water/ reports/southafrica/articles.cfm?ID=10554 (accessed 12 December 2003).

Mehta, L. (2003) 'Problems of Publicness and Access Rights: Perspectives from the Water Domain', in I. Kaul, P. Conceiçao, K. Le Goulven and R. Mendoza (eds), *Providing Global Public Goods: Managing Globalisation*, Oxford: Oxford University Press.

—— (2004) 'From State Control to Market Regulation: behind the Border Policy Convergence in Water Management', IDS Working Paper No. 233, Brighton: Institute of Development Studies.

—— (2005) *The Politics and Poetics of Water. Naturalising Scarcity in Western India*, New Delhi: Orient Longman.

Mehta, L and Nshtona, Z. (2004) 'Dancing to Two Tunes: Rights and Market-based Approaches in South Africa's Water Domain', Sustainable Livelihoods in Southern Africa Research Report 17, Brighton: Institute of Development Studies.

National Treasury (1999) 'Provincial and Local Government Finances', *National Budget Review 1999*, Republic of South Africa, Chapter 4, http://www.treasury.gov.za/documents/budget/1999/review/chapter_4.pdf (accessed 7 May 2004).

—— (2004) 'Provincial and Local Government Allocations', *National Budget Review 2004*, Republic of South Africa, Chapter 7, http://www.finance.gov.za/documents/budget/2004/review/Chapter%207.pdf (accessed 7 May 2004).

Olver, C. (1998) 'Blueprint for the Business of Running Efficient Cities', *Sunday Times* (South Africa), 14 June 1998, http://www.suntimes.co.za/1998/06/14/insight/in04.htm (accessed 28 May 2004).

Pauw, J. (2003) 'Metered to Death: How a Water Experiment Caused Riots and a Cholera Epidemic', The Centre for Public Integrity, http://www.icij.org/water/report.aspx?sID=ch&rID=49&aID=49 (accessed 11 November 2003).

Plant, R. (1992) 'Citizenship, Rights and Welfare', in A. Coote (ed.), *The Welfare of Citizens: Developing New Social Rights*, London: Institute for Public Policy Research.

Schoonaker, B. (2004) 'Treated with Contempt', *Sunday Times*, 21 March.

SSA (2002) 'Measuring Rural Development: Baseline Statistics for the Integrated Sustainable Rural Development Strategy', Pretoria: Statistics South Africa.

Sunday Independent (2003) 'Attack the Problem not the Data: Report on the Number of People Affected by Water Cut-offs Was Based on Sound Methodology', 15 June 2003.

CHAPTER 4

Managing watersheds and the right to water: Indigenous communities in search of accountability and inclusion in Southern Veracruz

LUISA PARÉ AND CARLOS ROBLES[1]

The nature of the problem

Ecological degradation and economic injustice are often the result of the extraction or transfer of natural resources from poorer to richer, more influential regions. Dams, highway constructions and other major public works projects frequently generate conflict over natural resources that can be linked to a lack of accountability and adequate compensation mechanisms to address the impacts of natural resource extraction and exploitation. The story told in this chapter is one of imbalances of power between local communities and local, regional and national institutions; and of the conflicts and accountability problems related to these imbalances. The tensions that arise between these actors centre on the right to water; who exercises it and how; and the barriers to realising that right. A key issue that emerges in this case is the difficulty in realising the right to water and establishing accountability over how watersheds are managed, given the complex sets of actors and overlapping institutions and histories involved.[2]

Research for this chapter was carried out in the watershed of the Huazuntlán river (a tributary of the Coatzacoalcos) in southern Veracruz on the coast of the Gulf of Mexico, an area that provides 75 per cent of the water for industrial and human use in two petro-industrial urban areas with over half a million inhabitants, Coatzacoalcos and Minatitlán. To supply water needed to fuel the oil industry along the coast of southeastern Mexico, water from the watershed is captured at the Yuribia dam (above the town of Tatahuicapan) in the rural mountainous rain forest region and transported for 60 kilometres by aqueduct to the cities below.[3] The compensation that these cities pay (or do not pay) to the indigenous communities living in the watershed is at the heart of a long history of conflict that has developed between these communities and the urban public water authorities.

This extraction accounts for water scarcity, both for urban dwellers and for rural people, because it has not been accompanied by the sustainable management of the watershed territory. After heavy rains, urban households often lack water for three days because of the excess of sediment that clogs the dam and water treatment facilities. This problem is related, on one hand, to a model of development that promoted forms of land use unsuitable to tropical soils, such as the extension of large-scale cattle ranching (Tudela 1989; Ewell and Poleman, 1980; Lazos and Paré 2000). On the other hand, it is related to inadequate planning and fragmented (sectorialised) public policies, and a centralised system of decision making. Decentralisation reforms in Mexico are intended to create spaces for public participation and accountability mechanisms, but these are often only consultative and not representative, and lack a permanent institutional life (Ribot 2002; Blauert 2004).[4]

Against this background, this chapter will examine the different strategies used by indigenous communities to realise the right to water and, in seeking compensation for water transfer, to build accountability in the way that the watershed is used and managed. It considers the governance issues, changes in perceptions of water and rights, mechanisms for participation and accountability (or their absence), and the conditions that prevent or lead to successful mobilisation for accountability. What this chapter reveals is that building accountability and co-responsibility between numerous actors with diverse and contradictory interests requires an ongoing process of negotiation and engagement through both formal and informal channels. For the rural indigenous groups living in the watershed, establishing accountability and protecting their right to water involves new challenges in establishing horizontal relationships of co-responsibility. These have to emerge within the communities themselves around the responsibility for maintaining the watershed, as well as between the indigenous communities, the urban municipalities and the reserve management. Our argument about accountability, therefore, is that the governance of (scarce) water requires a variety of mechanisms that can help to reconcile competing notions of accountability and correlate the associated rights and duties (see Mehta, Chapter 3). This chapter will show how traditional indigenous values can provide the basis for constructing a new, more solidly grounded culture of accountability.

The chapter includes a methodological and conceptual framework; a mapping of the social actors involved in water governance, and of their interests and perceptions; a description of the institutional and legal framework for water management and the gaps in mechanisms of accountability; and a discussion of the claims made by community organisations, and the resulting contestations, in the struggle to establish accountability. The chapter ends with some reflections on our role as researchers working to promote participatory and accountable natural resource management practices, and some conclusions about when particular strategies for demanding accountability around the right to water are successful. As an example of this, we present the strategy we designed in partnership with community groups for compensation of the environmental services they are providing.

Multiple strategies for natural resources management: a conceptual framework

In Mexico, the neoliberal development model's privileging of market forces has accelerated environmental destruction and the erosion of traditional local institutions. Major development projects have often deepened regional inequalities and the urban–rural gap as well as increasing social and political exclusion and poverty. The absence of an framework to address these inequalities is due to a lack of developed accountability mechanisms and rules, the poor enforcement of those that do exist, and the persistence of a political culture based on client–patron relationships (Paré 1975).

When communities lose control over their land, environmental degradation and poverty increases. In this case study, the transformation of land use, from slash-and-burn indigenous maize production into cattle ranching, has brought about not only the disruption of the rainforest landscape but also major social, cultural and political transformations.[5] Some authors define 'resilience' as the capacity of ecosystems to absorb disturbances or recuperate from natural events such as floods (Berkes 2004). But the capacity of ecosystems to regenerate is also influenced by the relationship between environmental and social change, and by social actors and institutions. In this case study, the relationship between environmental degradation and community institutions has an important influence on accountability issues.

Traditional notions of accountability are mostly limited to the obligation of governments to explain and justify their actions to citizens (Day and Klein 1987; Schacter 2000) and to electoral issues of ensuring 'free and fair elections'. A narrow notion of accountability, as discussed in the introduction to this volume, is often reduced within a good governance agenda to 'transparency',[6] focusing on the right to information. But a broader concept of societal accountability, as we saw in Chapter 2, 'involves social mechanisms outside the electoral sphere in which social movements supervise the legality of procedures carried out by politicians and public officials' (Smulovitz and Peruzzotti 2000: 32–3).[7] Also helpful to our discussion is the concept of co-governance for accountability, which 'confuses the boundary between state and society: in addition to co-producing specific services and pressuring government from the outside, social actors can also participate directly in the core functions of government itself' (Ackerman 2004: 451).

In terms of our case study, accountability is not reduced to a vertical claim by people against the state, but involves a two-way relationship in which different actors mutually claim their rights, and also define their obligations. Achieving accountability is not a question of merely creating institutional arrangements from above, but a process that requires new forms of negotiation and institutional arrangements for natural resource management that can benefit both those living within the protected areas and those outside them (Gaventa 2004).

Currently, and in relation to water specifically, there is a paradigm shift in the way that natural resources are seen. Water has moved from a common good to a tradable commodity (see Mehta, this volume), a shift that often distracts from community responsibilities for natural resource management. For example, in Mexico, payment for environmental services is seen, by the social movements organised around the opposition to mega projects and hydroelectric dams, as another attempt to privatise natural resources. In the final section of this chapter we describe our own experiences in relation to payment for environmental services, and examine the conditions under which it can provide better institutional arrangements that improve environmental conditions and livelihoods.

Starting with the premise that people are not necessarily a threat to ecosystems but can be a force for conservation (Buck et al. 2001), it has been our intention to carry out a joint enquiry with communities into arrangements over water use and how indigenous people have confronted the situation they face. Our concern is not only to increase academic understanding but to generate reflections that contribute to effective collective action, and to identify alternative solutions, consistent with strategies of civil accountability described in Chapter 2.

As action researchers and active promoters of proposals for how accountability could be improved, we saw our role as part of a creative process of collective learning (Leeuwis 2000) (see Box 4.1, p. 95).[8] Towards this end, we organised a range of activities including fora, workshops, focus groups with local actors, training programmes and community resource mapping. Sharing history, culture, environmental policies and landscape assessment with the local population opened the doors to an intercultural dialogue, which helped to create a common vision of the problems. Working on 'both sides of the equation' (that is, through dialogue with both government institutions and communities) aims to increase 'the receptivity of voice or responsiveness by the state' (Gaventa 2004: 17), although there was often resistance on the part of government institutions. In the conclusion to this chapter, we refer to the lessons learnt: the successes, difficulties and failures of this approach in building a new culture of accountability that connects rural and urban relationships to water management.

Mapping the different actors involved: conflicting uses, interests and perceptions

Figure 4.1 gives a picture of how the fluidity of water connects a variety of social actors. On its way down from the mountains in the reserve, the Texizapa river provides water for more than 13,000 people at local level. The Tecomaxochapan sacred spring has been transformed into a reservoir for the village of Tatahuicapan. Since 1985 the Yuribia dam has been diverting 800 litres per second from the Texizapa river to the industrial cities on the coast.

The current conditions of the watershed are not favourable to its conservation on a long-term basis. Pesticides, slash-and-burn agriculture on hills inclined at more than 35 per cent and cattle ranching produce erosion, pollution and sedimentation. The shrinking water volume seems to be of major concern to all the actors involved, including the people who live in the cities (especially the poor communities, who pay a disproportionately high cost for water), residents of the downstream villages, cattle ranchers using land on the reserve, and the urban municipalities authorities that control water distribution.

In Tatahuicapan, water is free and is seen as a common good. However the ecological conditions for resource management are now subject to individual or family-based decisions because the supportive societal norms either do not exist anymore or are not respected. The resilience of the system under these conditions is at risk. The fluidity of water streaming down the watershed is mirrored in the different interests and perceptions of different users regarding the nature of water and how it

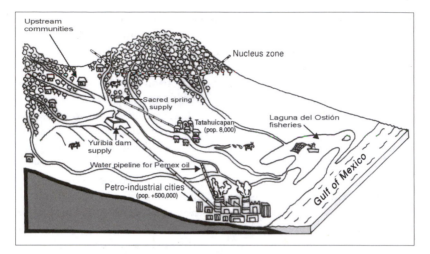

FIGURE 4.1 TEXIZAPA WATERSHED CATCHMENT: DIFFERENT WATER
SUPPLY USES

should be used. Indigenous groups now claim the right to reciprocity for
water extraction, and thereby to development, whereas the urban poor
see water as a basic right. Indigenous communities base their claims to
water on cultural and mythical tradition, as well as on specific livelihood
needs. In the cities, people have no idea of the ecological problems
upstream, the causes of water scarcity, or the threats regarding future
supply. They perceive water service as expensive and inefficient; in
moments of shortage, their interests and rights appear to be in conflict
with those of the rural providers.

Table 4.1 helps to show the multiple actors and competing interests
involved, including ourselves, as researchers.

Conflicting interests and perceptions over water

In order to understand the range of conflicting interests between so many
different actors around the management of the watershed, how claims
have developed and what strategies were used in different moments to
build accountability, we sketch out a brief history of the institutional
changes at local level, their effects on land use, the transformation of the
rainforest, and perceptions of water. Across the region there is a strong
sense of identity tied to the land. This is partly because at the end of the
nineteenth century, before the Mexican Revolution, indigenous people

TABLE 4.1 MULTIPLE ACTORS AND COMPETING CLAIMS

Key accountability conflicts	Actors involved	Competing claims to water/watershed
Access to water	*Ejidos*/Ranchers	Agriculture
	Urban municipalities	Extraction for drinking water
	Rural municipalities	Drinking water/sacred resource
	Petrochemical industries	Extraction for industrial use
Distribution of water	Rural municipalities	Dam on municipal territory, watershed includes *ejidos*
	Urban municipalities	Water shortages affect urban residents
	Reserve management	Conserving rainforest
Watershed maintenance and conservation	Rural municipalities	Sustainable livelihoods
	Urban municipalities	Periodic compensation to rural municipalities for watershed mainte-nance
	Reserve management	Rainforest conserva-tion and livelihood protection
	Universities/NGOs (including ourselves)	Environmental conser-vation, poverty reduction
	Federal and state government	Environmental conser-vation, economic development

lost part of their land to large landowners. Through agrarian reform, land was partially recuperated, but is now under the legal status defined by the state (*ejido* land tenure).

Prior to 1960, *ejido* land was owned in a communal way and traditional authorities – elder council, village chief (*jefe de pueblo*) – coexisted with *ejido* authorities recognised by the Agrarian Affairs Department (Veláz-quez 1997). The main crops were maize and beans. Water was perceived by the indigenous peasants of Tatahuicapan as a common good and local rules for its protection were strictly enforced through sanctions such as publicly exhibiting the offender or charging fines.[9] For example, logging was banned on common land, and river banks remained forested. Sporadically, Tatahuicapan cattle ranchers ran for the municipal presidency, and began to gain more influence.

Over the next twenty years, significant colonisation occurred as land was taken over, fenced in and virtually privatised into individual plots as government programmes gave priority to cattle ranching.[10] But small indigenous cattle ranchers fought to redistribute the land that had been monopolised, won a significant court case, and began to gain political force. Water was still perceived as a common good, with shared rules for access, independent of the individualisation of land holding. In losing power at local level, big ranchers also lost their positions in the municipal governments, and this contributed to their loss of control over land they had gained in the previous decades.

When the Yuribia dam was built in 1985, a large popular movement put pressure on the state government to respond to claims for education, health and public construction works for this marginalised area.[11] After the dam was seized by villagers from the whole watershed area in 1985, the city government of Coatzacoalcos signed an agreement where, in return for water, it would provide the necessary investment to improve urban infrastructure and services in Tatahuicapan. When the city later reneged on the agreement, further mobilisation by the residents of Tatahuicapan led to negotiations for additional concessions. Shutting down the valves of the dam was the best way that they could find to make their voices heard, and the success of this strategy has meant that water has become a weighty factor in the mechanics of social and political pressure.

Water has also gained an economic and a socio-political value for Tatahuicapan. Because the dam is on land owned by Tatahuicapan, the town itself has gained political clout and economic importance. Now in Tatahuicapan water transfer from the watershed to the cities is seen not only negatively but as an important instrument of negotiation. But despite concessions on services such as clinics and roads, no agreement was reached between the urban and rural municipal governments about watershed management. This brief description illustrates how perceptions of water have evolved following changes in landholding systems and patterns of water use.

Water management: gaps in mechanisms of participation and accountability

The fluid nature of water disperses its management between as many different institutions as the territories it crosses, resulting in atomisation of public interventions (land, water, forestry, agriculture, fisheries) and problematising greater inclusion and horizontal linkages between rural communities. The question of who is accountable to whom and on which issues becomes very complex as it involves multiple layers and chains of actors and institutions. In the next section, a short description of actors' interests and dynamics will help to contextualise our work as action researchers and the proposal to local government discussed later.

The dynamics of local institutions[12]
Specific conditions in the villages present a challenge to the adequate management of resources. It is through community institutions that the federal and state government applies its social, environmental and productive policies and programmes. For some indigenous people, water is sacred because they believe that revered spirits inhabit rivers and streams: this religious perspective is in paradoxical conflict with the poor management reflected by common practices such as pollution, deforestation and unsustainable fishery practices.[11]

At the local level, the most important spaces for public participation are the assemblies (by *ejido*, village and barrio) and the working commissions. Changes in these institutions wrought by external programmes and actors have reduced communal capacity to avoid negative impacts on their environment by creating or validating norms. Loss of community control is closely linked to changes in landholding systems, which have moved from communal to private tenure in 40 years. For instance, the government plan to regulate land tenure, the Programme for Secession of Ejido Rights, has contributed to the loosening of the assembly's powers to regulate land use, including sales and purchases. This practice has now expanded to include outsiders, who are not interested in local institutions such as the village assembly. Since the municipality was created, land-based governance institutions (*ejido* assembly, *comisariado ejidal* and vigilance council) have become isolated and have fewer connections with other local and regional institutions. Different political parties fight to control either the municipal government or agrarian authorities such as the Ministry of Agrarian Affairs. The current municipal government, in office for a three-year term, has become a protagonist in the politics around watershed management. But while the current municipal government is open to cooperation, the continuity of plans and possibilities for collaboration with non-governmental actors are subject to power shifts within and between political parties.

Although traditional indigenous community structures are being eroded, they still maintain principles of reciprocity and cooperation (Mauss 1967, Durstom 2002), as well as the necessary trust for the tasks required (Durstom 2000). These practices should not be romanticised, but they are important in understanding how accountability can function at the local level. For example, the *tequio* is a traditional institution used for public works based on *mano vuelta* (exchange of non-paid labour among peasants). While increasingly less common, these traditions do persist. Although the term 'accountability' does not exist in local indigenous culture, the values of reciprocity and cooperation, and the constant consultation between local authorities and the assembly on overarching issues, constitute a form of accountability in practice. Municipal government must respect decisions taken at the general public assembly. It is also on the basis of these values that villagers demand information from local authorities regarding their actions. However, there have been cases when accountability at the local level has broken down. For example, when the local water committee did not provide information on how fees villagers paid for the network maintenance were being used, people stopped paying and refused to participate in the committee's assemblies.[13] Local institutions are in constant interaction with external actors, including both the federal and state government, concerning social policies, financing and other issues. These interactions are regulated by a legal framework. The way that the legal framework is enforced, however, often does not contribute to the consolidation of long-term institutional arrangements based on consensus between the different actors involved. The next section examines this problem.

Governmental institutions

In Mexico, the legal framework for water is governed by the Law of National Waters and supported by other statutes such as the Environmental Equilibrium and Protection Law and norms related to water quality. According to the national constitution, water resources belong to the Mexican state. The National Water Commission is a semiautonomous federal authority, which is part of the Ministry of Environment. The official position of the federal government is that community participation should play a key role in the sustainable management of water. The National Hydraulic Programme for 2001–6 includes institutionalised social participation in water management through river basin councils, commissions and committees amongst its objectives. Among diverse strategies to achieve the sustainable management of water in Mexico is that of 'inducing societal recognition of water's economic value, and to consolidate organized society's participation in water management' (NHP 2001).

At the national level, 26 river basin commissions have been created to represent diverse users. However, providers from the catchment sites are not represented on these commissions. The authorities of the mountain villages such as Tatahuicapan are often unaware of the existence of their right to participate in this commission. They have not been included, although it is precisely the space where the integration between environmental, forestry and water policies could be addressed. There are some questions as to the scope for participation in the river basin commissions: this participation is relative and limited as the law confers on the National Water Commission the authority to decide whom to invite. This feature allows the Commission's officers to manipulate the balance of power and to direct decisions towards objectives already established at other levels (Castelán 2002: 183–4).

Sub-watershed and micro-watershed committees could be an important planning instrument but, throughout the country, very few have been created or function when they do exist. At the time of writing, we were still awaiting a response from a state government agency we invited to help with the formation of such a watershed committee in Texizapa. Each ministry defines its strategy without real coordination with other actors (even if legal instruments and formal agreements require holistic approaches). The result is that policies are not only uncoordinated but often contradictory. Water management institutions such as the Municipal Water and Sanitation Commission and even the National Water Commission seem to believe that their job starts from the tap down, as opposed to starting with watersheds where water is produced. Until very recently, these institutions did not coordinate their policies with the agencies in charge of the environment in the watershed such as the Management of the Reserve, the Federal Secretary for Environmental Protection and the Ministry of the Environment and Natural Resources. This fragmented vision erodes the capacity of government agencies (for both water provision and water use) to protect the ecosystems. According to the Coatzacoalcos Municipal Commission for Water and Sanitation, water supply is not guaranteed for more than eight years, yet there is no coordinated water policy for the whole mountain area. Neither have the municipalities and *ejidos* within the watershed issued norms or regulations for the protection of water resources.

The accountability issue in all of this relates to the difficulty of enforcing existing laws and procedures for a better-planned system, including coordinated institutional interventions that would benefit both the cities and rural municipalities through the creation of arrangements to mitigate future conflicts between rural and urban communities. Building accountability is difficult because local institutions lack information about their entitlements within this legal framework, and higher authorities lack political will to listen to the voice of indigenous people, even when they have sound proposals. Within this context, there is no simple recipe for creating accountability, nor will accountability be achieved merely by designing improved institutional structures. Instead, power inequities need to be confronted and new cultures of accountability nurtured.

Power struggles between these institutions are in evidence. The remit of the National Water Commission involves significant powerful interests and money. Conservation institutions such as the Ministry of the Environment and Natural Resources have smaller budgets than the ministries of Energy, Finance or Economy.[14] In a context of weak accountability and a lack of participation, it is not easy to create policy on local agreements for water conservation, or develop oversight and monitoring mechanisms that could lead to greater accountability. Given this landscape of institutional actors, the next section will explore the strategies used at the local level to build more accountable management of the watershed.

Conflicts, claims and strategies

Since the dam was built in 1985, Tatahuicapan has struggled to obtain the enforcement of state commitments concerning education, communication and health services. When the state did not deliver on these commitments, groups from Tatahuicapan cut the water supply to the cities by closing off the dam valves, which has led to further conflict. The main demand behind these cuts was and still is constructed around reciprocity as the basis of a fair exchange (water for services). However, what has developed is a cycle where conflict breaks out between the residents of Tatahuicapan and the cities' water authorities. Village residents cut the water supply or take other similar measures, and the cities respond by appeasing the residents with short-term benefits that do not address the underlying problem of sustainable watershed management. Through this pattern of conflict–negotiation–conflict, marginalised indigenous groups have obtained some short-term benefits, alleviating some social pressure for broader or more substantive changes.

However it does not always work out well for the political mediators. In 1985, when the community stopped the dam construction, community mobilisations overwhelmed the leaders. When people found out what type of negotiations their local authorities had agreed to regarding the construction of a health centre, they kidnapped the leaders and interrupted the construction until state authorities came to negotiate again. Traditional community practices of accountability required the leaders of the movement to exert pressure for compliance with the agreements.

The lack of accountability of the existing municipal authorities of Mecayapan (to which Tatahuicapan belonged at that time) in negotiations with the cities over their commitments to provide services to the villages resulted in the inhabitants of the watershed developing a strategy for direct action. In October 1993 some four thousand indigenous people, armed with bows, arrows and machetes, closed the valves of the dam and left the cities without water for three days. Four years later the new municipality of Tatahuicapan was recognised by the state Congress, which meant that the government had a responsibility to provide services to the municipality. Each case of direct action by indigenous groups against the dam is answered by the urban municipal governments with immediate material concessions, such as paving a road or contributing money towards a school. These responses do not address the underlying causes of conflict. The delay in the delivery of these concessions fuels the cycle of social mobilisation, which sometimes leads to violence. Water has become a tool to exert pressure on the government, and some groups in Tatahuicapan have clearly come to believe that cutting off the water supply is the only way to draw government attention to their needs.

It is difficult to discern if the city government's delay in introducing institutionalised accountability, such as formal procedures for compensations, is deliberate. The fact that urban authorities have managed to deal with such uncertain institutional arrangements for over 20 years shows that city governments were not under much pressure from their citizens to provide information about what really goes on in the water catchment areas and how the city water authority invests the funds from the fees paid for water. In the absence of predictable rules and durable institutions, the residents of Tatahuicapan (the weaker party) occasionally have been able to hold the city hostage in order to speed up the process of legal recognition of their territory as a separate municipality. The cost of this unpredictability for urban consumers is that they have had to put up with water shortages because city authorities do not honour agreements made with the rural mountain communities, and because the sustainable management of the catchment area seems not to be in the political interests of any of the institutional actors involved. The dynamics of conflict over water, and the strategies used by indigenous groups in Tatahuicapan to force government actors to deliver on their commitments, illustrate how accountability is a two-way relationship. Thus having adequate institutions in place does not necessarily lead to accountability in the absence of citizen action.

Building accountability through shared responsibility: a plan built through action research

Over the past three years of participatory research, we engaged in dialogue with the local government in Tatahuicapan to generate new concepts and practices for more accountable institutional arrangements over the long term. In our experience, Leeuwis's argument that solutions to the dilemma of contradictory interests are possible when the actors involved can create spaces for negotiating strategies, and find tools to strengthen trust, faces some significant challenges (Leeuwis 2000). Changes in some of the institutional relations analysed above, which are embedded in a context of conflict, clientelism, exclusion, lack of coordination, and the absence of spaces for participation, require new forms of negotiation and institutional arrangements. For instance, in practice, the government only pays compensation in some years and not in others. And as no conservation plans exist, the compensation funds are not invested in reforestation or sustainable land management projects, but in urban services in Tatahuicapan. The army manages government reforestation programmes without significant participation by local people. Only the district head municipality is allowed to participate in negotiations over the reforestation programme. The remainder of the villages in the watershed are excluded from this process.

The adoption of new political practices that can contribute to greater accountability is possible only if there is political will on both sides. Participatory governance is an alternative that can lead to increased accountability to marginalised groups, but it cannot be 'simply achieved from above with new policy statements, but … requires multiple strategies of institutional change, capacity building, and behavioural change' (Gaventa 2004: 5). This section will explore the advances that have been made in building accountability and realising the right to water, in part through our own efforts as action researchers.

Over the past three years, we have developed an agenda around building mechanisms that would lead to greater accountability and sustainable management of the watershed, involving both rural and urban poor. We have started planning meetings in the villages to organise a regional committee to facilitate a redistribution of decision-making power to local and regional levels. This committee will also help to build trust between users and providers, and between rural and urban poor and government institutions. With the institutionalisation and long-term perspective of local and regional agreements where local actors have representation, the risk of conflict is diminished. A fund will be administered by the watershed committee, on the basis of land management plans, administering and monitoring the funds for the watershed restoration.[15] This proposal creates the possibility of financing rural development by taking into account the externalities in the cost of water. Several mechanisms, including payment for environmental services, taken either from the users' fees or from subsidies, would support development infrastructure and sustainable production.

Our approach to increasing accountability is summarised in a manifesto now signed by both local government institutions and community groups: *A Strategy for Common Survival: Water and the Relationship between Tatahuicapan, Coatzacoalcos, Minatitlán and Cosoleacaque*. It synthesises many discussions with all of the key actors involved, and represents a shift from the traditional form of negotiation because it is contingent upon the willingness of representative stakeholders from both the cities and the villages to discuss new arrangements of rules.

This shift towards increased dialogue between urban and rural political institutions does not exclude the possibility of social mobilisations. As Gaventa has argued, the possibility for social mobilisation is an important element in building accountability:

> Given that inequalities in power often exist, the struggle to attain authentic and meaningful voice by community leaders may involve conflict, as well as collaboration. While some approaches to partnership overemphasise consensus building to the exclusion of conflict, others point out that conflict and collaboration often must go hand in hand. (Gaventa 2004: 16)

But the contents of the new proposal address both spaces for citizen participation, and compensation mechanisms for watershed management.

Traditionally, in exchange for water, rural indigenous communities demanded development in kind: schools, roads, health centres and basic services. Now cash is required to finance watershed restoration. The president of the Tatahuicapan municipality, in his only appearance at the commission before his term ended, announced at a river basin commission meeting that part of the resources obtained from the fees paid for water would be deposited in a municipal fund as a form of 'social investment for sustainability' to finance projects for the watershed restoration.[16] This proposal has some advantages over the mainstream approach of payment for environmental services, as we explain below.

The federal government has initiated a 'Payment for Hydrological Environmental Services Programme'. However, in the Tuxtlas watershed, the failure of the government to deliver the payment promised during the first year in that part of the reserve provoked rejection by the local communities. The main problem with the programme (which entails a five-year period of obligatory conservation of forest cover) is that, rather than involving people in community participation for sustainable management, the programme offers individual contractual relationships between the government institution and the local authority that do not always deliver the correct amount of funds to the registered owner of the land. Significant internal conflicts have resulted from this ill-conceived approach.

Our alternative proposal involves community agreements and mechanisms to establish permanent norms and responsibilities. The participation of all the main actors – including watershed villagers, local rural authorities, urban municipalities, state and regional water bodies, the reserve director and local NGOs – in the fund's decisions would guarantee accountability. Despite the conciliatory nature of the president of Tatahuicapan's speech at the Coatzacoalcos river basin commission meeting, the main official response was to deny the commission the ability to deal with these demands, which would become a responsibility of the urban municipalities.

Accountability mechanisms

The tools to share decision making and enforce accountability that have been developed by the municipal president of Tatahuicapan and our team include an effective legal framework, mechanisms of technical/environmental monitoring, and a social audit. While these are very specific institutional steps, they are being taken in conjunction with wider measures to build trust and dialogue between the different actors

BOX 4.1
LESSONS LEARNT ABOUT RESEARCHING ACCOUNTABILITY

Throughout the case described in this chapter, we played different roles, sometimes simultaneously. Sometimes we were interviewers, or advisers in resource management and farming techniques, and at other times our role was to provide information and lobby government officials. But we always worked towards the objective of trying to reconstruct trust between the rural indigenous communities with water institutions in the cities. Based on this wide range of activities and our long history of engagement in processes at the local level in Veracruz, we highlight here some of the key lessons we learned about researching accountability.

- *The importance of understanding historical and cultural context.* When we walked together with men and women from Tatahuicapan to their sacred spring for the first time, we were able to learn about the different perceptions of men and women, young and old, about the causes of deforestation and the different approaches to solving it. This experience showed how our vision for accountable management of the watershed is just one among many.

- *Creating new parameters for negotiation.* This requires ongoing discussion between different cultural perspectives and different values, and that all the actors involved should respect these differences. The values of reciprocity and cooperation, and a vision of the common good were important assets that communities brought to their struggles for greater accountability and the right to water.

- *Respecting the pace of political and social change.* When involved in interviews with bureaucrats within the water management authorities in the cities, sometimes we felt we were getting ahead of the local government rhythm of change and it was necessary to slow down. There is a risk that research can undermine existing processes of representation, and take on roles that are not legitimate.

involved. The legal framework must reflect local and regional agreements; a technical monitoring will verify the responsible use of resources
according to the management plan; and a social audit will ensure social
equity among the rural stakeholders.

Although this will be a long-term process, some results are already
discernible. Improvements in village sanitation have been made, such as
fencing in pigs that pollute local water supplies and spread disease. A
geographical information system and management plan for the watershed
communities now serves to raise funds and as a reference for monitoring
results. Alliances with urban actors have raised awareness of the cause of
problems and willingness to cooperate with this plan.

The three-year term for local government is short and processes to
create a new culture of accountability can easily be interrupted. In our
view, our most important achievement to date has been the formation of
experimental groups of men and women that have opened discussion at a
community level about how to develop an environmental agenda. These
groups are now engaged in finding representatives to take forward their
proposals, and to influence public policies. They have formed an
environmental citizen committee to discuss water management with the
cities and different institutions.

Conclusion

This chapter has shown how informal strategies for demanding accountability have a central role in securing the right to water. We can now
offer some key conclusions about improving accountability within this
context.

Contradictions between local perceptions of rights

Conflicting legal frameworks within the existing web of economic and
political power make it very difficult to institutionalise accountability
mechanisms. The principles that underpin indigenous institutions, such
as reciprocity and cooperation, can be reframed in terms of the management of the common good. They can also perpetuate conflict and lead to
a crisis of governance. In the past, some situations have led to successful
mobilisations while others have presented difficulties. Even when the
city governments respond to accountability claims by the indigenous
communities, their impact has been fleeting and has not helped to forge
new mechanisms for long-term accountability. The responses of cities
and the reserve management did not address underlying inequalities in
ways that would help to avoid future problems in water supply.

Long-term strategies for accountability

The negotiation process must be seen as a middle-term and long-term strategy dependent on many internal and external factors. The three-year terms of the municipal government are not long enough to consolidate new institutional arrangements, which emerge in large part through a slow process of consensus building, both internally and with external institutions.

Changing both sides of the equation

In order to increase the possibilities of a partnership or dialogue between actors with different degrees of power, changes are required on the government's side to create deliberative spaces open to all actors and respectful of the different perceptions, views, needs and proposals of others. For the community, there are also great challenges. On one side the water issue has to be perceived in a generalised way as a problem that concerns not only the cities but also the villagers' welfare and responsibilities. Much more has to be done to enable the villages to improve the management of their own water resources.

Building alliances for accountability

What is needed is increased awareness, both in the urban municipal governments and in the communities within the watershed, about what is necessary to improve the management of water resources. The strengthening of alliances between different levels and forms of government – even within Tatahuicapan, between the municipal government and the *ejido* – is an important first step for consensus to be built around a sustainable development plan. These processes offer hope that the cycles of conflict and environmental degradation that impede the realisation of the right to water in both rural and urban contexts can be ended. The formation of the watershed committee and the recent establishment of a plan for watershed management and restoration with the municipality of Coatzacoalcos may signal a new phase in conflict resolution and environmentally sustainable management, where the rights to water in both rural and urban areas will be protected.

NOTES

1 Luisa Paré and Carlos Robles are attached to Instituto de Investigaciones Sociales, Universidad Nacional Antónoma de Mexico (UNAM) and Desarrollo Comunitario de los Tuxtlas Asociación Civil (DECOTUX AC), respectively.

2 For example, within the area of the biosphere reserve (see Note 3) and the wider watershed, there are a variety of landholding patterns. Land tenure is both *ejido* and

communal. Over 1,500 *campesinos* (peasants) in eight villages, mainly Nahuas and Popolucas, inhabit the area. Some are the descendants of the indigenous population that has occupied the area since prehispanic times. *Ejido* is a form of social ownership in which land, previously held by powerful landowners or the nation, is given to peasants who, until the 1992 constitutional reforms, could not sell it (only inherit it). An *ejidatario* is a person entitled to this type of property.

3 The region is part of a biosphere reserve created in 1998, the Reserva de la Biostera de las Tuxlas.

4 Most of the actual decentralisation reforms are characterised by an insufficient transfer of powers towards local institutions, under strict control of central government. Often local institutions do not represent the communities, nor are they accountable towards them.

5 In Tatahuicapan, over a period of 30 years, the extent of grassland converted from rain-forest increased by 300 per cent (Lazos 1996).

6 Transparency, now a popular idea with many social movements, is limited in the Mexican legislation to the obligation for governmental agencies to publish basic financial information on their web pages and the right of citizens to demand and obtain this information.

7 'By focusing on the workings of traditional mechanisms of accountability, such as elections or the division of powers and the existence of an effective system of checks and balance among them, these diagnoses tend to ignore the growth of alternative forms of political control that rely on citizens' actions and organizations' (Day and Klein 1987: 1).

8 In action research or participatory research, community groups are not research objects but subjects who participate in the definition of the objectives of the whole process.

9 Interviews with elder Nahua peasants.

10 In 1960, five cattle ranchers controlled 57 per cent of the existing stock (Lazos 1996).

11 A pre-Hispanic myth was revived during the excavations for the dam, when the machinery hit a huge serpent, a Nahuat symbol for water. In keeping with the legend, the machine's operator died of fright. The serpent was taken to the capital zoo. As told to us by an older member of the community: 'It was the male; the female serpent remained to protect the spring.' The operator's symbolic death re-established a kind of reciprocity that allowed the water to be removed (after demands were met). See Blanco *et al.* 1992.

12 Here we adopt Leach *et al.*'s (1997) concept of institutions, 'as regularised patterns of behaviour that emerge from underlying structures or sets of rules in use'.

13 Interview with the head of the Tatahuicapan water supply.

14 In 2005, the Ministry of the Environment and Natural Resources had a US$1,542 million dollars budget; Finance US$2,162; Rural Development US$3,376; and Energy US$2,396.   http://www.shcp.sse.gob.mx/contenidos/presupuesto_egresos/temas/ppef/2005/ index.html

15 This plan includes agroecological alternatives such as agroforestry, intensive cattle ranching, soil conservation and the establishment of community norms concerning access to natural resources.

16 'Social investment for sustainability' involves raising funds for conservation and restoration of the resources that underlie the compensation for environmental services.

REFERENCES

Ayuntamiento de Tatahuicapan and Carlos Robles (2003) *Una Estrategia para la Sobrevivencia Común: el Agua y la Relación entre el Municipio Indígena de Tatahuicapan y la Región Industrial de Coatzacoalcos–Minatitlán, en el Sur de Veracruz, México.* Santiago de Chile: Fondo Chorlaví.

Ackerman, J. (2004) 'Co-Governance for Accountability: Beyond "Exit" and "Voice"', *World Development*, Vol. 32, No. 3, pp. 447–63.

Berkes, F. (2004) 'Knowledge, Learning and the Resilience of Social-Ecological Systems', paper prepared for the Panel 'Knowledge for the Development of Adaptive Co-Management'. IACSP '04 Conference, Oaxaca, Mexico, August.

Blanco, J. L., Paré, L. and Velásquez, E. (1992) 'El Tributo del Campo a la Ciudad: Historias de Chaneques y Serpientes', *Revista Mexicana de Sociología*, Vol. 54, No. 3, pp.131–7.

Blauert, J. (2004) 'Espacios de Consulta o de Decisión? Los Consejos de la Política Ambiental Regional en México, X', paper at IASCP '04 Conference, Oaxaca, August.

Buck, L. E., Geisler, C. C., Schelhas, J. and Wollenberg, E. (eds) (2001)Biological Diversity: Balancing Interests through Adaptive Collaborative Management, Boca Raton, FL: CRC Press.

Castelán, E. (2002) *Las Presiones Sobre los Recursos Hídricos en México*, Mexico DF: Centro del Tercer Mundo para el Manejo del Agua.

Cortéz, C. (2004) 'Social Strategies and Public Policies in an Indigenous Zone in Chiapas, México', *IDS Bulletin*, Vol. 35, No. 2 (April), pp. 76–84.

Day, P. and Klein R. (1987) *Accountabilities: Five Public Services*, London: Tavistock.

Durstom, J. (2000) 'Qué es el Capital Social Comunitario?', Serie Políticas Sociales, No. 38, Comisión Económica para América Latina (CEPAL), Santiago de Chile.

—— (2002) *El Capital Social Campesino en la Gestión del Desarrollo Rural: Díadas, Equipos, Puentes y Escaleras*, Santiago de Chile: Comisión Económica para América Latina (CEPAL).

Ewell, P. T. and Poleman, T. T. (1980) *Uxpanapa Reacomodo y Desarrollo Agrícola en el Trópico Mexicano*, Xalapa, Veracruz: INIREB.

Folke, C., Carpenter, S., Elmqvist, T. *et al.* (2002) *Resilience for Sustainable Development: Building Adaptive Capacity in a World of Transformations*, Rainbow Series No. 3, Paris: International Council for Scientific Unions (ICSU),
http://www.sou.gov.se/mvb/pdf/resiliens.pdf

Gaventa, J. (2004) 'Representation, Community Leadership and Participation: Citizen Involvement in Neighbourhood Renewal and Local Governance', study prepared for the Neighbourhood Renewal Unit, Office of Deputy Primer Minister, Institute of Development Studies, draft, February.

Lazos, E. (1996) 'La Ganaderización de dos Comunidades Veracruzanas: Condiciones de Difusión de un Modelo Agrario', in L. Paré and M. J. Sanchez, *El Ropaje de la Tierra: Naturaleza y Cultura en 5 Zonas Rurales*, Mexico City: Plaza y Valdéz Editores/ Universidad Nacional Autónoma de México.

Lazos, E. and Paré, L. (2000) *Miradas Indígenas Sobre una Naturaleza Entristecida. Percepciones Ambientales entre Nahuas del Sur de Veracruz*, Mexico City: Plaza y Valdéz Editores/Universidad Nacional Autónoma de México.

Leach, M., Mearns, R. and Scoones, I. (1997) 'Environmental Entitlements: a Framework for Understanding the Institutional Dynamics of Environmental Change', Discussion Paper 359, Institute of Development Studies, Brighton.

Leewis, C. (2000) 'Reconceptualising Participation for Sustainable Rural Development:

Towards a Negotiation Approach', in *Development and Change*, Vol. 31, No. 5, pp. 931–61.

Mauss, M. (1967) *The Gift: Forms and Functions of Exchange in Archaic Societies*, New York: Norton.

Mearns, R. (ed.) (1996) *The Lie of the Land: Challenging Received Wisdom on the African Environment*, Oxford: James Currey Publishers Ltd.

Mehta, L. (2000) 'Problems of Publicness and Access Rights: Perspective from the Water Domain', working paper, Institute of Development Studies, Brighton.

National Hydraulic Programme 2001–6 (2001) Mexico DF: CNA, Ministry of the Environment and Natural Resources.

Newell, P. and Bellour, S. (2004) *El Mapeo de la Transparencia o Responsabilidad Social: Orígenes, Contextos e Implicaciones para el Desarrollo*, Cuaderno de Investigación No. 2, Xalapa: IIS-UNAM-UAM-IDS.

Paré, L. (1975) 'Caciquismo y Estructura de Poder en la Sierra Norte de Puebla', in B. Roger (ed.), *Caciquismo y Poder Político en el México Rural*, Mexico DF: Siglo XXI Editores.

Paré, L., Robles, C. and Cortéz, C. (2002) 'Participation of Indigenous and Rural People in the Construction of Developmental and Environmental Public Policies in Mexico', in Gaventa, J., Shankland, A. and Howard, J. (eds), *Making Rights Real: Exploring Citizenship, Participation and Accountability*, IDS Bulletin, Vol. 33, No. 2, pp. 83–90.

Ribot, J. C. (2002) *La Descentralización Democrática de los Recursos Naturales: la Institucionalización de la Participación Popular*, Washington: World Resources Institute.

Sachs, I. (1994) 'Urban Futures: Six topics for MOST', Management of Social Transformation programmes (MOST), United Nations Educational, Scientific and Cultural Organisation, www.unesco.org/most

Schacter, M. (2000) 'When Accountability Fails: a Framework for Diagnosis and Action', Policy Brief 9, Institute on Governance, Ottawa.

Sen, A. (1995) *Nuevo Examen de la Desigualdad*, Madrid: Alianza Editorial.

Smulovitz, C. and Peruzzotti, E. (2000) 'Societal Accountability in Latin America', *Journal of Democracy*, Volume 11, No. 4 (October), pp. 147–58.

Tudela, F. (ed.) (1989) *La Modernización Forzada del Trópico: el Caso de Tabasco*, México DF: Proyecto Integrado del Golfo, El Colegio de México.

Velásquez, E. (1997) 'Configuración y Reconfiguración de la Comunidad Indígena: el Caso del Parcelamiento de "Ejidos Comunales" en la Sierra de Santa Marta, Veracruz', paper presented at Social Sciences Doctorate Programme Seminar, El Colegio de Michoacán A.C.

Wainwright, H. (2003) *Reclaim the State: Experiments in Popular Democracy*, London: Verso.

CHAPTER 5

Conflicting rights, environmental agendas and the challenges of accountability: social mobilisation and protected natural areas in Mexico

CARLOS CORTÉZ AND LUISA PARÉ[1]

This chapter explores the contradictions between the agendas and accountability strategies of different social actors in two protected natural areas (PNAs) of rainforest in Southern Mexico. Different interests and perceptions over the actors' rights are at the root of these contradictions, which undermine the construction of accountable practices around conservation and sustainable development strategies in PNAs. The two case studies are both situated in south-east Mexico: the Tuxtlas Biosphere Reserve in Veracruz, and the Montes Azules Integral Biosphere Reserve in Chiapas. These cases highlight questions about how to establish formal accountability mechanisms for defining development policies for environmental resources.

Divergences over land rights and knowledge rights have resulted from historical power imbalances, institutional complexity, and the different political and economic interests of the actors involved. Conflicts over land rights centre on disputes about how land rights are guaranteed and how land is used. Conflicts over knowledge rights, on the other hand, have emerged from different views about 'traditional' or 'indigenous' knowledge, who has the right to knowledge about plants, medicine and other resources in the rainforest, and how these resources should be used. Given these conflicts over land and knowledge rights, and the institutional and historical complexity that underlies them, this chapter explores the difficulties in building meaningful accountability. What this chapter shows is that divergent and contradictory views of rights over resources can lead to and sustain conflict that makes building accountability extremely difficult.

The challenge of establishing accountability mechanisms in natural reserves in Mexico is sharpened by an underlying and fundamental tension: the different actors involved in the PNAs have radically divergent views and discourses about the nature of the resource (the environment) that should be protected and thus of the rights that follow from their competing conceptions. The most important actors involved in PNAs are federal, regional and local governments, multilateral and local NGOs, transnational corporations, universities, indigenous communities, and community-based organisations. For some of these actors, such as conservationist NGOs, natural resources should be conserved and protected because of their intrinsic value, while for others, such as transnational corporations, natural resources are considered as economic goods. Priorities for the indigenous population are access to land and territorial rights, which in some cases they were entitled to before the creation of the reserves.

Cooperation between these different actors is necessary to reach environmental, economic and social objectives, but it is not very common and has been unstable when it occurs. This can be explained in part by the lack of trust between different actors, which is an underlying factor that contributes to the difficulties in building accountability. The obstacles to accountability are compounded by the absence of spaces for participation in the way these resources are controlled and managed, where the different views of nature and the environment could also be expressed and at least partially reconciled. This chapter will explore how diverse interests generate conflict, contributing to a lack of accountability in the way that the environment is controlled and managed. It will also explore examples of when different actors have succeeded or failed in constructing accountability, where accountability is understood as a two-way relationship in which different actors mutually claim their rights and define their obligations (Gaventa et al. 2002).

The main issues at stake are, on one hand, that indigenous people have traditional as well as constitutional rights to their land, and, on the other, that they have physical access and knowledge rights to the natural resources contained there. However, these rights seem to be in conflict with the conservationist agenda, advanced by both the federal government and environmentalist international NGOs (INGOs), which asserts the need to conserve remaining natural resources. The approach to creating PNAs to achieve this goal has been pursued without establishing adequate procedures for the participation of the local population, or consideration for how to protect livelihoods – yet both these requirements are essential to making rights real as part of a broader agenda of human development.[2] This omission is important in the light of the different understandings of the environment that lie at the heart of some of the conflicts over rights and the lack of accountability in southern Mexico. Arturo Escobar's (1999) categories of different discursive formations on resource management are useful in terms of classifying these different understandings of nature as a resource because the range of views he presents are those expressed by the key actors in these cases:

1 The *globally centred* perspective is shared by most NGOs from the North, and is based on representations of threats to biodiversity. The extinction of species is a main focus. Nature is seen as a global resource that must be protected. This perception is related to three concepts: conservation, sustainable development and benefit sharing (either through intellectual property rights or other mechanisms).[3]

2 The *sovereignty* perspective, advocated by some governments, focuses on the ability of Southern countries to negotiate the terms of treaties and biodiversity conservation strategies. Nature is seen as a resource that individual countries should control, a principle that has been affirmed by successive environmental treaties.

3 The *biodemocracy* perspective focuses on democratic control of biological resources. The social movement against biodiversity prospecting, discussed in this chapter, would be an example of a social movement based on a biodemocracy perspective. Nature is seen as a resource belonging to communities who have traditionally held the land where the rainforests exist.

4 The *cultural autonomy* perspective is part of a critique of neoliberalism, and emphasises different cultural approaches to nature and the need for an intercultural dialogue. Many indigenous movements in Mexico and Latin America have adopted this perspective, including the Zapatistas in Chiapas. Other groups, less politically motivated, also try to conserve their modes of livelihood on the basis of a specific type of relationship with their environment. For example, one movement opposes the PNAs as top-down approaches to conservation, and advocates community-run reserves as an alternative. From this standpoint, autonomy from the government is a necessary precondition for demanding collective rights in a diverse and heterogeneous society. Nature is seen as a politically contested resource, with joint responsibilities for its conservation.

Each of these discourses about nature also connects to the co-construction of separate discourses and practices of accountability – with different approaches to who should control 'nature', the way the environment should be used and managed, and which rights claims should be upheld.

This case shows how different views about environment and nature, as well as conflicts over specific rights to concrete resources, contribute to a context in which institutional change alone cannot bring about accountability. Instead, competing and overlapping interests must be reconciled through a politics that brings these different perspectives to the fore. This chapter will focus on how social movements and political mobilisations around specific rights claims have a key role in constructing accountability through these means.

The first section of this chapter includes some general information about the institutional and legal frameworks and public policies in PNAs, and some key characteristics of both reserves. The second section explores the conflicting interests of different actors around land rights, and the implications of these differences for accountability. The third section focuses on conflicts between the actors' perspectives of knowledge rights, and identifies some accountability gaps in the relationships between the different actors involved. Finally, this chapter will explore some of the consequences for accountability of these conflicts over rights, and some of the changes that could lead to increased accountability and improved governance.

The institutional and legal framework of public policies in PNAs

In Mexico in the 1960s, when agrarian reforms led to demand for more land, the agricultural frontier moved out towards the tropical rainforests, the last refuge for landless peasants who were seen as a threat to large landowners' interests in different regions. From the 1960s to the 1970s different laws and programmes were implemented in order to colonise the rainforests, which were then transformed into grasslands: this process increased the diversity of ethnic groups living in these regions.

But from the 1980s, pressure from conservationist INGOs was mounting on the Mexican government to take steps to protect rapidly dwindling areas of rainforest. As a result, a series of PNAs were created across Mexico during the 1980s and 1990s. Many of the PNAs have been established in regions with a dense population. When reserves are created, the first policy tools used are the establishment of conservation and management zones (nucleus and buffer zones) and the definition of governance plans for the reserves.[4] The nucleus zone must be free of productive activities, while in the buffer zone local communities can engage in ecotourism or other environmentally sustainable activities. When reserves are created, land rights can be suspended on the basis of public interest. Reserve decrees have been criticised for being imposed without the participation of the communities affected by their creation, for not respecting promises of indemnities, and for the constraints the reserves place on local people's livelihoods, which is a factor that inhibits effective accountability relationships between the different actors involved. At a workshop on PNAs in Chiapas in February 2005, one participant explained:

> Our right to be consulted and to be part of the decision-making process in regions declared biosphere reserves is denied to us. We reject pressures made in different ways for relocation and disguised as peaceful – as they do not guarantee a future with dignity for us.

The essence of the actual conflicts between different actors' interests and agendas around PNAs cannot be understood without reference to the Plan Puebla Panama (PPP). The PPP, a mega-project for the economic integration of south-eastern Mexico and six Central American countries, is intended to promote investment, infrastructure and socio-economic and human development. As reactions to the PPP show, the creation of PNAs is seen by some as part of a politically contested process of gaining control of natural resources. The Mesoamerican isthmus, situated in the south-eastern part of Mexico, including Chiapas and Veracruz, is of immense strategic value as natural resources (oil, biodiversity and water) are plentiful. With generally high levels of poverty in the area, cheap labour is also abundant.

Over the past five years, in regional and international meetings held in Mexico and Central America, several social movements have wholly rejected the PPP. For example, the political leadership of the Zapatistas considers the PPP to be part of a geopolitical strategy designed to control natural resources and exploit the local labour force, to the detriment of the culture, territorial control and rights of the indigenous people (Resistencia Ciudadana al Plan Puebla Panamá 2002). This chapter will explore in greater detail two cases of PNAs where control of natural resources is being disputed: the Montes Azules Reserve in Chiapas and the Tuxtlas Biosphere Reserve in Veracruz.

Biosphere reserves in tropical rainforests: from agricultural frontier to biodiversity's last boundary

The Montes Azules Integral Biosphere Reserve, Chiapas

Three decades ago, the Mexican government, motivated by international environmental concern for conservation, created the Montes Azules

Integral Biosphere Reserve (Montes Azules Reserve) covering 331,200 hectares in the Lacandona rainforest in Chiapas. The reserve is located in the Usumacinta basin, which contains 30 per cent of the country's water resources and has the greatest levels of biodiversity in North America. But since the creation of the Montes Azules Reserve, the situation in Chiapas has changed dramatically with the emergence of a well-organised and militarised social movement, which is challenging the government's policies on the PNA.

Eleven years ago, in January 1994, on the same date that the NAFTA (North American Free Tree Agreement) came into force, the Ejercito Zapatista para Liberacion Nacional (Zapatistas) emerged as an armed movement in Chiapas, denouncing the situation of indigenous populations in Mexico and demanding changes at national level. Social mobilisation has been instrumental in pushing for changes in state-level legislation, and has also led to the creation of autonomous municipalities and *juntas de buen gobierno* (Good Governance Councils) as part of this process.

Since 1994, the government's response to the Zapatista movement has varied from a strictly military response to political negotiations, although these were suspended several years ago. The government has vacillated, sometimes accepting that the demands are just but at other times accusing the Zapatistas of manipulation by external interests. It has both dismissed the Zapatistas as a purely localised movement, and allowed Zapatista political leaders to present their position at the National Congress Tribune in 2001. Changes at national and state government level in 2001 have now slightly modified this perspective (Cortéz 2004). Despite the highly variable relationship between the Zapatistas and the Mexican government, the Zapatistas have come to play a central role in the politics of accountability around the Montes Azules reserve.

Tuxtlas Biosphere Reserve

Situated on the Gulf of Mexico coast in Veracruz, the Tuxtlas Biosphere Reserve was created in 1998 and covers 155,220 hectares (see Chapter 5). Within the boundaries of the reserve are over 121 poor rural communities, with a total population of 350,000 (including three medium-sized towns). Indigenous groups, including Nahuas and Popolucas, have lived in this area since pre-hispanic times. As in Chiapas, public policies promoting resettlement and cattle ranching have accounted for the destruction in about 50 years of more than 85 per cent of the original forest (Lazos and Paré 2000). Many previous initiatives to create a PNA in the region (1937, 1979, 1980) had no impact at all as they were only formal declarations without any specific policies for implementation. The reserve created in 1998 is intended to promote the sustainable management and conservation of the Tuxtlas region. With water shortages affecting lowland urban areas with their petro-chemical industries, and flash flooding taking lives in the mountainous watershed, a general consensus had been reached that something needed to be done.

There are serious environmental concerns behind the creation of both of these reserves. But the process of establishing the reserves has generated conflict between competing sets of rights – and thrown into relief the radically different views of the main actors involved regarding nature as a resource. The lack of opportunities for participation by these different groups in the management of the reserves also contributes to the lack of accountability and the high levels of mistrust. These factors together have contributed to an extremely complex situation, one in which it is very difficult to establish lines of accountability. The next section will explore more closely the creation of the reserves as a source of conflict over land rights, and the strategies of poorer groups to claim their rights in response.

Competing claims and land rights

Montes Azules
The complex land tenure pattern in the Lacandona rainforest is the result of two processes. On one hand, for many decades the government's agrarian ministry has granted different groups endowments to the same lands, creating conflicts between them. On the other, many indigenous families have settled within the reserve area without governmental approval and claimed land for themselves according to traditional land tenure practices. These processes have contributed to competing claims to land rights. In some cases, formal land rights granted by the government are in direct contradiction with each other, and in other cases formal land rights clash with informal claims by indigenous people who are actually living on the land.

Without taking into account the reasons for emigration of indigenous people into the reserve, many government officials (including the director of the National Ecology Institute) and NGOs such as the World Wildlife Fund (WWF) and Conservation International have accused the recently settled population in the Biosphere Reserve of being responsible for environmental destruction caused by slash-and-burn agriculture and the shift to cattle ranching. In April 2000, WWF and a group of ecologists, concerned about conserving the rainforest in the reserve, called upon the Mexican government to stop the destruction of rainforest by indigenous people. The government and some conservation NGOs demanded their eviction, by force if necessary. In response, the federal government began to implement a plan to relocate the population to new settlements in locations outside the reserve, in order to relieve environ-mental pressure on the rainforest. While the conservationist NGOs and certain elements of the government advocate the forced resettlement of indigenous people living in the reserve area, indigenous groups are claiming the right to the land within the reserve.

An official from the Agrarian Ministry pointed out in an interview that the range of actors interested in Montes Azules makes it the most complicated reserve in Chiapas – with the most pressing environmental problems. Transnational companies (Grupo Pulsar), the World Bank (GEF in the Tuxtlas), international NGOs (Conservation International in Chiapas), the United States Agency for International Development (USAID), national or regional NGOs and academic institutions are all important actors.[5] The federal and local governments and indigenous groups settled around and in the reserves are also central actors.

A land rights and environmental sustainability round table was created in 1988 as part of an inter-institutional agreement between the federal and the state governments to reach workable solutions to the competing land rights and environmental problems.[6] But the interests, positionality, and negotiation capacity of the different actors involved are not equal. Some indigenous groups have been able to negotiate the conditions for their resettlement and protect their land rights. Others, particularly those who have only recently settled in the reserve, have very little capacity to negotiate.

The fundamental dispute between environmental conservationists and indigenous groups claiming land rights within the reserve has not been resolved. The underlying causes for this tension have been oversimplified by the polarised debate. According to the special officer from the Agrarian Reform Ministry in Chiapas:

> the causes of emigration to the rainforest must be considered in order to be able to define the most adequate responses…. [This perspective] created some internal dissent because the environmental sector was interested only in the irregular settlements, while we proposed to look at what is happening in the buffer zone in order to find out if we are creating conditions to allow people to have alternative livelihoods…. Many of the existing settlements in the Montes Azules reserve were generated by the land reform and the governmental policies…. This means that the deforestation process in Montes Azules was related not only to the illegal occupations of the reserve but to other issues.[7]

DEMANDS AND RESPONSES

The different groups established in the reserve have responded in different ways to this pressure from government and conservationist NGOs to relocate. Some have been willing to negotiate with the government and accept resettlement, while others have negotiated the recognition of their right to remain in the nucleus zone of the reserve. Other communities (especially those linked to the Zapatistas) have refused to negotiate with the government or give up their rights to the land within the reserve.

In contrast with the government's 'globally centred' perspective on the environment and nature, the principal demand of the Zapatista movement is the implementation of the San Andres Agreements signed by the Mexican government in 1994, accepting not only the recognition of indigenous people's rights and culture but also their territorial autonomy. One of the main factors in the breakdown of dialogue between the federal government and the Zapatistas is their different concepts of cultural and land rights. While the Congress Commission created to negotiate with the Zapatistas agreed on the central issues of cultural rights, the law approved in 2003 by the Congress dismissed this consensus and did not recognise the right to autonomy. This difference drove the Zapatistas to suspend negotiations and to resist all government-led neoliberal reforms. In the light of this general opposition, the Zapatistas consequently reject government-led environmental and development policies, including the attempts by the government to resettle people within the reserve area.

Although some of the Zapatista demands are related to land rights in the reserve, these land rights are linked to wider issues such as their cultural, social and political rights, self-determination, protection of their natural resources, and autonomy for the indigenous people within the national political agenda. For the Zapatistas, the Reserve is further evidence of the interests of global capital controlling natural resources, biodiversity and traditional knowledge. By having their land rights denied, the reserve settlers are also deprived of their rights to education, health and other services, which are tied to having land rights.

Tuxtlas

> The same federal government that gave us rights to the land was taking it away from us ten years later. (Peasant from a village in the Tuxtlas reserve)

In Tuxtlas, the creation of nucleus zones within protected natural areas has led to a range of effects on indigenous people's land rights: the expropriation of *ejido* land in its entirety,[8] the expropriation of a portion of village land, and the restriction of rights to communally held forests. In all, some 800 families have had their land rights affected by the creation of protected natural areas.

Although this land expropriation by the state has a legal basis (conservation in the public's interest), it directly clashes with the land rights granted by the state less than thirty years previously (see Paré and Robles, this volume). In the 1970s and 1980s, indigenous people in Tuxtlas received formal titles to their land after twenty years of struggle and attempts at land reform. In some cases, they received the formal rights to their land *after* the reserve decree, which then expropriated the same land for conservation.

In the process of land expropriation to create the PNA, the main grievance raised by the indigenous communities was the low price the government offered as compensation (US$200 per hectare, or less than a quarter of the land's commercial value). Losing land rights also meant giving up the rights to subsidies, which amount to half of the income of rural families in the region (Velázquez and Ramírez 2005; Leonard 2005). Communities rejected government reallocation offers as they meant emigrating from the region to locations without basic services such as roads, education and health facilities. Three of the villages filed injunctions against the government as a result of the land expropriations. But attempts to hold the state accountable for their actions in creating the reserve and perpetuating a situation of contradictory land rights have been impeded by the government's refusal to engage with communities:

> The government assumed that if they consulted people about the creation of the reserve, nobody would accept it. But there was no explanation, not even one attempt to create awareness or to negotiate. The same federal government that had given us the land was taking it away from us ten years later. For the majority of *ejidatarios* it was a betrayal. (Peasant from an expropriated community in Tuxtlas)

Conflicts between indigenous communities' rights to land and environmental conservation have been exacerbated by the top-down creation of protected natural areas. The lack of spaces for citizen participation in the creation and management of the reserve has contributed to increasing mistrust between the main actors involved and the politicisation of rights claims to land. Because of the reserve decree, there is an increased sense at the community level that the federal government has the responsibility to manage the reserve and resolve conflicts over land rights, but at the same time the communities themselves have increasingly fewer opportunities to contribute to the solutions to these problems. The strained relationships between key actors, and the apparently intractable conflict between rights, has important implications for accountability.

DEMANDS AND RESPONSES

For nearly five years the state government, responsible for the *ejido* land indemnities, was reluctant to enter into dialogue with the communities and resolve the conflicts over land rights. Two state elections (2000 and 2005) and the arrival of a host of new government officials has meant the suspension of previous agreements that had been reached between federal and state authorities concerning the reserve. The situation created by land expropriation and the fear of relocation rapidly became politicised as affected people turned to opposition political parties for solutions. In a vicious circle, state government repeatedly suspended negotiations because of this politicisation. Finally, after losing the injunction case in the courts, five years later, the communities accepted the low compensation price. In an attempt to defuse the situation, the state government construed the indemnities paid as a reward for communities' efforts at conservation rather than as compensation for expropriated land. But the conflict caused by the repeated delays in negotiations and the dispute over indemnities also undermined the ability of the federal authorities in charge of the reserve to promote sustainable development projects.

Other peasants and ranchers, on the contrary, would prefer the purchase by the state of the part of their land within the nucleus zone, as they cannot use this land productively. Although tree logging was illegal before the creation of the reserve, people saw the reserve as a threat to their land rights because they would lose formal rights to land they traditionally held. Some communities reacted to government attempts to ignore their previous land rights by threatening to burn the forests. Five years later a Payment for Environmental Services programme was launched, so that some communities would receive a small benefit (US$30 per hectare) for not cutting down the forest. The communities consider this an unsatisfactory offer and political rumours are spreading that the programme is a veiled attempt to privatise communal land. In contradiction with agrarian laws, and as one more example of lack of coordination between institutions even after the reserve decree, the Agrarian Reform Ministry gave individual titles to plots in the areas of the forest that had been communally owned. This contradictory policy strengthened a sense of individual rights to the forests within the nucleus zone which have now been cancelled as part of the reserve structure. This mistake deepened frustrations within indigenous communities and contributed to a sense of grievance over individual land rights. However, once again, the contradictions between the policies of different government agencies fuelled conflicts over the management of the reserve.

The increasing politicisation of government bureaucracies also serves to exacerbate disputes over land rights in Tuxtlas as mistrust between government officials at the state level is exacerbated by the differing political affiliations at various levels of government. In both cases, government slowness in resolving land problems linked to the creation of reserves has affected the lives of indigenous people living in communities within the reserves. In some expropriated communities, these issues have led to internal divisions within communities. While some rally around mobilisations or declarations against the reserve and in favour of its cancellation (Tuxtlas), others have invested indemnity payments to buy plots and turn to the reserve for investment funds. As we discuss below, a range of community-based strategies have emerged to address the lack of accountability and resolve the conflicts over land rights.

Knowledge rights and biotechnology research: hidden agendas?

The previous section has examined how conflicts over land rights have emerged around PNAs. Another important set of conflicts over rights has also developed as part of the trend towards conserving environmental resources: knowledge rights. Conflicts over knowledge rights in PNAs reflect radically different views of the environment: while government officials and conservationist NGOs see the environment as a resource to be conserved, some indigenous groups see the environment as part of their cultural heritage. Different (conflicting) rights are expressed here: the right of transnational pharmaceutical companies to invest in medicines backed by national laws protecting the rights of capital, the right of academic institutions to conduct research on the environment and use that knowledge, and the right of the local population to control how environmental resources are used, especially when the 'protection' of these resources does not result in any benefit for the communities themselves.

Natural resources are of strategic importance as a growing interest in genetics has changed the meaning of biodiversity for international corporations, especially the pharmaceutical and biotechnological industries.

The value of biodiversity is socially determined and elusive, as it depends on local as well as on scientific knowledge and does not require capital-intensive extractions of materials, as is the case with other natural resources (see Abah and Okwori, Chapter 10). As Baviskar points out, 'the process of decision making around resource-related issues often accords great weight to expertise, privileging technocratic knowledge' (Baviskar 2003: 5053). As in many other 'biodiversity hotspots', scientific research in the PNAs is now an issue of growing importance.

Within the context of the PPP, another reason to reject some projects that claim to be sustainable is that behind a discourse of protection lie real economical interests, which may be neither visible:

> We denounce the eviction and relocation policy and the imposition of PNAs, because it is in the interests of big transnational corporations such as Monsanto, Bayer, Aventis, Coca Cola, Nestlé, among others, interested in the appropriation of biological resources, of forests and water, all of which are of strategic value for our Nation.[9]

For some actors, actions linked with environmental protection that are promoted, organised or controlled by international organisations like the GEF, or leading INGOs like Conservation International or WWF, have important connections with transnational companies. These alliances are scientifically and technologically supported by academic groups, leading to conflation of the interests of transnational corporations with academic or scientific research initiatives. For some organisations working in PNAs, the principal interest of transnational corporations (chemical, pharmaceutical and biotechnological) and conservation NGOs is to identify biological material and patent it, so that it can be commodified. In the view of some of the indigenous social organisations, INGOs only offer incentives for rainforest conservation as a cover for bioprospecting ('biopiracy'), because the INGOs have prior agreements with companies to provide them with information gleaned through 'conservation'.

A general criticism by community groups is that actors engaged in bioprospecting do not consider indigenous people's rights, nor do they establish explicit lines of accountability and transparency with respect to these activities. The legal pressures and negative campaigning against people settled in the reserve on environmental grounds served the interests of other actors that can enter the reserve without similar restrictions. For example, the National Commission for Protected Areas does not regulate the intervention of researchers in PNAs very strictly. Official authorisation from the Ministry of the Environment and Natural Resources is required to collect samples in protected areas (Article 88), but the results of research are not available to the public without the researcher's agreement (SEMARNAT 2001: Articles 85 and 88).

In Chiapas bioprospecting has been the subject of important and ongoing discussion. As a result of public action by local and national civil society organisations, bioprospecting initiatives have been seriously questioned. In 1999, the ICBG-Maya project headed by the International Cooperative Biodiversity Group was revoked. This initiative, coordinated by the US National Institutes of Health, with participation from the University of Georgia and the Mexican academic institute Ecosur, was designed to do research on local knowledge of the medicinal properties of plants. Protest by the Indigenous Medical Organisations of the Chiapas State resulted in the suspension of the project. The position of some community-based organisations was set out in the San Gregorio, Biosfera de Montes Azules Declaration (2000):

> Indigenous people are not enemies of biodiversity, our culture is not destructive, as some ecologists have declared. Their critiques are welcome, but we also invite them to look for solutions to the problems of ecological destruction, marginality and poverty. Moreover, we call for the stewardship and the sustainable use and conservation of natural resources. And we denounce the genetic management of our environmental heritage by transnational and national enterprises through intellectual property rights. We call for trials, through the court system, on the patenting issue.

As recently as March 2005 this organisation, along with others, denounced a public consultation announced to discuss a biodiversity law proposed by the Chiapas state government. They argued that it was intended to legitimise bioprospecting by transnational corporations and to facilitate their control over biodiversity in Chiapas. In this perspective, the resettlement policy has been presented as part of a governmental counter-insurgency plan against the Zapatistas. Like conflicts over land rights, PNAs have become sites for disputes over knowledge rights. The interests of transnational corporations, conservationist NGOs, and academic researchers have become intertwined, and communities living in the reserve area are challenging this agenda. For those who see hidden agendas in the actions of scientific institutions and conservation NGOs, any proposal from these institutions is labelled as interventionist, and a violation of indigenous rights. Conflicts over knowledge rights contribute to lack of trust and antagonistic relationships between poor, rural indigenous groups and the government. The next section will explore how these various conflicts over rights impede attempts by community-based and civil society organisations to build mechanisms for accountability.

Challenges for building accountability: the politics of rights and resources

The foregoing sections have explored how the creation of PNAs has fuelled conflicts over rights within the context of disputes over the meaning and appropriate use of the environment as a resource. The institutional politics driving the different actors involved undermines the possibility of establishing accountability mechanisms. This section will review some of the interests that various civil society and community-based organisations have in terms of building accountability, and the obstacles that have emerged.

In both reserves, there is an array of organisations that have been active for years around land rights reform and other political demands, and have developed important expertise in agro-ecology, health and education. Before government programmes began to address these issues, community-based organisations had taken the lead in promoting environmentally sustainable practices, although the impact of these efforts was reduced by contradictory public policies and institutional infighting, as described earlier. These groups have been pursuing a range of strategies in order to resolve the conflicts over rights in the reserves, and increase accountability in the way that the environment is managed.

But these organisations do not represent a single position. Community-based organisations' perspectives are expressed in diverse agendas and practices, through different alliances, and from the local to the global level. These agendas include the recognition of cultural and political rights, as well as the implementation of specific development programmes. Some of these organisations are now receiving funds from government or from international NGOs (for initiatives such as CO_2 capture, and in Payment for Environmental Services initiatives) to strengthen sustainable production either for local use or for the global market. These organisations have had an important role in attempts to contribute to increased accountability around the management of the environment as a natural resource.

Both in the Montes Azules and the Tuxtlas reserves, some civil society organisations from academic, NGO or political backgrounds are more concerned with environmental issues and local development than with joining the national and international movements against neoliberal policies. With funds available from different government agencies and international non-governmental organisations, they carry out projects and initiatives to involve local people in the process of defining their own agendas and development plans. Others, more concerned with global issues and networks, provide information on wider environmental issues such as biopiracy, attempts to promote genetically modified organisms and megaprojects such as the PPP; these groups are involved in mobilisation to build community representation in wider forums. Yet another group of community-based organisations prefer to avoid collaboration with government programmes as they see them as incompatible with their own political positions, and do not want to risk government co-option of their constituency. In turn, some sectors of government see autonomous organisational processes as a threat.

There is considerable diversity in the types of community-based and civil society organisation involved in addressing the conflicts over rights and lack of accountability that have been highlighted by the creation of the PNAs. But they have had only mixed success in achieving these goals. Some community-based organisations are directly engaged in resolving these conflicts over rights. In Tuxtlas, in order to pressure the government to deliver the payment of indemnities, some of the indigenous groups in the affected communities changed strategies. They abandoned attempts at local mobilisation, filed a second injunction for the cancellation of the reserve, and joined a wider national movement against PNAs, mostly defined in opposition to the PPP megaproject. While the disputes over land rights remain unresolved, indigenous people occupy their land 'illegally'.

In Chiapas there have been lengthy negotiations over the complex landholding problems. The high levels of distrust in the whole process have been used by other social actors, such as environmental NGOs, to scale up the resistance to the PPP megaproject agenda. Possible government evictions of people from their land are denounced as a government strategy to privilege transnational corporations' bioprospecting interests. Because of constant protests against the possible eviction of people from the Montes Azules Reserve, some federal officials demanded that the Agrarian Reform and Environmental ministries change their policies in order to protect the indigenous peoples' rights established in the ILO 169 Agreement. (The International Labour Organisation's Convention Concerning Indigenous and Tribal Peoples in Independent Countries entered into force on 5 September 1991.) So far the state government has refused to comply. The lack of agreement between different parts of the government contributes to the gap in accountability around the management of the environment, and while there is no agreement over land rights, conservation projects have been put on hold.[10]

Meanwhile, the Zapatistas have declared an impasse. In October 2004, the Zapatista political leadership defined its position in a public statement:

> Due to the offensive of paramilitary groups … dozens of indigenous families had to move from their land and from small villages in the Montes Azules Biosphere. During this time they have been in a terrible situation, far from their original land, but displaced Zapatistas have been careful to obey our laws that require the protection of forests. However, the federal government, hand in hand with multinationals, intends to take control of the richness of Lacandonan rainforest. They have threatened once again to remove with violence all the settlements in the area, including the Zapatistas. *Los compañeros* and *compañeras* of different threatened communities have decided to resist, for as long as the government does not sign and respect the 'San Andres Agreement'. (Report from the Clandestine Indigenous Revolutionary Committee – Commander General of the Ejército Zapatista de Liberación Nacional (EZLN), Sub-comandante insurgente Marcos)

The cases of the Montes Azules and Tuxtlas reserves show how extremely complex institutional relationships and the overlapping interests of different actors can lead to increasing conflicts over rights. The question is what kind of accountability relationships can be established to avoid this type of clientelist approach to sustainable management of the environment. In the current situation of conflict, it is not possible to develop viable environmental and economical alternatives and build trust between community organisations and the government.

Conclusions

This chapter has shown how uneven relationships between the different actors and interests in the PNAs can undermine the construction of common agendas for conservation and development, and mechanisms for accountability. At the heart of this situation are different perspectives on rights and the nature of environment as a resource. The lack of spaces for participation in the institutions that manage the environment, especially within the PNAs, is also an important factor that restricts the potential for increased accountability.

PNAs are not always and everywhere a source of conflict and uncertainty. In many circumstances they represent an opportunity for local development and a better livelihood for poor communities. The integration of the local population into the sustainable management of the environment cannot be widely guaranteed at present, in large part because of the lack of recognition of their land and knowledge rights, and the lack of spaces for participation in the decision making that affects these rights. A participatory scheme should integrate local people's concerns and experiences with natural resource management and protection, while respecting their land rights through fair compensation and consensual relocation when unavoidable.

When decisions concerning PNAs are left in the hands of experts, progress towards a sustainable development model is minimal and the building of consensus around conservation very slow. On the other hand, when, as a result of social action, spaces for negotiation are opened and an intercultural dialogue is facilitated, the resolution of conflicts becomes possible, and problems can be solved (as in the case of the round table on land rights and environmental sustainability in Montes Azules). From the cultural autonomy standpoint, a condition for intercultural dialogue, and therefore for accountability, is that actors recognise each other as equals, and acknowledge each other's cultural, social and political rights.

The conflicts generated by the creation of both reserves have to do with lack of consultation and participation in reserve management. To reach the PNA objectives, it would be necessary to guarantee the participation of the different interest groups from the beginning, to involve them in a permanent way in activities and budget planning. Many factors, such as political interests at the local and regional level and internal contradictions or tensions between community-based organisations, make it difficult to construct participatory spaces in a short time. In both cases, the legally mandated regional reserve management councils either have not been formed, or, when formed, have been under the operational control of government agencies.

The cases in this chapter show that when institutional mechanisms and policies are insufficient to resolve disputes over rights and establish accountability, it is difficult to reach consensus between different actors to build common agendas around conservation and sustainable development. The lack of strong institutional coordination is also a source of social unrest and contributes to the loss of confidence in and lack of support for government conservation programmes. However, building greater accountability is not just an administrative issue that can be solved by changing rules or establishing certain guidelines. It is fundamentally a question related to power, and the struggle between different political interests.

Relationships characterised by the absence of co-responsibility, the lack of adequate institutions with the capacity to fulfil their functions, and the active presence of distrust, mean that accountability is limited on multiple levels. However, it would be naive to reduce the problem of accountability to questions of designing and establishing the correct procedures and participatory spaces. What we are facing is the existence of different visions regarding the nature of the environment in general and indigenous rights in particular. This explains why policies aimed at environmental sustainability, such as PNAs or Payment for Environmental Services programmes, are seen by some as part of the Plan Puebla Panama, and rejected for this reason.

The key implication for accountability from the cases examined in this chapter is that the competing and conflicting rights around resources, derived from radically different understandings of nature and subsequent discourses of accountability, are essentially irreconcilable through institutional change. It is in the politics and political mobilisation around rights claims that these differences about nature can be engaged. The steps taken to promote more accountable relationships demonstrate a certain capacity of the state to respond to people's demands. This shift has been possible because of the high degree of mobilisation by different community-based and civil society actors. But even acknowledging these advances, a culture of accountability is not deeply embedded, as shown by the refusal of the government to give information about megaprojects such as the PPP, which has provoked confrontation with community-based organisations.

The recent social movements focused on changing intercultural relations in Mexico, especially the Zapatistas and the indigenous movements, represent a political and cultural challenge to building accountability – and demonstrate the conflictual nature of cultural politics. An alternative autonomous position requires a new kind of dialogue between different cultural perspectives, one that obliges the different actors involved to state explicitly their social, economical, cultural and political interests, and assume co-responsibility for natural resources protection and social development. Accountability could then become not only a one-way relationship between indigenous groups and the government, but a two-way relationship involving respect for rights and responsibilities for all the actors involved.

NOTES

1 Carlos Cortéz and Luisa Paré are researchers with the Universidad Autónoma Metropolitana-Xochimilco (UAM-X) and Instituto de Investigaciones Sociales, Universidad Nacional Autónoma de Mexico (UNAM), respectively.

2 The human development approach is the process through which people's options and their functions and capacities are increased (a long and healthy life, access and

knowledge of their resources for a healthy life (UNDP 2000).

3 For instance, many environmental policy instruments such as carbon sequestration and the Clean Development Mechanism (CDM) are focused on reforestation in the South towards fulfilling the commitments of the Kyoto Protocol. Many of the projects derived from the CDM, however, do not take into account the structural causes of deforestation and loss of biodiversity in the South.

4 Environmental policies in Mexico are the responsibility of the Ministry of Environment and Natural Resources and among its policies is the System for Protected Natural Areas, managed by the National Commission for PNAs, which is responsible for the environmental protection of 7 per cent of the national territory. Regional Development Programmes, Global Environment Facility and European Commission funds, among others, are the main financing sources for PNAs.

5 UNAM in both reserves, Ecosur in Chiapas and a state university in Veracruz, in addition to foreign universities.

6 Interview with Martha Cecilia Díaz Gordillo, February 2005.

7 *Ibid*.

8 *Ejido* is a form of social property in which land, previously held by big landowners or the nation, is given in usufruct to peasants who, until the 1992 Reforms to the Constitution and Agrarian Law, could not sell it (only hand it on as an inheritance). An *ejidatario* is the person entitled to this type of property.

9 Second Encounter on PNAs, Chiapas, February 2005.

10 Neither in Chiapas nor in Veracruz were there processes of consultation for the declaration of the reserve, although according to the government's legal framework such a process is obligatory.

11 Disseminated on 13 October 2004 by the Mexican newspaper *La Jornada*.

REFERENCES

Baviskar, A. (2003) 'For a Cultural Politics of Natural Resources', in *Economic and Political Weekly*, Vol. 38, No. 48, pp 5051–6.

Coordinación General del Plan Puebla Panamá (2002) Proceso de Organización, Planeación y Resultados, Plan Puebla Panamá, June, Mexico DF: Presidency of Mexico.

Cortez, C. (2004) 'Social Strategies and Public Policies in an Indigenous Zone in Chiapas, Mexico', *IDS Bulletin*, Vol. 35, No. 2, pp. 76–84.

Escobar, A. (1999) *El Final del Salvaje. Naturaleza, Cultura y Política en la Antropología Contemporánea*, Bogotá: Instituto Colombiano Agropecuario and CEREC.

Foro de Información, Análisis y Propuestas (2001) 'El Libre Comercio y Asuntos Transfronterizos: el Pueblo es Primero Frente a la Globalización', *mimeo*, México DF.

Gaventa, J., Shankland, A. and Howard, J. (eds) (2002) 'Introduction – Making Rights Real: Exploring Citizenship, Participation and Accountability', *IDS Bulletin*, Vol. 33, No. 2.

Lazos E., and Paré, L. (2000) *Miradas Indígenas sobre una Naturaleza Entristecida. Percepciones sobre el Deterioro Ambiental entre los Nahuas del Sur de Veracuz*, Mexico City: Plaza y Valdéz Editores/Universidad Nacional Autónoma de México.

Leonard, E. (2005) 'Titularización Agraria y Apropiación de Nuevos Espacios Económicos por los Actors Rurales; el Procede en Los Tuxtlas, Estado de Veracruz", in E. Leonard, A. Quesnel and E. Velásquez (eds), *Políticas y Regulaciones Agrarias: Dinámicas de Poder y Juegos de Actores en Torno a la Tenencia de la Tierra*, Mexico City: Institut de Recherche pour le Développement (IRD), Centro de Investigaciones y Estudios Superiores en

Antropologia Social (CIESAS), and M. A. Porrúa Grupo Editorial, pp. 297–325.

Massieu, Y. and Chapela, F. (2002) 'Acceso a Recursos Biológicos y Biopiratería en México', *El Cotidiano*, Vol. 19, No. 114 (July–August), pp. 72–87.

Moguel, J. (2001) 'Claroscuros del Plan Puebla Panamá: de Cómo se Escamotean los Derechos Indios y se Traslada el Debate a los Presuntos Temas del Desarrollo', in A. Bartra (ed.), *Mesoamérica, los Iios Profundos. Alternativas Plebeyas al Plan Puebla Panamá*, Mexico City: El Atajo Ediciones.

Newell, P. and Bellfour, S. (2004) 'El Mapeo de la Transparencia o Responsabilidad Social: Orígenes, Contextos e Implicaciones para el Desarrollo', Cuaderno de Investigación No. 2, Instituto de Investigaciones Sociales, Universidad Nacional Autónoma de Mexico (UNAM), Universidad Autónoma Metropolitana (UAM), Development Research Centre (DRC)–Institute of Development Studies (IDS).

Resistencia Ciudadana al Plan Puebla Panamá (2002) *Serie Acción Ciudadana en las Americas*, No. 2 (September).

SEMARNAT (2001) *Reglamento de la Ley General del Equilibrio Ecológico y la Protección del Medio Ambiente en Materia de Areas Naturals Protegidas*, Secretaría de Medio Ambiente y Recursos Naturales (Ministry of the Environment and Natural Resources).

UNDP (2000) *Human Development Report*, New York: United Nations.

Velázquez E., and Ramírez, F. (2005) 'Las Impugnaciones Locales a las Políticas Estatales de Conservación de los Recursos Naturales: el Caso de la Reserva de la Biosfera Los Tuxtlas, Veracruz', paper presented at AMER, Vth Congress. Balance y perspectives del Campo Mexicano a Una Década del TLCA y del Movimiento Zapatista, Oaxaca, 25–28 May.

CHAPTER 6

From protest to proactive action: building institutional accountability through struggles for the right to housing

CELESTINE NYAMU-MUSEMBI

When are struggles for basic rights by weak social groups able to have an impact on public institutions and make them more responsive and accountable?[1] This chapter responds to this question by drawing from the experience of an ongoing struggle by council tenants in Mombasa, Kenya for decent housing conditions, secure tenure, functioning urban services, and an end to the grabbing of public land in the municipality.[2] Lessons from social movement literature suggest that in assessing the impact or effectiveness of such struggles it is necessary to pay attention not only to internal factors such as how the movement is organised, what resources it is able to mobilise, and the terms in which it articulates its claims, but also to external factors such as the nature of the state, the configuration of public institutions and the broader political context (Tarrow 1998; McAdam, Tarrow and Tilly 2001). In a paper exploring how citizens' exercise of voice may more directly influence policy and service delivery, and how public institutions can be more 'client-focused', Goetz and Gaventa employ a framework that breaks down this combined analysis of internal and external factors into three key questions (Goetz and Gaventa 2001: 10):

1 What is the social, cultural and economic power of the group? (This interrogates the extent to which there is a united and well-organised constituency that is able to articulate its entitlements clearly, able to attract allies in strategic places, and enjoys broad social support for its claims.)
2 What is the nature of the political system? (This interrogates the depth of procedural and substantive democracy: the manner in which executive, legislative and judicial power is organised, and the genuineness of political party competition based on ideas and programmes.)

3 What is the nature of the state and its bureaucracies? (This interrogates the extent to which there is a professional and relatively autonomous civil service, a level of commitment to reform in the bureaucratic culture and practice, and pro-poor responsiveness.)

These questions provide a useful framework for taking stock of and accounting for gains and losses of the council tenants' ten-year struggle in terms of ability to have an impact on public institutions and make them more accountable. But first, what is the context of the struggle: who is involved and what are the main issues?

Background

The city of Mombasa is Kenya's sea port and its second largest city, with a population of about 700,000.[3] The city has an officially acknowledged housing crisis (Central Bureau of Statistics 1999: 15). The worst manifestation of the crisis is in the slums that have mushroomed in the city over the last ten years. But equally visible is the severe deterioration in the quality of existing low- and middle-income housing, which is also in short supply. Most people in this income group have only two options to choose from: on the one hand, the 'Swahili' type houses[4] (built out of mud and mangrove poles) occupied by several families, each household having a single room.[5] Cooking and toilet facilities are communal, with no proper sanitation services as they are located in unplanned, semipermanent settlements. On the other hand, council-owned estates constructed in the colonial era that have not seen much maintenance since the mid-1980s. Among these estates are Tudor, Changamwe and Mzizima, where the tenants' associations' mobilisation work began.[6]

The tenants' associations from these three estates joined together in November 2002 to form the Shelter Committee of ILISHE[7] Trust, an umbrella organisation bringing together community-based groups in the Coast province. The Shelter Committee helps to mobilise other council tenants facing similar problems with the aim of ultimately getting all 18 council estates involved and active in the struggle. The tenants' struggle can be summed up as being about four issues: decent housing conditions, functioning urban services, secure tenure and fighting the grabbing of public land.

Decent housing conditions
Under the terms of the lease agreement, the council has an obligation to maintain the houses. The council has not undertaken routine maintenance

tasks such as painting of the exterior, or repairs and replacements of the fixtures, since the early 1980s. Tenants are forbidden to make any 'alterations or additions whatsoever' to the flat or 'any fixtures and fittings therein' without the council's consent. The council's established practice of withholding consent notwithstanding, those tenants who can afford it have been forced by circumstances to resort to self-help measures such as replacing sinks, toilets, doors and windows, and even improvised wooden staircases. However, for tenants living in blocks with shared ablution facilities, the deterioration has not seen such mitigation; these tend to be poorer tenants and also it would take the agreement and financial contribution of several households to tackle these problems.

Functioning urban services

The city has been in economic decline for the last ten years (Gatabaki-Kamau et al. 2000: 1). This economic decline was made worse by politically motivated clashes just prior to the 1997 elections. Key sectors of the economy, such as tourism, suffered huge setbacks, as did the urban infrastructure.[8] Water and sanitation services are poor in the city as a whole, but low-income areas are hardest hit. Estates such as Tudor have not had running water since 1995, a situation made worse by an ongoing dispute between the council and the state-operated National Water Conservation and Pipeline Corporation. Yet the tenants have continued to pay for water and sewerage services they do not receive, since these charges are included in their rent charges. Here, too, the tenants have resorted to self-help measures. A women's group in Tudor estate sank a borehole that sells water to the residents. People also buy water from vendors who cart water around the estates.

Secure tenure

As tenants with written lease agreements, the council tenants are more tenure-secure than most low-income residents of Mombasa. But tenure security is much more than having an official document: council tenants do not *feel* secure. Corrupt practices in the council's department of housing, irregular practices such as rigging waiting lists, and back-dated eviction notices used to evict people without the benefit of the notice period required by the tenancy agreement all contribute to the feeling of insecurity. The tenants speak of an increasing trend of people having to *teremka* (go down the slope) literally and figuratively into the *muoroto* (slum) on the periphery of the estate because they have either been unable to pay the rent, or unable to fight off an irregular reallocation of their lease to another tenant favoured by some council official or councillor. Thus the search for tenure security is expressed first and fore-most in demands for an end to corruption. The search for tenure security also takes the form of demands for transfer of ownership to the tenants.

Fighting the grabbing of public land
In Kenya it is impossible to talk about the crisis in public housing without talking about land grabbing and therefore about corruption among bureaucrats and politicians. 'Land grabbing' has defined Kenyan politics, particularly in the 1990s, according to the Ndung'u Commission, which was set up in July 2003 to investigate illegal/irregular allocations of public land (Government of Kenya 2004). Land grabbing refers to irregular allocation of land set aside for public purposes, or any government-owned land, to private individuals or corporations. Many allocations did not follow the procedure laid down in the Government Lands Act. Allocations followed the exception rather than the rule: regular allocation procedure should go through an Allocation Committee. An exception permits the president (a power delegated to the Commissioner for Lands) in exceptional circumstances to bypass the allocations committee and give a direct grant through a letter of allocation. This became the standard procedure, doing away with scrutiny in all allocations.

Mombasa council tenants' mobilisation efforts sprang from resistance to land grabbing, since Mzizima and Tudor estates were threatened with this fate in the mid-1990s. The council's plans to sell off the estates were foiled by a combination of high-profile campaigns by the tenants and a hitch in the financing arrangements.

The next three sections analyse the tenants' struggle through the lens of an adaptation of the framework suggested by Goetz and Gaventa to respond to the central question: when are struggles for basic rights by weak social groups able to impact on public institutions and make them more responsive and accountable? The next section will address how to assess a group's social, cultural and economic power, which is necessary to hold public institutions to account.

What is the social, political, cultural and economic power of the group?

Social and political power
This can be assessed on two counts: first, does the struggle have broad membership so as to command social legitimacy? Second, does it offer incentives for people to join and stay engaged in collective action?

It is important to understand the membership of social movements. Who is in the tenants' struggle? Is its membership broadly representative of council tenants in Mombasa? As has already been stated, the struggle originated in three estates. The Shelter Committee formally started outreach activities in the other council estates in 2003. By December 2004 eight other estates had been added to the number. However, this represents a swelling in numbers rather than organic growth into a movement. It was precipitated by response to an immediate threat: in July 2004 the tenants received letters from the National Housing Corporation telling them that they would henceforth be required to pay their rent to the corporation, and also that the rent would be increased. This is on account of a dispute between the council and the corporation over outstanding amounts that the council owes to the corporation. The tenants mobilised and through ILISHE instructed a lawyer, who has since managed to secure a temporary injunction to prevent the National Housing Corporation from collecting any rent, pending hearing of a case filed by the tenants to determine whether the council or the corporation is the landlord.[9]

The links between the Shelter Committee and these eight estates are through key individuals rather than a critical mass, and therefore broad ownership of the struggle is something that needs to be cultivated. Discussion on how to expand the structure of decision making in the Shelter Committee so as to accommodate them is still at an exploratory stage. In terms of geographical spread, therefore, it is fair to say that the membership has not been broad enough to include a majority of the people affected by the issues central to the struggle.

Even within the three estates in which the struggle is most active, more could be done to achieve broader inclusiveness. With the discontinuation of the savings scheme there is no register of members as such, and so it is difficult to say with certainty how many are 'paid-up' members of the tenants' association in each estate. There is an identifiable core group that stays active, but mobilisation in the bulk of the estates has peaked and plateaued, depending on whether there was some imminent threat that called for unified resistance.

Does membership cut across divides? In terms of socio-economic class the group is relatively homogeneous. Therefore the divides that have mattered most are ethnicity and political party affiliation. The joint Shelter Committee has managed to function relatively smoothly, notwithstanding diversity in ethnic origin and political party affiliation. Coast province is characterised by a very particular politics of ethnicity that polarises 'indigenous' coastal peoples (*watu wa pwani*) and people from up-country (*watu wa bara*). The politically instigated clashes that preceded the 1997 general elections were fuelled by this polarisation. Political party affiliation broadly follows this pattern. The area has been a key stronghold of the former ruling party, KANU (the Kenya African National Union, in power for the last 40 years until the 2002 elections), and therefore coastal peoples are presumed to be KANU loyalists. Up-country people are presumed to support the former opposition, now in the governing coalition.

Tensions along these lines occasionally manifest themselves in relationships among the tenants and with external actors. There has been talk about the disruptive effect of the election campaigning seasons, when some tenants' association officials double up as party activists. If they undertake door-to-door recruitment exercises for their party, will people not identify them with that party the next time they come on a mobilisation exercise for the estate's tenants' association? There was one acknowledged incident of a tenants' association becoming deadlocked for months over unresolved differences between two officials belonging to rival political parties that had clashed during the campaign. This has subsequently been resolved following open discussion at the joint Shelter Committee level and binding arbitration.[10]

In order for the group to acquire and maintain membership it needs to show that it has something to offer. They need to demonstrate this to persons who remain aloof in the estates in which the tenants' associations have been active, as well as to the estates that have not experienced tenant organisation. Those active in the struggle cite solidarity and the amplification of voice (*kupaza sauti kwa pamoja*) as the most significant benefits of belonging to the tenants' struggle. One other benefit cited is membership in ILISHE Trust, which promises support in the form of connections to professional organisations (legal aid providers, for example), access to the media, and a means to secure funding (even though the latter is not guaranteed). What is lacking is a clear articulation and popularisation of the ultimate vision or desired outcome of the struggle, whether that be winning the right to own their houses or clarity in and implementation of the council's obligations to maintain the houses and deliver services. Clear articulation of the long-term goal is important in view of the weight of immediate disincentives to joining this type of struggle. Housing in Mombasa is difficult to come by. Therefore council housing – with all its problems – is still desirable. Many would not want to jeopardise a tenancy status that is already precarious and expose themselves to reprisals in the form of evictions or, even worse, job losses for those tenants who are also council employees. People need to be persuaded that there are long-term benefits that make the risks in the short term worthwhile.

Cultural power

'Cultural power' is a useful label for exploring a group's ability to influence public discourse on the issues that define the struggle. To paraphrase Goetz and Gaventa (2001: 41), it refers to the effective use of the media and other public forums to gain support for their cause and to shame and praise officials; the group's ability to successfully challenge presumptions (especially official presumptions) about the group and their struggle; and the ability to build credibility by combining protest with constructive engagement.

USE OF MEDIA TO GAIN SUPPORT AND TO SHAME AND PRAISE

The tenants' struggle has used the media and public forums quite effectively, particularly when a specific threat was imminent. It was a high-profile media campaign that thwarted the council's secret plans in 1997 to relocate Mzizima tenants (who are low-cadre employees of the council) so as to make room for a private housing development that would price out low-income earners from that neighbourhood.[11] In 2000 Mzizima tenants made their case before a presidential commission that had been set up to propose changes to the land law system.[12] Media publicity had earlier exposed planned evictions intended to make way for similar redevelopment in Tudor estate.[13] Tudor tenants credit their campaign for the decision by the National Social Security Fund to withdraw from negotiations for the financing of the redevelopment, which essentially halted the council's plans. In 1995 a concerted media campaign made the council shelve plans for a steep hike in rent, averting the full hearing of a court case that the tenants had initiated to challenge the rent increase.

The tenants now need to strategise for a more proactive media strategy that goes beyond mainstream media, particularly for the purpose of reaching into council estates in Mombasa. In order to win broad public support for reform of public housing policy nationally, the struggle also needs to be presented in terms of a vision for broader social transformation, articulating the struggle as being about offering an alternative vision rather than simply securing gains for the immediate constituency (Hunt 1990).[14] For instance, the campaign to resist private real estate developers is being pursued not only on the basis that tenants who cannot afford high rents will be displaced, but more broadly to ensure city policies that put people's basic shelter rights ahead of profits.

Shaming and praising of officials could be sharpened and made more evidence-based. In tackling land grabbing, for instance, Changamwe residents carried out impressive investigative work and compiled a list of the reference numbers of all the illegally allocated plots, along with the names of the people to whom they had been allocated. Missing from the list, however, were the names of the officials involved in the allocations. The obstacles to obtaining this information are enormous (as the Ndung'u Commission found out), but determined groups have been able to obtain it through a combination of formal and informal networks.

CHALLENGING PRESUMPTIONS

The importance of challenging presumptions (especially official presumptions) about the group and its struggle cannot be overemphasised. In official discourse the tenants are perceived as no more than ungrateful beneficiaries of heavily subsidised housing. The tenants' own account is that it is they who subsidise the council: with the council's failure to carry out routine maintenance since the mid-1980s, tenants have been forced to carry out major repairs at their own expense to make the houses habitable, knowing full well that the council will never reimburse these 'unauthorised repairs', nor will they be able to remove fixtures they have installed at the end of their tenancy, as this will be treated as vandalism.

This is common knowledge among the tenants, but in public discourse on council housing it is not. Making it more explicit could change the way in which 'subsidy' is understood, thus legitimising the tenants' alternative account. Literature on social movements and rights suggests that, in order for weaker social groups to be able to institutionalise and consolidate their gains, they must work towards legitimising their alternative vision so that it becomes the 'hegemonic' position (the taken-for-granted way of thinking or doing things) (Hunt 1990).

BUILDING CREDIBILITY BY COMBINING PROTEST WITH CONSTRUCTIVE ENGAGEMENT

Has the tenants' struggle worked to build credibility by combining protest with constructive engagement? It has been easier for the council tenants to agree on what they are against than to agree on a shared vision for proactive action. Whereas many who are active in the Shelter Committee see the ultimate aim of the struggle in terms of being able to purchase the houses from the council, there are some who will be content if the council carries out repairs, involves the tenants by allowing them to contribute through their labour and ideas, and takes this contribution into account in calculating the new rents so that the resulting rent increment is not too large.[15] There is also lack of agreement on the eligibility criteria for purchase, with some holding the view that only residents of at least ten years' standing should be allowed to participate (ILISHE 2002: 22). It will be necessary to carry out a detailed assessment of views among the residents so as to determine what vision is broadly representative. Engaging the council and other relevant public institutions on a constructive agenda will require the identifying and crafting of the key message, so that it can be targeted at the institutions most likely to intervene effectively. It will also require clear ideas for action, in the form of concrete, carefully budgeted proposals to the council.

Economic power

In the mid-1990s and into the late 1990s the tenants' associations in the three estates operated savings schemes, both to finance the struggle and to build up a funding base that would enable them to leverage financing for the purchase of the houses. These schemes have since lapsed. Except for *ad hoc* collections to deal with emergencies, there is no effort to fundraise among the membership. Now, since the joint Shelter Committee is one of the constituent committees of ILISHE Trust, ILISHE fundraises among donors and then makes allocations among the various areas of work. The tenants' work has made a significant contribution to ILISHE's funds by winning the 2002 Body Shop Award for Human Rights, which brought US$75,000 to the organisation. It is fair to say that the initial determination to build financial self-sufficiency through savings in preparation for the eventuality of purchasing the houses has been replaced by a reliance on fundraising from donors through ILISHE on a 'project' basis. The award served to weaken further the previous emphasis on linking grassroots mobilisation with building up savings. On the whole, the economic power of the tenants' associations is very weak, made worse by fluctuations in the number of people actively involved in the struggle.

What is the nature of the political system?

The following features of the political system have had significant implications for the tenants' struggle: political party competition; the relationship between central and local government; public institutions' accountability to Parliament; and the degree of protection of citizens' rights from the excesses of politicians and bureaucrats.

Political party competition

In an ideal situation, parties compete on the basis of programmes and ideologies, and therefore social movements are able to form strategic alliances with any party whose agenda is congruent with the movement's goals so as to advance their struggle. The situation in Kenya is far from this ideal. Party politics since independence has lacked genuine competition among alternative policies. Following ten years of legally imposed single-party rule, Kenya has had three multi-party elections: in 1992, 1997 and 2002, the last of these unseating KANU (from central government as well as from Mombasa) for the first time in 40 years. Even though the major parties publish manifestos, their political rallies and public discourse in general is dominated by ethnic posturing rather than by issues (Gatabaki-Kamau *et al.* 2000: 75; Southall and Wood 1996; Mutunga 1999). The politics of ethnicity has acquired a peculiar sharpness in Mombasa and in Coast province generally since the clashes of the 1997 elections, intended to flush out *watu wa bara* (up-country people who are not regarded as indigenous to the coastal region).

This context cannot be ignored in analysing citizen engagement with public institutions. The areas in which the council estates are located are densely populated and therefore any organised group constitutes an attractive vote bank for local politicians and aspirants. The tenants' struggle has not escaped the politics of ethnicity. Among the tenants there are suspicions that the reason why the council has paid no attention to the state of the estates is because the majority of tenants are *watu wa bara* – up-country people.

The political climate plays a big role in determining the types of strategies citizens' collective action will adopt. In a party-based political system that is not defined by issues and programmes, patronage sets in. There have been moments of setback in mobilisation efforts, when the respective tenants' associations that make up the joint Shelter Committee were in disagreement about whether to align their interests (and therefore political support) with a particular politician.

Relationship between central and local government

The relationship between central and local government in Kenya has been marked by determination by the former to control local affairs. The Local Government Act, which defines the functions of local authorities, gives a lot of oversight powers to the Minister for Local Government. For instance, local authorities need the Minister's approval for their budgets, employment decisions and the setting of local rates (such as property rates), as well as the Attorney-General's approval for any by-laws enacted. The 1998 Local Authorities Transfer Fund (LATF) Act requires central government to designate 5 per cent of income tax revenue to local governments, which is then allocated among the various councils on the basis of population and subject to the councils' submission of a detailed budget and service delivery plan (Smoke 2004). This allocation, in addition to local rates and licence fees, makes up most of the local councils' revenue.

With few sources of revenue and an unpredictable flow of central government allocations,[16] municipal councils are still expected to provide a wide range of services. The pressure on local governments to raise revenue locally in meeting their service delivery mandate means that Mombasa municipality will be very reluctant to relinquish ownership of council estates that bring in a predictable and regular (though meagre) share of their revenue. It does not help that the economy of the city as a whole has been in decline since 1990 and therefore revenue from business licences and service charges has been falling (Gatabaki-Kamau *et al.* 2000: 1). Income from council housing accounts for 10 per cent of the council's revenue.[17] The biggest expenditure item is salaries for the council's bloated workforce and the councillors' generous allowances.[18] The irony was not lost on the tenants when a newspaper story on a council decision to increase rents by 30 per cent was published alongside a story on the councillors' vote to increase their own allowances by about 50 per cent.[19]

The relationship between central and local government is complicated further because the local government structure exists side by side with a provincial administration system under the Office of the President. This system is governed by a hierarchy that operates in a top-down fashion from Provincial Commissioner to District Commissioner, to a divisional administration at the sub-district level, then to a chief at the location level, assistant chief at the sub-location level and headman at the village level. The lines of authority and responsibility are not clearly defined and conflicts between councillors or council bureaucrats and district officials have often been bitter.[20]

The council tenants encountered this tension in their fight against the grabbing of public land. After obtaining the details of 'grabbed plots' they tabled these lists before the Municipal Physical Planning Liaison Committee, which set up a task force chaired by the District Commissioner, comprising the Municipal Engineer, Provincial Commissioner and Physical Planning Officer – a mix between council bureaucrats and provincial administration officials. The task force confirmed that these plots had indeed been irregularly allocated and that the buildings erected on them did not comply with the building code, primarily because many of them blocked off access to public amenities. The task force recommended revocation of the building approval. This revocation needed to be issued by the Town Clerk. The plot owners are wealthy and politically well connected, both on the local and national political scene. The Town Clerk was reluctant to take any action that the councillors would not approve of. Two months later no action had been taken. In April 2001 the tenants' association in Changamwe estate wrote to the committee requesting permission to demolish an illegally erected wall on one of the grabbed plots that was blocking a road, since the committee was afraid to take action against the grabbers. After a month of waiting in vain for a response from the committee, the residents mobilised and demolished the offending wall. In May 2001 the Provincial Commission wrote an urgent letter to the Town Clerk directing him not to approve any building plans for that plot, or 'any transaction that would provoke residents'.

In terms of protocol, the Provincial Commissioner has no authority to direct the Town Clerk. However, the Provincial Commissioner has a mandate to 'maintain law and order' within his jurisdiction, and the riotous demolition of the wall had turned this into a 'law and order' issue. The District Commissioner serving in Mombasa at the time (DC Rotich) was particularly responsive to citizens' complaints about land grabbing, and the tenants and other groups took full advantage of this and drew in the provincial administration whenever they could.[21] It is quite ironic that citizens would turn to the infamous provincial administration (reputed to be a top-down authoritarian and unresponsive structure) to reign in the excesses of their elected representatives (councillors). This should caution against too much faith in representative democracy as a means to secure accountability and responsiveness.

Public institutions' accountability to Parliament
If political accountability were functioning well, the tenants would be able to get their local MP to raise the issue in Parliament through questions to the Ministry of Local Government and/or Ministry of Lands and Housing and expect that action would be taken, for instance to compel the council to come up with a plan for proper maintenance of the estates or a plan for instituting a tenant purchase scheme. The tenants do not consider this to be a serious option because local MPs have been implicated in land grabs in the previous regime. Tough talk against corruption in the current regime notwithstanding, no action has been taken against them. Some MPs previously served as councillors and did nothing about poor housing conditions in the estates, and therefore the tenants seriously

doubt that they can be relied upon to champion their cause in their new capacity as MPs. There is also a perception that approaching Parliament in Nairobi is a circuitous route, far removed from their reality, and there is no guarantee that the Ministry of Local Government will take action, let alone that the council will act on any directive the Ministry might issue. However, this route is worth a try, if for nothing else at least for the sake of building up a record and strengthening the case for more direct forms of accountability on the basis that the conventional representation-based system for political accountability has failed to serve citizens. The tenants' own proposal for Citizens' Committees in every ward as a forum for ongoing engagement with MPs and councillors expresses a desire for more direct forms of political accountability, but a case needs to be built up for them.

Protection of citizens' rights

Political power must be configured so as to ensure that the boundaries of the state–citizen relationship are observed and that citizens' rights are protected against the excesses of politicians and bureaucrats. In the case of council housing, protection is very weak and council tenants are rendered vulnerable. Kenya's constitution does not provide for a right to adequate housing[22] or a right to an adequate standard of living. However, these are internationally recognised in the International Covenant on Economic, Social and Cultural Rights, to which Kenya is a signatory.[23] A draft constitution produced in March 2004 after a broadly consultative process of constitutional review does make proposals for recognition of a broad range of economic and social rights, including housing, but it is not possible to predict whether or when this new constitution will be enacted.[24]

There is no statute dealing with housing. The Housing Act (Chapter 117 of the Laws of Kenya) relates narrowly to the activities of the National Housing Corporation. A proposal is underway to enact a Housing Act that deals with housing broadly (Draft Sessional Paper 2002). Kenya has not had a national housing policy since 1967 (Sessional Paper No. 5 1966/7). The most recent population and housing census indicates an urgent need for such a policy in view of a major housing crisis in urban areas (Central Bureau of Statistics 1999). An updated policy is only in the process of being drafted by the Department of Housing, and is yet to be presented in Parliament for endorsement (Draft Sessional Paper 2002).

The legal and institutional framework governing council tenancy specifically is also inadequate. There is no national legislative framework regulating the manner in which councils manage housing. This is left to each council's own by-laws, and many councils have not even enacted specific by-laws to deal with housing. Although the Minister for Local Government in 1995 issued a legal notice in 1995 stipulating standards of habitability for buildings, these relate to new construction and there is no provision for their retroactive application to existing housing, nor any clear indication that local councils are also bound by the order as owners of buildings, in addition to being the enforcers of the order.[25]

The laws that are intended to regulate landlord–tenant relations are not applicable where the government is the landlord. Councils as landlords are exempt from these general laws that spell out the obligations of landlords to their tenants. In addition, the law makes it less likely that council tenants will seek redress to hold councils to account. Government bodies (including local authorities) are exempt from the application of the Rent Restriction Act. The Rent Restriction Act sets up a Rent Restrictions Tribunal, which offers a cheap procedure for resolving disputes in a forum that is easier for low-income tenants to access. A low-income tenant is defined as any tenant paying less than Shs. 2,500 a month – just under US$40. Under this law, a low-income tenant cannot be evicted or have their rent increased without an order from the Rent Restrictions Tribunal (Bodewes and Kwinga 2003: 227). The exemption of government-owned housing from the jurisdiction of the tribunal means that low-income tenants of council housing are easier to evict. If they wish to challenge their eviction they must pay for the more expensive court process, which they are rarely able to do, not only on account of cost, but for fear of reprisals and loss of the lease altogether.

The argument for a change in this aspect of law is strengthened in the face of the breakdown of accountability mechanisms at the level of council and central government responsibility. Council tenants are effectively denied access to justice. In order to protect the rights of council tenants as citizens a mechanism for redress is necessary, even if it is not judicial redress. This could take the form of an ombudsperson for public housing, or a special dispute resolution tribunal that deals with such disputes involving government housing and government land.

In order to play a significant facilitative role in the institutionalisation of gains made by struggling groups, rights must be understood and employed as part of a broader strategy of political contestation (Hunt 1990: 318, 319). A clear legal framework setting out rights and responsibilities in concrete areas goes a long way. However, a struggle that focused narrowly on securing legal recognition of a right to adequate housing, for instance, would be missing the opportunity for broader political engagement. Such engagement would entail articulating a link between inadequate (or lack of) housing and disenfranchisement: how it begets other forms of deprivation such as generalised insecurity, inability to access quality health and education services, gross under-investment of city government revenues in those areas, and citizens' lack of voice over the way in which the city's or state's revenue is spent (Appadurai 2001: 28).

What is the nature of the bureaucracy?

How responsive is the bureaucracy to the citizens who rely on its services? Is the bureaucracy professional and relatively autonomous? Does it have systems of fiscal and administrative accountability that function reasonably well?

Degree of responsiveness and autonomy

Conventional understanding expects the relationships of responsiveness and accountability to function as follows: bureaucracies involved in service delivery will be responsive to citizen needs, and accountable to elected officials (Goetz and Gaventa: 2001). This expectation presumes that the bureaucrats have a measure of autonomy and that there exists a clear separation of powers between the civil service bureaucracy and the system of elected representatives. But bureaucrats in councils do not enjoy autonomy from councillors, and the functioning of the bureaucracy that runs council housing illustrates this. The council housing docket falls within the Directorate of Housing. But proposals by the director have to be endorsed by a resolution passed by the councillors. The tenants' associations learnt the hard way about the effect of the tangled relationship between bureaucrats and politicians in the council. One local councillor was very supportive of the tenants' efforts to get the estates converted into Tenant Purchase Schemes. The councillor managed to get the director of the housing development department on his side, and also cultivated support among a few more councillors. They planned to table a draft resolution at a full council meeting. Some tenants who are also council employees claim that the reason the proposals were never presented to the council is because as soon as the mayor got wind of it he summoned the director of housing and told him in no uncertain terms that if he tabled those proposals before the council he would be dismissed. Technically the mayor has no power to dismiss the director, since the director, like all civil servants, is recruited through the Public Service Commission, which is a central government body. He is therefore answerable to the Ministry of Local Government and not the council.

However, it is not uncommon for mayors and councillors to use their influence to get civil servants dismissed or transferred to less attractive postings.

In this type of setting bureaucrats cannot afford to be responsive to citizens if to do so jeopardises their careers. Even leaving aside meddling mayors, the set-up gives no incentives to council bureaucrats to pay attention to complaints, views or suggestions of service users, because their terms of service are not linked to performance. The line of accountability only goes upwards to the Ministry, and no reference is made to citizens' assessment. Little wonder, then, that building alliances with bureaucrats has not been a feature of the council tenants' struggle. It would not make strategic sense for a movement to invest in cultivating long-term relationships with bureaucrats whose own tenure is so precarious.

Fiscal and administrative accountability

How efficient are the bureaucracy's systems of fiscal and administrative accountability? Fiscal accountability through formal systems of auditing and financial accounting for the use of public resources is extremely weak. Ideally, fiscal accountability would mean relying first on the council's own internal auditing procedures to detect abuses, and, second, on the general review function performed by the office of the Comptroller and Auditor-General, who reports to Parliament on the use of public resources in all government agencies, including local authorities. The tenants are able to estimate the revenue that the council gets from the rent they pay, but their demands that the council make public its expenditure statements have met with no response from the council. This information is essential in enabling the tenants to build a case showing that it is possible for the council to carry out essential and urgent repairs (to leaking roofs, for example), and that tenants' offers to make labour contributions would make such repairs feasible. The tenants' suspicion is that the council routinely deploys revenue from the rents to pay salaries and has no plan setting aside a portion of the revenue for routine maintenance of the estates, a perception that is not helped by frequent worker strikes or strike threats over delayed or missed salaries.[26] Complete lack of transparency in the management of council finances only fuels such suspicions.

There is some hope as awareness spreads about the Local Authority Transfer Fund (LATF) and about the requirement that, as a condition of accessing the fund, councils develop a Local Authority Service Delivery Action Plan (LASDAP) in a participatory process that involves citizens in identifying priority projects. However, central to enabling meaningful direct citizen participation is the ability to access information on how the council operates. There is no provision for monitoring the implementation process.

Administrative accountability operates through procedures that require bureaucracies to operate within their defined mandate and to report to ministers and legislatures. So in this case the directorate of the housing development department would be required to report to the Ministry responsible for housing, which would in turn be accountable to the relevant parliamentary committee, for instance the Public Investments Committee since the estates are public property. No such reporting appears to be required of the directorate. As a first step, such a report would provide an inventory of all housing owned by the council, which is important in the face of allegations that some have been 'privatised' informally; individual bureaucrats and councillors have sold them off or are collecting personal rents from them. That the Ndung'u Commission was unable to get such an inventory does suggest that councils have something to hide. The Commission complains that, of all the public institutions it had to interact with, local authorities were the most uncooperative. The Commission requisitioned from each local authority comprehensive lists of all public utility lands in its jurisdiction, as well as a list of all allocations to individuals and companies. The information supplied was grossly inadequate and the Commission concedes that it was unable to establish the full extent of land grabbing in areas administered by local authorities (Government of Kenya 2004: 39). This suggests that serious implementation of a simple reporting requirement has the potential to shake up the opaque council bureaucracy and expose irregularities.

The issue of land grabbing exposes administrative accountability failures at higher levels implicating the Commissioner of Lands and the Office of the President. As noted in the beginning, checks and balances such as the use of an Allocations Committee have been dispensed with in favour of unfettered allocation powers personified in the President or Commissioner. With respect to public land within townships the Commissioner of Lands is authorised to make such land available for sale subject to four conditions.[27] The first condition – only if such land is not required for public purposes – has evidently been breached. In Mombasa's council estates incidents of the sale of functioning marketplaces, school playgrounds, road reserves and parking lots attest to this. Second, the Commissioner must satisfy himself/herself that the land has been subdivided into plots clearly designated as suitable for residential or business purposes. This too has been breached: in Tudor, for instance, a commercial building with shops and bars has been built right in between residential blocks. Third, any buildings constructed on the plots must conform to specified building conditions. This must be verified by the Town Planning Officer and Town Engineer. This has been breached, as evidenced by structures on road or railway reserve land and others blocking off access to public amenities. Fourth, the land must be sold through an auction, preceded by advertisement and balloting 'unless the President otherwise orders in any particular case'. Records show that no auction for sale of public land has been held anywhere in the country in the last 50 years, and there is no documentation of a presidential order exempting specific plots from auction (Government of Kenya 2004: 11). A reasonable interpretation would presume that such presidential order must be in writing, even though the statute does not say so. It is difficult and futile to distinguish between allocations that had presidential exemption (issued verbally) and allocations made by low-level functionaries on the pretext of such presidential permission.[28]

Ultimately, the overall expectation that public land allocations will be in the public interest has been gradually eroded as the scrutiny mechanisms have disappeared altogether.[29] The Ndung'u Commission confirmed and substantiated Kenyans' suspicions that public land allocations were being used to reward political loyalty and to buy votes. The Commission found that allocations would intensify in the build-up to a general election (Government of Kenya 2004).

The tenants' fight against land grabbing draws attention to issues of scale in struggles for accountability: weak groups organising at the local level will focus on local manifestations of a problem, their immediate experience of deprivation of rights, but the accountability failures are on a nation-wide scale. The local-level organising may at best change the behaviour of local powerful individuals or officials, but without changes in the policy environment that makes corrupt behaviour possible, even such slight gains at the local level become difficult to sustain.

Conclusion

The analysis of accountability and responsiveness in citizens' engagement with public service delivery institutions in the case of the Mombasa council tenants' struggle, through the lens of the framework proposed by Goetz and Gaventa, shows a gap between ideals and context-specific realities. It becomes clear why, after ten years of struggle, the only victories that the tenants can point to have been about staving off the worst harms. These are not small achievements by any measure: keeping well-connected business interests at bay is remarkable. However, their efforts have not imprinted a legacy on the public institutions they have engaged with – in the form of a positive change in policy at local or national government level, for instance, or institutionalised changes in the specific practices and procedures of the Housing Development Department or municipal council. This absence of a lasting legacy is explained by a combination of the factors explored above, namely: the group's fluctuating social and cultural power and narrow economic base; inability to sufficiently distance the group from a politics of patronage and ethnicity and cultivate a new way of engaging; and a bureaucracy in which accountability systems have broken down and public officials have no incentive to be responsive to service users. With respect to the problem of land grabbing, issues of scale make it difficult for the tenants' localised actions to have impact on accountability failures on a national scale.

Inevitably, the tenants' ongoing struggle will continue to face one key dilemma: they need sustained action for long-term institutionalisation of accountability mechanisms in the larger political context and in the relevant bureaucracies that play a major role in shaping the struggle. Yet struggles for basic rights often have a sense of urgency about improvement in one's condition, and therefore in order for people to join and stay committed there must be some indication that this will materialise sooner rather than later. This is not easy to resolve, but it seems there is no shortcut to gradually building a genuine movement: the shift from protest to proactive action is imperative.

NOTES

1 Throughout this paper, the term 'accountability' is understood as comprising two dimensions: answerability (that public officials/institutions are under obligation to justify their actions) and enforceability (that sanction follows failure to account and failure to perform and that citizens have redress for harm suffered) (see Newell, Chapter 2). Responsiveness is used in the sense articulated by Goetz and Gaventa: 'the extent to which a public service agency demonstrates receptivity to the views, complaints and suggestions of service users, by implementing changes to its own structure, culture and service delivery patterns in order to deliver a more appropriate product' (Goetz and Gaventa 2001: 6).

2 The author is part of a team of Institute of Development Studies (IDS) researchers that has had close interaction with the Mombasa council tenants for three years (since 2002). Part of the participatory action research involved facilitating their strategic planning. It is hoped that the reflections in this chapter will make further contributions to that process of shaping a strategic vision for the struggle.

3 The last population census was held in 1999. Mombasa's population then was 643,168, with 181,849 households (Central Bureau of Statistics 1999: 15).

4 This is the most common type of housing available. The particular history of land tenure

and administration in the coastal region has produced a high incidence of absentee landlordism, so it is common to find that the owner of the house is not the owner of the land, but collects rent from tenants who each rent a room and share bathroom facilities. Technically their tenure is insecure because they could be evicted and the structures demolished should the landowner claim the land back.

5 This single-room living arrangement is not unique to Mombasa. The 1999 census found that 59 per cent of urban households nationally live in a single room. In the capital city, Nairobi, the figure is 67 per cent (Central Bureau of Statistics: 1999: 18–19).

6 Unless otherwise stated, the information presented here about the estates was generated by the Tenants' Associations from historical profiles, collective mapping exercises and interviews with key informants such as elderly residents and one active member of Changamwe Village Development Association who is a retired councillor and therefore had access to the council's archives. Their findings were then presented and discussed at a workshop in April 2003 which the author helped to facilitate. See 'Sharing Experiences and Mapping out Strategies for Advancing the Struggle for Shelter Rights' (Joint workshop for Tudor, Mzizima and Changamwe Tenants' Associations – Mombasa, Kenya, 15 and 24 April 2003).

7 ILISHE stands for 'Ilimu Sheria', Kiswahili for 'legal awareness'.

8 Following the 1997 clashes, average hotel occupancy fell to 26 per cent. The tourism sector suffered further setbacks with the embassy bombing in 1998. As of 1999, average hotel occupancy had fallen to 11 per cent (Gatabaki-Kamau et al. 2000: 2). The bombing of an Israeli-owned resort at the coast in 2002 further devastated Mombasa's economy.

9 Personal communication with Justus Munyithia, counsel for ILISHE, 18 April 2005. The case reference is Wilson Ndolo and others v Municipal Council of Mombasa and National Housing Corporation, Chief Magistrate's Court Case No. 4542 of 2004.

10 There is a tricky balance to strike between staying politically engaged as individual citizens free to form party or other affiliations, and at the same time building up (or at least not undermining) the inclusiveness and social legitimacy of the struggle. Open discussion is a good start and needs to become a regular practice, not just in response to extreme cases. In addition, perhaps it is time the group agreed to some general principles on their members' political engagement: for instance, agreeing not to use the tenants' association's name to further partisan activities, and not wearing party insignia to tenants' association events.

11 See Miano Kihu, 'We'll Resist Eviction by Council, Vow 114 Families', Sunday Nation, 24 October 1999.

12 Memorandum of Mzizima Staff Housing Estate to the Commission of Inquiry into the Land Law System in Kenya (the Njonjo Commission), 6 July 2000.

13 See Daily Nation, 19 July 1994.

14 Employing a Gramscian framework of analysis, Hunt refers to this process as one of counter-hegemony: 'the process by which subordinate classes challenge the dominant hegemony and seek to supplant it by articulating an alternative hegemony' (Hunt 1990: 312).

15 This divergence of views emerged at a review meeting held at ILISHE, Mombasa, 14 December 2004.

16 LATF is expected to make central government remittances more predictable but this is not yet the case. Using population as the basis for allocation is rigid and does not respond to changing needs, and is also contested (Smoke 2004).

17 The other revenue sources are: rates (taxes on land) 44 per cent; service charges 19 per

cent; market fees and commercial rents 10 per cent; business licences 8 per cent; other revenues (from user fees for health services, for example, or nursery school fees) 9 per cent (Gatabaki-Kamau *et al.* 2000).

18 Salary arrears are a frequent cause of confrontation between the council and its employees. See, for example, 'Council Unable to Pay Arrears', *Daily Nation*, 4 January 1995.

19 See 'Council Increases Rents', *Sunday Nation*, 9 July 2000, p. 4. The same story also exposed institutionalised nepotism in employment, whereby each councillor had a quota of employees to bring in, and some councillors had exceeded their quota, resulting in overemployment and causing a bitter row at the council meeting.

20 One source of conflict is with respect to a policy that was introduced in 1983, the District Focus for Rural Development. Under this policy, a District Development Committee is given the power to approve all development projects funded by the central government, even when those projects are proposed by the local authority (Government of Kenya 1987; Smoke 2004). The District Development Committee is chaired by the District Commissioner and in several cases DCs who did not have good relations with elected councillors have frustrated local authority projects.

21 See 'Squatters Paid Shs. 2.4m' *Daily Nation*, 10 April 2001; ILISHE Trust 2002.

22 The UN Committee on Economic, Social and Cultural Rights defines 'adequate housing' to include secure tenure. The other defining features are: availability of services (such as water, heating, lighting, refuse disposal), affordability, habitability (protection from damp, cold, heat, rain, structural hazards), accessibility (especially to vulnerable groups such as physically disabled, elderly, children), location (proximity to employment, schools, health services), and cultural adequacy. See UNCESCR, *General Comment No.4, Right to Adequate Housing*, 1991, available at http://www.ohchr.org/english/bodies/cescr/comments.htm

23 Kenya's constitution recognises a right to private property under Section 75 of the constitution, but this has been interpreted narrowly to refer to a right to compensation for compulsory acquisition of property by the state.

24 See http://www.kenyaconstitution.org.

25 *Kenya Gazette Supplement No. 44*, Legal Notice No. 257, The Local Government (Adoptive By-laws) Building (Amendment) Order, 7 July 1995.

26 See 'Council Unable to Pay Arrears', *Daily Nation*, 4 January 1995.

27 Sections 12–15 of the Government Lands Act, Chapter 280 of the Laws of Kenya (revised edition 1984).

28 In the absence of transparent processes, fraud has characterised the public land allocation system. Examples include: direct allocations by the Commissioner of Lands without presidential delegation of powers; allocation of government land that was already alienated for other purposes; multiple allocations of the same piece of land; forged letters of allocation bearing the President's name (which the Commissioner of Lands then acts upon to confer title); and even fake documents of title (Government of Kenya 2004: 75).

29 Similar breaches of procedure became the norm in dealing with 'special lands' – lands protected by law on account of their ecological integrity, cultural significance and strategic importance such as forests, wetlands, historical sites and lands set aside for research and scientific installations (Government of Kenya 2004: 15). Breaches also plagued settlement lands purchased by the government for purposes of settling landless people.

REFERENCES

Appadurai, A. (2001), 'Deep Politics: Urban Governmentality and the Horizon of Politics', *Environment and Urbanization*, Vol. 13, No. 2, pp. 23–43.

Bodewes, C. and Kwinga, B. (2003) 'The Kenyan Perspective on Housing Rights', in S. Leckie (ed.), *National Perspectives on Housing Rights*, The Hague: Kluwer Law International, pp. 221–40.

Central Bureau of Statistics (1999) *Kenya 1999 Population and Housing Census: Analytical Report on Housing Conditions and Household Amenities*, Nairobi: Government Printer.

Gatabaki-Kamau, R., Rakodi, C. and Devas, N. (2000) 'Urban Governance, Partnership and Poverty: Mombasa', Working Paper No.11, Birmingham: International Development Department.

Goetz, A. M. and Jenkins, R. (2004), *Reinventing Accountability: Making Democracy Work for Human Development*, Basingstoke: Palgrave Macmillan.

Goetz, A. M. and Gaventa, J. (2001) 'Bringing Citizen Voice and Client Focus into Service Delivery', IDS Working Paper No. 138, Brighton: Institute of Development Studies.

Government of Kenya (1987) *District Focus for Rural Development*, Nairobi: Office of the President, Government of Kenya.

—— (2002), Draft Sessional Paper on Housing, Ministry of Land and Housing, unpublished.

—— (2004), *Report of the Commission of Inquiry into the Illegal/Irregular Allocation of Public Land*, Nairobi: Government Printer.

Hunt, A. (1990), 'Rights and Social Movements: Counter-Hegemonic Strategies', *Journal of Law and Society*, Vol. 17, p. 309.

ILISHE Trust (2002) 'Land and Shelter Rights Struggles of Communities', unpublished mimeograph, ILISHE Trust.

McAdam, D., Tarrow, S. and Tilly, C. (2001) *Dynamics of Contention*, Cambridge: Cambridge University Press.

Mutunga, W. (1999), *Constitution Making from the Middle: Civil Society and Transition Politics in Kenya*, Nairobi: Swedish Department for Research Cooperation (SAREC).

Smoke, P. (2004), 'Kenya: Erosion and Reform from the Centre', in D. Olowu and J. Wunsch (eds), *Local Governance in Africa: the Challenges of Democratic Decentralization*, London: Lynne Rienner Publishers.

Southall, R. and Wood, G. (1996) 'Local Government and the Return to Multipartyism in Kenya', *African Affairs*, Vol. 95, No. 381, pp. 501–27.

Tarrow, S. (1998) *Power in Movement: Social Movements and Contentious Politics*, Cambridge: Cambridge University Press.

CHAPTER 7

Rights to health and struggles for accountability in a Brazilian municipal health council

ANDREA CORNWALL, SILVIA CORDEIRO AND
NELSON GIORDANO DELGADO

The right to health is enshrined in Brazil's 1988 constitution, dubbed 'the Citizens' Constitution' for giving legal form to the demands mobilised in the struggle for democratisation. The realisation of this right is intimately linked with the pursuit of accountability. The architecture of the Brazilian health system has at its foundation an acknowledgement of the contribution that citizens can make to equitable and efficient service delivery through their role in mechanisms of accountability. The right to health is instantiated in the monthly meetings of *conselhos de saúde*, health councils, at municipal, state and national level, in which representatives of civil society come together with health workers and representatives from the municipal government to audit health spending and approve health plans. Endowed with the power to make binding decisions, the *conselhos* are mandated by law to approve budgets, plans and accounts before monies can be released from the federal coffers.

The health of the population is a fundamental resource for the nation; and maintaining national health systems that can deliver services to the mass of the population, especially those who can least afford health care, is of symbolic as well as political and economic importance. Yet the provision of public health services also requires resources. It involves significant investment and management of public monies, and difficult decisions over allocations of ever-diminishing budgets. Throw in the complications of a mixed health system, where there is statutory acknowledgement of the limits of state provision and the need to contract out particular services to the private sector, and add historic distrust on the part of citizens in the probity of its bureaucrats, and the interplay between the realisation of rights and demands for accountability become all the more complicated.

This chapter is about how citizens in the small north-eastern Brazilian municipality of Cabo de Santo Agostinho, in the state of Pernambuco, have sought to realise the right to health through efforts to exact accountability from their municipal government. It tells the story of the evolution of the town's municipal health council, and reflects on some of the challenges for the realisation of the right to health that persist. It begins by introducing the health councils, their structure and functions, and the political context out of which they arose. It then goes on to explore the origins and evolution of the municipal health council in Cabo. Focusing on some of its successes and shortcomings in the pursuit of accountability, the chapter reflects on some of the challenges faced by citizen actors in pursuing the right to health through these institutions.[1]

Brazil's health councils: new democratic spaces?

Popular participation in the governance of health services has been on the international health agenda since the 1970s (Loewenson 1999). In many of the co-management and consultative institutions established as part of health sector reforms, citizens are provided with opportunities for involvement in discussion, and sometimes in decision making, over making the delivery of health services more effective (Cornwall, Lucas and Pasteur 2000). Less commonly found are institutions that offer citizens a role in deliberation over health policy and the nature of health service provision, matters that are often retained as functions of the state. Rarer still are institutions that endow social actors – not merely individual citizens but the representatives of organised civic associations – with the legal right to approve budgets and health plans, and play a part in ensuring accountable governance. This is the function of Brazil's innovative participatory health councils (Coelho 2004; Coelho and Nobre 2004; Coelho, Pozzoni and Cifuentes 2005). Operating at each of the three levels of government – municipal, state and national – the health councils lend shape to a set of norms and institutional arrangements for the provision and governance of health care that provide new opportunities for citizens to engage directly in holding the state to account for their right to health. Each municipal and state government in the country is obliged to have a health council, with a structure that is predetermined by national decree.

The Brazilian health system – the Sistema Único de Saúde (SUS) seeks to embody the basic principles of universality, equity, decentralisation and *controle social*, a term which constitutes only part of what the word 'accountability' has come to mean in English. Health councils are organs of accountability in a number of senses.[2] They are sites for the pursuit of fiscal accountability, in which citizen representatives can literally audit the accounts of the local government, and pick up and pursue any anomalies. They are also sites for answerability, as public sphere institutions to which public officials are obliged to present accounts and explanations for health spending. And they are sites that provide citizen groups with a direct interface with health policy decision makers at every level, and which serve – in theory at least – to maintain the accountability of these public officials to diverse publics. They are open to members of the public and, whilst only elected councillors have the right to vote, all present have the right of voice.

Brazil's health councils represent a form of governance institution that has gained considerable popularity in recent years as a space for 'cogovernance' (Ackerman 2004). Writing on the challenges for accountability of these new governance institutions, Cornwall, Lucas and Pasteur (2000) suggest that one of their most pressing challenges is overcoming embedded hierarchies that are so much a feature of the health sector, especially in the constitution of expertise and 'ignorance'. In Brazil, an unusual confluence of influences has made these dynamics more complex. For the generation of medical professionals now in senior positions within the public health system and in non-statutory health organisations, the national health system and its participatory institutions was the fruit of a long and intense struggle by the radical public health movement (the *movimento sanitarista*) of the 1970s and 1980s, in which many of them took part as medical students. A deep commitment to public health and to the right to health arose out of this movement, and inspired a generation of visionary doctors, whose agency has been so crucial at every level to the success of democratising health reforms.

The system of participatory health councils was envisaged by the health reformers who mobilised for its institutionalisation both as a means of creating an interface for civil society with the government and as a further political means of democratising Brazilian society, by stimulating the engagement of associations, movements and other forms of popular organisation with the process of governance. The councils were seen as providing a complement to the representative democratic system, involving representation of a different kind – of civil society organisations rather than elected politicians. The councils are composed according to strict rules of parity. Civil society organisations constitute 50 per cent of the council's representatives. They are elected by civil society delegates at municipal conferences or in municipal assemblies.

Representatives of health workers make up 25 per cent of the council's members, and include primary health care auxiliary nurses and outreach workers, doctors and specialist health workers. The last 25 per cent is made up of representatives from the municipal health secretariat and contracted-out service providers, consisting of the Secretary of Health, and managers of municipal hospitals and clinics in the public and private sector.

The notion of *controle social*, literally 'social control', represents at once the idea of 'the people' controlling what is rightly theirs *and* the enlistment of publics in the auditing of health spending. The term is often taken to extend to citizen engagement in health policy and planning, and to represent the right to participate at every level and in every aspect of health sector decision making. Yet in practice, as we go on to suggest, there are limits to citizen participation in this context that confine the possibilities for engagement to a narrower auditing role.

Background

The municipality of Cabo de Santo Agostinho, with a principally urban population of just over 150,000 people, lies in the Greater Recife area in the state of Pernambuco. The town is an important economic centre because of its strategic location, its established industrial facilities and its expanding service sector, especially in the tourism, health and retail sectors. Despite those economic potentialities, Cabo de Santo Agostinho has low human development and infant development indices, substantial populations of people below the poverty line and a high rate of illiteracy. Its mixed epidemiological profile reflects the diseases of poverty and those associated with urban living, such as cardiovascular and degenerative disease. Health services are provided at neighbourhood health posts, and by referral to municipal and private hospitals in the town of Cabo de Santo Agostinho itself. The successful implementation of a national primary health care programme – which involves teams of community health agents, who are linked to health posts staffed by a doctor and nurses, doing regular house-to-house visits – has brought marked improvements over the last seven years in a range of health outcomes, from a drop in the infant mortality rate (from 41/1000 to 18/1000) to reduced hospital admissions figures.

Cabo has a rich history of social movement mobilisation, dating back to agrarian struggles, the engagement of the progressive Catholic church, informed by Liberation Theology, during the period of the dictatorship, and a strong feminist movement with regional and national connections.

Immediately after the return to democratic rule, a progressive democratic party held the municipal government until shortly after the first wave of implantation of the *conselhos*. A diversity of social movements, NGOs and corporate social actors exist in both urban and rural areas in the municipality. Some of these are long-standing organisations, supported by the progressive Catholic church's work with base communities. Others came into being as a result of the first wave of democratisation in the late 1980s with support from the municipal government, and continue to benefit from municipal government *subvenções* (literally subsidies, grants to support their activities). Others still are directly contracted through *convênios*, statutory agreements, with the municipal government for the delivery of social and health services. There are around 130 registered civil society organisations in the municipality, and many more small community-based organisations dealing with issues in their immediate locality. The character of the state and of civil society, the nature of mutual dependencies and of cross-cutting links that exist across their borders, mediated by the church and by political parties, is extremely significant in making sense of the struggles for accountability in the municipality.

Cabo's municipal health council: laws, structures and purpose

Cabo's municipal health council (*conselho municipal de saúde*, CMS hereafter) was officially inaugurated by Municipal Law 1.687 on 12 May 1994, according to Federal Laws 8080/90 and Law 1840 /90. It was established with the following goals:

1 To define municipal health priorities;
2 To establish guidelines to be followed when making the municipal health plan;
3 To act on making strategies and controlling the application of the health policy;
4 To propose criteria for financial and budget planning and application of the municipal health fund, auditing transfers and use of resources;
5 To follow, evaluate and audit health services provided to the population by public and private institutions with SUS service contracts in Cabo;
6 To define quality criteria for the functioning of public and private health services within the SUS;
7 To call the municipal health conference every two years, together

with the executive, according to the Lei Orgânica da Saúde (Basic Health Law).

Cabo's CMS is made up of 20 members and 20 substitutes, distributed as follows: 10 service users; 5 health professionals; 3 public managers; 2 representatives of private services with contracts with SUS. Its legal status is that of a collective body of public administration linked to the executive branch of government. The CMS meets once a month for 3–5 hours, meetings are open to the general public and take place in a central location in Cabo, in a building – the Casa de Conselhos ('House of the Councils') - provided by the municipal government.

The CMS was established in Cabo just as the progressive Partido do Movimento Democrático Brasileiro (PMDB) government lost office to the conservative Partido da Frente Liberal (PFL). In its initial years, there was little opportunity to develop its potential. As in many parts of Brazil, the council came to be an extension of the municipal government, filled with appointments made by government and serving as a mechanism for rubber-stamping the government's decisions. This period of crisis was extremely significant in shaping the current CMS. Popular movements, progressive Church interests, unions and the feminist movement joined forces in a popular front to pressurise the municipal government to democratise the health council. The return of progressive government in 1997 was accompanied by the recruitment of an energetic, radical reformer into the position of Secretary of Health, and the revitalisation of the CMS and reforms to the health system that ushered in what is today's SUS in the municipality.

While citizens can attend and have rights of voice in health council meetings, councillors are elected as representatives of civil society organisations. Terms are for two years, renewable for a further term. In 2000, the health council elected its first civil society chair – one of the first in Brazil, where it is usually the municipal health secretary who takes up this position. During 2000–2, intense discussions within the CMS gave rise to internal regulations that sought to further democratise the action of the council. Rules of representation were evolved to ensure a diversity of communities of place and of interest, with half of the civil society seats being allocated to representatives of neighbourhood associations and the remaining half to those representing particular interest groups, such as the women's movement, the black movement and disabled people. These efforts culminated in the largest municipal health conference held to date, in 2003, at which new councillors were elected by several hundred delegates who had been elected at pre-conferences in four regions of the municipality. Ranging in age from their early 20s to their late 60s, most of Cabo's councillors are lower-middle-class or working-class, on average having no more than secondary schooling and often only primary level education. During 2003–5, the council's civil society complement consisted of civil society organisations as diverse as an Afro-Brazilian cultural centre, a herbal medicine non-governmental organisation (NGO), an association representing 'progressive' elements of the Protestant church, a Catholic workers' movement and a feminist NGO, along with residents' associations from all over the municipality. To extend the health council's scope yet further, in recent years efforts have been made to inaugurate local health councils in neighbourhoods in the municipality.

The health council is notionally autonomous and thus independent of the municipal government. In practice, however, it is reliant on the secretariat of health to provide resources for it to function effectively, including paying for the costs associated with administrative support. This support is critical to the council's viability, as the administrator not only keeps records of meetings, prepares documents for councillors to read and convenes meetings, but also reminds the councillors of the meetings, keeps them up to date with any changes in policy at state or national level that are communicated to her by councillors involved at those levels, and helps to organise training, transport of councillors and logistics for participating in events such as conferences. Charged with functions that require both significant investments of time and money, this infrastructure and resourcing is critical – underfunding undermines both the possibility of the council being able to exercise social control effectively, and the trust that members have in the seriousness with which their work is taken by the government.

Council members are entitled to demand access to public health accounts and explanations about certain investment and spending decisions, as well as to pay visits to clinics, health units, and hospitals to carry out spot checks. An auditing committee, composed of two CMS councillors and a member of the public, is charged with carrying out a number of such checks, examining stock cupboards for expired or badly stored medicines and inspecting the facilities. The mandate of the councillors extends beyond that of a watchdog, however, in their function as representatives of broader community interests. One of their tasks is to consult broadly amongst their constituents about local health plans, and to become directly involved in organising biannual health conferences, where such plans are opened to discussion. Councillors' own perceptions of what being a member of the CMS entails varies significantly, as does the way in which they frame their role in relation to the task of holding government to account. In a participatory workshop, councillors gave the functions of the health council as follows:[3]

- To facilitate popular participation in health public policies; to define priorities, audit resources and evaluate results.
- To develop projects as well as to audit what is approved by the council.
- To promote social control, with popular and democratic participation.
- To contribute to the system's better functioning, with popular participation.
- To enforce peoples' rights, already guaranteed by SUS.
- To audit users' demands for good service.
- To exercise social control through organised civil society, playing a central role and directing public policies for the sector.
- To jointly discuss and establish the best options for public policy.
- To propose and to follow public policies.
- To be a deliberative body where members have the opportunity to audit and to contribute to health policies.
- To provide citizens with conditions conducive to participation in public health policies in the community.
- To contribute to the management, auditing and construction of health policy.

A lack of clarity over what the role of the council ought to be, and what its limits actually are, is one of the factors that hampers the work of the council. Newly appointed councillors are sent on training courses, of variable quality, which teach them the basics about what their role involves, and instruct them in the various technical procedures that are part of health budgeting and planning. This is, however, a rather rudimentary education: necessarily so, as the costs of providing such training are significant. Councillors talked about how useful and important the training they had received was for them, and how much they valued opportunities to go on further courses and attend events in the nearby metropolis, Recife, including state-level conferences on a range of health-related topics. For those who had been able to take up these opportunities, they were regarded as an invaluable opportunity for personal as well as professional growth, expanding their horizons and bringing them into contact with similar people from other municipalities. Not everyone, however, is interested in taking up these opportunities or able to do so, and there is a general feeling in the council that people do not have enough of an idea of what exactly they are there to do.

People enter the council with expectations that are shaped by their previous experiences, whether in political parties, social movements or their own communities. Their own interpretations of what *controle social* ought to be all about play a part in defining what for them are the appropriate concerns of the council, as well as the boundaries of their own interventions in this space. How do these different perceptions of the function of the health council play out in practice? The next section explores some of the everyday dynamics of the health council, and the meanings of accountability and rights that citizen representatives, health workers and managers bring to their engagement with the health council.

Accountability in practice

The everyday business of the CMS ranges from listening to presentations by organisations who deliver services, to being informed about the plans of the municipal health secretariat, to discussing specific incidents that have been reported by members of the public concerning the provision of health services. There is little deliberation on matters of health policy; health plans are prepared by the government, without any attempt to engage the participation of health councillors in their formulation, and presented to the council for their approval, along with periodic presentations of the accounts. There is equally little expectation on the part of health councillors that they will be involved in the health policy and planning process, even though some see their responsibility in these terms.

Examination of the minutes of the CMS for the last three years reveals a series of patterns of interaction between health bureaucrats, citizens and health workers. One is a pattern of information provision followed by question and answer, which generally involves one of the managers, and most often the Secretary of Health. There is often little or no deliberation over the issues brought for consultation, nor does there appear to be any expectation of a more broad-ranging discussion: they are presented as matters of fact, questions are asked, and the matter is closed. This is the way that the municipal health plans tend to be treated. Another pattern is one of clarifying or contesting the way in which things are being done by debating whether something should be on the agenda, whether the council needs to have a position or a policy, and so on. At times, this appears to be about the council exploring the boundaries of what they are expected to do, at times about finding ways of working more effectively. Yet another interaction is more adversarial, generally involving denunciations of the quality of care or lack of services available in public health facilities, but also extending to critique of particular medical staff or failures to provide certain services. Rarely does this turn into constructive debate as to what to do about it, taking a more predictable pattern of making a complaint, and the complaint being recorded.

The minutes of the health council meetings support the impressions that we gained from our conversations with representatives. Users talked of the need for persistence, of wearing down a reluctant bureaucracy until they gave in to demands; managers spoke of the frustration of dealing with users who clearly did not understand either technical issues or the bigger picture; and workers spoke of the difficulties they faced in meetings, being unable to speak out against managers, but equally feeling on the receiving end of the criticisms levelled by users in their denunciation of health service provision. These tensions are played out in the space of the meeting. Styles of interaction echo the different purposes that the council serves, from the adversarial, distrustful stance of user representatives in contests with the state through to the posture of consultation, with users and workers listening to and asking questions of the managers, to a more collaborative relationship, with users and workers making suggestions together, and management agreeing with them. These different purposes are held in a permanent tension and create significant paradoxes for what participation in the council comes to mean to different members.

Deliberation in the council often appears to be less about content than procedure; quite what councillors actually understand deliberation to mean says more about their perceived role in auditing and authorising decisions than in deliberating the nature of health policy and the content of health plans, as the following quote from a user representative illustrates:

> We are not a consultative body; we are a body that deliberates. The manager has his/her own planning team ... he or she makes an action plan, what is going to be spent on health ... he or she comes here and presents to us what is going to be spent within the plan for each account. It comes to us, we take a good look at it and then we say if we approve the plan or not. If it is approved the government can go ahead with it, it can spend the money approved ... it is up to me, as a councillor, each three months, to say where it has advanced, because accounts are rendered every three months.... The council audits them really closely, members have the right to go to take a look for themselves; if it is wrong, we can stop it. That is the role of the council.

Framed in this way, realising the right to health involves making sure the municipal health secretariat and the medical staff they employ do their job: discussions rarely stray outside the frame of what that job is defined as by the government. There are strict rules that are set by central government about the proportion of money that should be spent on primary care, and guidelines and models for the delivery of care at that level that municipal governments can opt out of, but doing so may present political risks, which are better avoided. Municipal health secretariats can, however, contract out a greater proportion of secondary and tertiary care to the private sector, if they wish, and pursue health plans that give less priority to the health rights of the poor. As one union activist – a former CMS representative and a regular and vocal figure in CMS meetings – pointed out, it was the job of the CMS to hold the government to account for the resolutions made in the health conference, not to make policy. Yet even he conceded that the long shopping list of promises that constituted these resolutions necessitated prioritisation, and that the lack of citizen engagement in that prioritisation process potentially undermined the prospects citizens had for holding the government to account for its role in realising their right to health.

The worlds of the bureaucrat and the citizen tend to intersect most on questions of probity, and very rarely around issues that might be regarded as 'technical'. There have been notable exceptions. The current chair combed through the epidemiological report for the previous year and found a large number of untreated cases of one prevalent condition, which he brought to the health council as a concern. It was, however, not a concern that was debated: he simply informed them that he had composed a letter to the authorities noting the incidence of this condition, and calling for more attention to be paid to providing effective medical treatment. It was evident that his own technical knowledge did not extend to knowing exactly what that treatment might be – unlike treatment activists in other contexts, including parts of Brazil, who would be able to demand specific medication. What mattered, for him, was putting on the record that not enough was being done: a form of interaction with the authorities that was as familiar to him, from his activist background, as it was to a number of his fellow councillors. It needs to be remembered that he, like many user representatives, has rudimentary education and does not come from a medical background. To take up an issue like this is in itself evidence of the kinds of changes that the CMS has made possible. It is, however, an exception: many of the most effective challenges to the municipal health secretariat tend to come from people with medical training, who are able to directly pursue lines of argumentation that are simply not available to ordinary citizens.

Making a difference

Despite difficulties and contradictions, CMS actors have been relatively capable of taking initiatives, speaking out, expressing criticism, proposing and resisting in their role as civil society representatives. Acting autonomously, they have sought allies in social movements and within the state on certain issues of mutual concern, such as outsourcing of services. Common political sympathies – such as anti-privatisation sentiments – create bridges across the health council, and have worked to strengthen the power of the CMS in seeking to withstand the tide of marketisation that threatens the public health system. Where the municipal government's policies are in the interests of poorer members of the community – and this could be said, by and large, for the Partido Popular Socialista (PPS) government that was in office when we carried out this research – then this auditing role within the broader ambit of a SUS that delivers on its promises of equity and equality makes management and political sense. Yet much comes to depend on the character of individual bureaucrats, as on the broader agenda of the municipal government. The scope for conflict and co-option is as present in these spaces as that for collaboration, and civil society representatives may adopt a range of strategies for engagement, which put them into conflict with each other.

Shifting alliances and commonalities between health bureaucrats, health workers and user representatives complicate attempts to categorise actors as part of bounded interest groups. These alliances take shape in other spaces – the space of the party office, the church, the neighbourhoods in which councillors live. Party affiliation may make more of a difference when it comes to some issues; belonging to a common faith may matter more when it comes to others. Debates in the space of the council call on these allegiances, and on cultural styles familiar from other spaces: they are often characterised less by the kind of detached rational argumentation that is evoked in the writings of deliberative democrats than by other processes of persuasion that are laden with power, whether bound up with personal loyalty, religious belief or belief in superior knowledge or expertise, and political strategies and tactics that make the CMS an intensely political arena.

When councillors were asked what difference the council had actually made to the well-being of people in the municipality, the answers were often couched in terms of the kinds of successes claimed by the municipal health secretariat. Health bureaucrats emphasised the importance of the CMS in creating a bridge with civil society, as much as some acknowledged the limitations that civil society representatives had in understanding the complexities of health provisioning. For a number of the user representatives, the successes of the CMS were closely identified with making the health system function better: they pointed to the successes of the CMS in dealing with demands to guarantee service provision and improve the quality of care, thus contributing to the accomplishment of municipal health plans and improving basic health care units, access to tests, specialised outpatient centres, social mobilisation for municipal conferences, and the establishment of local health councils.

There seems to be a broad acknowledgement by the actors involved that the existence of the council has made some contribution to reducing the practice of clientelism and exchange of favours as the predominant form of access to health services in Cabo. Similarly, there has been an increase in public recognition and identification of privileges existing in the sector as well as the possibility of fighting to end them. Yet a number of current as well as former user representatives were much more circumspect about the successes of the CMS. Yes, they said, there had been gains: the council is an institution worth having. But they highlighted a wide range of concerns, from the 'party-isation' of the space of the council, to the compacts between government and user representatives benefiting from service contracts that complicate prospects for accountability, to the lack of voice of more marginal members, silenced as much through fear of the repercussions of speaking up as through their own lack of confidence in what they might have to say. For some, these factors neutralised the potential of the council as a mechanism of *controle social*; for others, they were an inevitable part of it, something which required constant vigilance as well as active strategies for its further democratisation.

A further dimension of reflections on the council concerns the gap between the ideals of the SUS and the realities of scarce resources, and the difficulties of ever overcoming the barriers to access experienced by those with complex and expensive conditions that simply could not be treated effectively at this level because of shortcomings in the ways services are articulated. These raise larger concerns about the very way in which the SUS is organised, and about the tensions between democratising priority setting and the medical exigencies with which planners of public health have to deal in order to be able to contribute to guaranteeing the right to health.

Realising the CMS as an accountability space

Even when the practice of participatory governance institutions does not meet the expectations that were created as part of the political struggle that led to their institutionalisation, most case studies conducted in Brazil stress their 'positive impact on the process of construction of a more democratic culture in Brazilian society' (Dagnino 2002: 162). The significance of this impact cannot be underestimated in a country with such an entrenched authoritarian tradition as Brazil, which combines state centralisation with local clientelism, and where economic modernisation and the location of Brazil within international capitalism has been conducted under an authoritarian regime, worsening its elitist and exclusionary character. Institutionalised participatory spaces such as the CMS contribute, by and large, to the collective political effort to democratise the implementation of public policies in Brazil, since (1) they confront elitist conceptions of democracy, (2) they challenge authoritarian conceptions about the primacy of 'technicians' and 'the technical' in state decision-making processes, (3) they challenge state monopoly over the definition of what is public and what the public agenda should be, and (4) they contribute to reducing clientelism and to more transparency in government actions (Dagnino 2002).

From what we gathered in Cabo, the signs are there that the process of creating spaces for accountability is having some effect on the culture of politics, with the hope expressed by some councillors that the expansion of local councils will serve to further open, and broaden, spaces for participation. It is evident, however, that simply creating spaces for citizen participation is no guarantee that old political practices will not simply be reproduced within them (Cornwall 2002). The council is an intermediary space. It is one that lies in between a series of other spaces: those of associations, of the bureaucracy, of health providers, of political parties and a range of other social and governmental actors. It is one threaded through with relationships, with party political alliances, clientage relationships and tensions. Social actors representing civil society are far from autonomous *vis-à-vis* a municipal government which gives many of them small grants to support their activities, and has contracts with others to deliver services. Neither civil society nor the state can be thought of as constituting a homogeneous bloc; and amidst the universe of civil society organisations in Cabo there exists tremendous diversity in terms of capabilities to engage in these spaces, as much as in their own internal democracy and accountability and claims to legitimacy, which further complicate their interactions within the space of the council.

To be effective in holding the state to account, health councils require a range of resources – the provision of which goes beyond the means and the responsibility of civil society members. Funds are needed to support the everyday functioning of the council, to provide a space to meet and someone to organise meetings, keep records and notify councillors of any pertinent changes in policies or upcoming events that require their attention. Financial resources are also required to support the training of representatives, not just from the users' segment – who require information on the structure and functioning of the health system, and on interpreting accounts and budgets to be effective – but also from the health workers and managers' segments, to equip them with the capabilities to participate in this kind of forum. Beyond these material resources, there are further technical and symbolic resources that are critically important if councils are to have 'teeth'. Active participation by user and health worker representatives is often not matched by commitment from managers, whose inaction and perceived lack of respect for councillors undermines the potential of the CMS as a space for accountability.

Although managers often voice professions of intent and eulogies regarding the importance of citizen participation in *controle social*, their conduct is perceived by many user representatives to reveal a very different attitude. The municipal government was charged by some user representatives with failing to provide adequate and timely information; seeking to drive through plans and budgets at short notice; giving councillors very little chance to find out and debate what they entailed; and exerting 'pressure' at key decision-making moments. There is a significant consensus among user representatives – shared by some health worker councillors – that the lack of value given to the CMS by the bureaucracy acts as a critical brake on its effectiveness. There remains amongst bureaucrats a very real tension between the legitimacy the CMS can offer them, and a perception that 'the council wants to be the manager', displacing what they see as properly their prerogative in making decisions about public health.

Contests over the meaning of *controle social* lie at the heart of the ambivalent relationship between managers, workers and users in the CMS. Conflicts and tensions between users and managers can be interpreted in terms of contestation over two distinct although not entirely incompatible conceptions about accountability through participation. One conception (commonly held by managers) sees participation as a model for the management of public policies and another one (generally that of users) understands participation as a process of democratisation of those policies. Of course, that does not mean that managers are not interested in democratising the process, or that users do not see management as relevant. But it does shed light on why the demarcation of issues as 'technical' becomes so important in the conflicts that arise in spaces of *controle social* over public policies, and it is linked precisely to the struggle for effective power sharing between state and civil society actors in those spaces. On one hand, acknowledging the legitimacy of politicising the technical is a way for civil society actors to demand power sharing. On the other hand, the constant reaffirmation of the essentially technical character of decisions is an argument enabling state bureaucracy to retain maximal power. Which direction the balance tilts in will depend on actors' political forces in distinct scenarios, and the result is always provisional.[4]

Conclusion

For all the shortcomings people identified – and there were many – everyone we spoke to, without exception, viewed the CMS as critical to the very possibility of accountability, and as an institution worth preserving no matter what difficulties were experienced in making it effective. People across the board – from the director of a maternity clinic to a temporary auxiliary health worker, to a worker at a programme for black youth, to the founder of a centre for herbal medicine – all felt that being part of this institution had provided them with opportunities for hearing new perspectives, learning new things and contributing to improving public health in Cabo. The very newness of this institution, and its counter-cultural nature in a political context marked by pervasive authoritarianism and clientelism, means that the potential for change may only be realised over a much longer term. The challenges are many, from changing the very dispositions of political society to transforming relationships in a sector marked by the hegemony of hierarchies of expertise. But there is every indication that, slowly, the CMS is beginning to make a difference, turning users into citizens who are aware that access to decent health services is not a favour, nor a privilege, but a right, and transforming a culture of clientelism into a culture of accountability.

Realising that right and enabling the cultural shifts that are required for accountability calls for continued efforts to change relations of power that enable managers to frame consultation and control the agenda, that deny lower-level health workers a voice, and that work to undermine the possibility of democratising health policy and planning. Overcoming these obstacles is a challenge that calls for new and imaginative ways of breaking and remodelling the old cultural patterns that limit the exercise of citizenship. As one councillor put it:

> When you begin to get the rights you have, and the way to seek those rights without the need for an intermediary, without favours or party-political

bargains, then you change the character of the life of a society into one in which citizens have awareness, in which you know what you are entitled to.

To fulfil their democratising potential, participatory governance institutions like health councils require more than citizen awareness and active citizen engagement – although this, and the further democratisation of the public sphere that would lend greater legitimacy and representativity to civil organisations, is a vital precondition for their role in making the work of *controle social* effective. What is also needed is an active, engaged and enabling state, a state whose bureaucrats recognise the role of accountability in democratic governance and who respect their obligations in creating the conditions and providing the resources that can facilitate citizen engagement – both material and symbolic. On one hand, efforts to enhance accountability need to reckon not only with an often idealised model of 'civil society participation' but with particular and shifting configurations of state–society relations, and the extent to which such configurations condition the possibility of accountability and require a range of potential strategies on the part of social actors – whether inside 'invited spaces' such as the health council or in 'popular spaces' outside them. On the other hand, they need to take account not only of the possibilities presented by enabling legislative and institutional frameworks, but also of pervasive political culture. There are, in short, no easy recipes, and for all the enabling conditions that would seem to exist in this case – supportive legislation, a municipal government that has at least provided some material support and had a public commitment to participation, a strong and organised civil society – the struggle for accountability in Cabo continues.

NOTES

1 This chapter is based on participatory research carried out in collaboration between the three authors – the ex-chair of Cabo's Municipal Health Council and director of the Centro das Mulheres do Cabo, a local feminist NGO; a political economist from the Rural University of Rio de Janeiro; and an anthropologist from the IDS, Sussex – and members of Cabo's health council and of the municipal administration. Parts of this paper are drawn from a longer paper (Cordeiro, Cornwall and Delgado 2004) prepared as part of the DfID-ActionAid Brazil *Olhar Crítico* ('A Critical Gaze at Practices of Citizenship and Participation in Brazil') project. Thanks to Alex Shankland for comments.

2 See Newell (Chapter 2) and Goetz and Jenkins (2004) on different dimensions of and interpretations of 'accountability', and Cornwall, Lucas and Pasteur (2000) on these issues with reference to the health sector.

3 Derived from cards produced at a participatory workshop held in Cabo on 12 April 2004 which included users' and health workers' representatives. Health managers chose not to attend.

4 In countries with authoritarian political cultures such as Brazil, it is probably more realistic to assume that the balance has a fatal attraction to state actors.

REFERENCES

Ackerman, J. (2004) 'Co-governance for accountability: beyond "exit" and "voice"', *World Development*, Vol. 32, No. 3, pp. 447–63.

Coelho, V. S. and Nobre, M. (2004) *Participação e Deliberação: Teoria Democrática e Experiências Institucionais no Brasil Contemporâneo* [Participation and Deliberation: Democratic Theory and Institutional Experiences in Contemporary Brazil], São Paulo: 34 Letras.

Coelho, V. S. (2004) 'Conselhos de Saúde Enquanto Instituições Políticas: o Que Está Faltando?', in V. S. Coelho and M. Nobre, *Participação e Deliberação: Teoria Democrática e Experiências Institucionais no Brasil Contemporâneo* [Participation and Deliberation: Democratic Theory and Institutional Experiences in Contemporary Brazil], São Paulo: 34 Letras.

Coelho, V., Pozzoni, B. and Cifuentes, M. (2005) 'Participation and Public Policies in Brazil', in J. Gastil and P. Levine, *The Deliberative Democracy Handbook*, San Francisco: Jossey Bass.

Cordeiro, S., Cornwall, A. and Giordano Delgado, N. (2004) 'A Luta Pela Participação E Pelo Controle Social: O Caso Do Conselho Municipal De Saúde Do Cabo De Santo Agostinho, Pernambuco', Rio de Janeiro: ActionAid/DfID.

Cornwall, A. (2002) 'Making Spaces, Changing Places: Situating Participation in Development', IDS Working Paper 170, Brighton: Institute of Development Studies.

—— (2004) 'New Democratic Spaces? The Politics and Dynamics of Institutionalised Participation', *IDS Bulletin*, Vol. 35, No. 2.

Cornwall, A., Lucas, H. and Pasteur, K. (2000) 'Accountability through Participation: Developing Workable Partnership Models in the Health Sector', *IDS Bulletin*, Vol. 31, No.1.

Dagnino, E. (2002) 'Democracia, Teoria e Prática: a Participação da Sociedade Civil', in R. Perissinotto and M. Fuks (eds), *Democracia. Teoria e Prática*, Rio de Janeiro/Curitiba: Relume Dumará/Fundação Araucária.

Goetz, A. M. and Jenkins, R. (2004) *Reinventing Accountability: Making Democracy Work for Human Development*, Basingstoke: Palgrave Macmillan.

Loewenson, R. (1999) 'Public Participation in Health: Making People Matter', IDS Working Paper 84, Brighton: Institute of Development Studies.

Young, I. M. (1996) 'Communication and the Other: Beyond Deliberative Democracy', in S. Benhabib (ed.), *Democracy and Difference: Contesting the Boundaries of the Political*, Princeton: Princeton University Press.

PART II • INVESTOR ACCOUNTABILITIES

Overview: Rights, resources and corporate accountability

PETER NEWELL AND JOANNA WHEELER

> The rapid expansion of global investment, production and consumption, in short, has collided in many places and in many ways with local communities. The collisions take place in both developed and developing countries.... Lacking the protection of either national or global norms and institutions, poor and marginal communities in developing countries are either left to suffer or fight or both. (Zarsky 2002: 2)

This section of the book explores the ways in which poorer groups mobilise to hold powerful corporate actors to account for their social, environmental and developmental responsibilities. We noted in Chapter 1 the way in which the state has assumed a central place in discussions about accountability in development amid the attention given to the good governance agenda. Embodying the technocratic approach to accountability that we are questioning in this book, the good governance agenda has privileged sound accounting, reporting and transparency as the central pillars of accountability. It is thus unsurprising that many such notions of accountability have been picked up and put into practice by the private sector. Indeed, there is an intimate relationship between the state and corporate accountability that lies at the heart of initiatives such as 'publish what you pay', recognising the key role of the private sector in attempts to combat government corruption.

Nevertheless, there is a broader and more fundamental accountability agenda that is neglected when we pose the issue in terms of sound financial management and clear reporting requirements. In a context of globalisation, businesses have assumed new forms of power which derive from the legal protection they now operate under as well as unprecedented access to new areas of the world. Investor agreements and global trade accords have enshrined these new powers, described by some as the 'new constitutionalism' (Gill 1995). While the rights of capital are more protected than ever before, the same cannot be said of the labour companies employ or the communities that host them. Questions about who regulates companies which increasingly operate beyond the control of any one state and who, therefore, is responsible when they fail to act responsibly, acquire central importance in development.

This raises issues about the ability of conventional tools of accountability to operate effectively in this new context and, in particular, to serve the needs of poorer and more marginalised groups. International regulation, and in particular international law, is seen to be weak and underdeveloped, and the capacity and willingness of states to regulate business have been thrown into doubt. Businesses themselves have proposed voluntary forms of self-regulation, but issues regarding their enforceability and scope have generated scepticism about whom they serve and how effectively. In this governance gap, NGOs, social movements and community groups have been constructing new mechanisms of accountability through a diversity of means. Though the breadth of strategies adopted towards this end demonstrates a remarkable diversity, and the range of both sectors and regions that we explore in this section of the book reflects a vast geographical canvas, the interesting, notable and politically significant point is the similarities and connections between the ways in which poorer groups in the global North and South are organising to put power into accountability.

Engaging allies across levels of decision making and beyond national borders, groups have mobilised through imaginative and incredibly broad repertoires of protest to register dissent, amplify voice and construct alternatives. Some strategies are aimed at enforcing rules and regulations set by others. Mobilisations around labour laws in the United States bear this out in the form of the living wage campaign and efforts to contest the racialised (non)-enforcement of environmental protection measures. Others are aimed at questioning deeper assumptions about who bears the costs and secures the gains from development. In the Niger delta, the contest is centred around the distribution of oil revenues, raising in turn complex and fraught questions of land ownership and entitlement, and magnifying ethnic divisions and sensitivities. In India, marginalised groups question why they are being asked to bear the social costs of adjustment by hosting large industrial projects that primarily benefit wealthier urban élites. Often, then, the issue at stake is the right to say no and the right to claim accountability. Positive rights that do exist are often systematically violated, or lack of awareness about their existence makes it easy for governments to overlook them.

Though played out through localised contests, these conflicts very rapidly assume much wider political dimensions. While garment workers in Bangladesh find their working conditions under scrutiny as a result of civil society campaigns about 'sweatshop' working conditions, activists in the North attempt to exert pressure on oil companies in order to change their operations in Nigeria. To some extent, companies force the spotlight on themselves, engaging in global claim making regarding their responsibilities and invoking the language of citizenship while continuing to be involved in controversial projects on the ground. The case of the National Thermal Power Corporation in India bears this out clearly.

The politics of promoting and ensuring corporate accountability is played out across many arenas simultaneously, therefore, implying a range of actors and raising awkward questions about where the lines of responsibility are drawn between state, market and civil society. The nature of the accountability contest inevitably changes according to the context, reflecting unique histories of conflict and distinct cultures of accountability. The materiality of the resources over which these contests and claims are fought brings into sharp relief questions of power over production and distribution, and, in so doing, raises questions of equity and justice. In Nigeria these controversies are often played out along ethnic lines. In the United States racial dimensions assume a higher profile in debates about environmental racism. Despite these differences, what we find are surprising similarities between the way groups mobilise to contest their fate as the social and environmental sinks that absorb costs associated with other people's development. From using 'weapons of the weak' (Scott 1985) and strategies of resistance, to various forms of engagement with formal institutions, what we see amid the empirical diversity is convergence around many of the themes we highlighted in Chapter 1 about the importance of cultures of accountability, the limits of strategies that rely upon change produced through the law, and the importance of viewing accountability struggles not as an end in themselves, but rather as a surrogate for the pursuit of a variety of forms of social and environmental justice.

REFERENCES

Gill, S. (1995) Globalisation, market civilisation and disciplinary neoliberalism *Millennium: Journal of International Relations* Vol.24, No.3, pp. 399–423.

Scott, J. C. (1985) *Weapons of the Weak: Everyday Forms of Peasant Resistance*, New Haven: Yale University Press.

Zarsky, L. (2002) 'Introduction', in L. Zarsky (ed.), *Human Rights and the Environment: Conflicts and Norms in a Globalizing World*, London: Earthscan.

CHAPTER 8

Corporate accountability and citizen action: cases from India[1]

PETER NEWELL WITH VAIJANYANTA ANAND,
HASRAT ARJJUMEND, HARSH JAITLI, SAMPATH
KUMAR AND A. B. S. V. RANGA RAO

We have a social responsibility to the community ... a moral responsibility ... we have to give something back ... we take this very seriously.[2]

We are being sacrificed for the national interest. We are the victims of this cause. What do we get in return?[3]

Given the imprecision of the term accountability as a guide to identifying who is responsible to whom and for what, it is unsurprising to find that in India, as in the other case studies featured in this book, competing notions of accountability feature prominently in conflicts over resources. Cultures of blame and shame collide amid a fog of claims and counterclaims regarding the respective responsibilities to one another of states, business, civil society and the communities at the centre of the conflict. Unlike the Nigerian case discussed in Chapter 10, the conflicts described below have been less violent in their conduct, less global in their scope, but no less political or intractable as a result.

Many companies, particularly multinational enterprises, are increasingly employing the language of citizenship to describe their relationship to society in the context of debates about corporate social responsibility. The limitations and dangers associated with corporate co-option of the language of citizenship, where entitlements are often claimed without assuming corresponding obligations, have been explored elsewhere (Newell 2002; 2005). In liberal notions of citizenship, rights claims are validated and mediated by the state. In the context of debates about corporate accountability, this becomes problematic in so far as the dual roles of the state as promoter and regulator of investment may create conflicting responsibilities. In circumstances in which the state fails to enforce the responsibilities of corporations under its jurisdiction, we may expect to find evidence of groups exposed to the harmful side of weakly regulated investment adopting their own self-help strategies to seek responsiveness from the corporations they host. The citizenship that is expressed by such actions is an active, living citizenship, a version of the concept that is often lost in more legal-constitutional and state-based notions of the term. Exploring the ways in which the poor seek to define and practise their own notions of citizenship should not, however, allow for a negation of the core responsibilities of the state towards its citizens, including the proper regulation of the social and environmental consequences of industrial development.

These competing notions of citizenship manifest themselves in contests over the nature of rights and responsibilities that apply to states, corporations and communities in the context that provides the case studies for this paper: India. While companies such as the National Thermal Power Corporation (NTPC) invoke a globally constituted notion of good corporate citizenship derived from the UN Global Compact (Global Compact 2005), the communities with which they are in conflict, employing a different and more localised notion of citizenship, invoke rights to work, to a secure livelihood and to a pollution-free environment. The claims they make refer to rights that the state is duty-bound to provide for its citizens, but in this case fails to enforce. The citizenship companies project through philanthropic acts and references to responsible conduct is a voluntary concept of 'good citizenship', in theory backed by rights and obligations articulated in legal statutes, in practice often not enforced.

This then is the link to accountability, a concept with two elements at its core: answerability and enforceability (see Chapter 2). The active forms of citizenship that groups express in the cases explored in this chapter aim to produce new forms of answerability: obligations to account for actions and to acknowledge the claims of communities. The particular focus here is relations between corporations and communities in three sites in India, though implicated in this relationship are many other actors from government as well as local NGOs, their national counterparts and the media. This focus provides interesting insights from the frontline of corporate accountability where communities confront corporations in situations of huge power disparity. The three case studies discussed here are, first, the controversy surrounding the NTPC power plant in Paravada, Visakhapatnam (Vizag), Andhra Pradesh; second, the struggles around the development of the Lote Industrial Area in Chiplun, Maharastra; and, third, conflicts around tribal rights and mining in Dumka, Jharkhand.

The first case concerns the siting and operation of the NTPC near the port city of Visakhapatnam in Andhra Pradesh (AP). The Simhadri Thermal Power Project (STPP) under the aegis of the NTPC was commissioned in Paravada, 40 kilometres from Vizag. The AP State Electricity Board signed a power purchase agreement with NTPC in 1997, and construction work started in 1998 after land was acquired from 13 villages spread over three mandals in Vizag district. The plant only started operating fully in May 2002. The company at the centre of this controversy, NTPC, is in many ways a national flagship company, a symbol of national pride, enjoying a significant degree of government backing. NTPC is not just a powerful player within Indian politics, but the sixth largest thermal power corporation in the world and a member of the UN's Global Compact.

The second case concerns the Lote-Parshuram Industrial Area, located in Ratnagiri district of Kokan region in Maharashtra. Following an announcement in 1988 by the Government of India of the development of 'growth centres', the Maharashtra Industrial Development Corporation (MIDC) was given the primary responsibility for selecting 140 sites for mini-industrial areas, acquiring land, and the planning and development of the basic infrastructure (Anand 2002). Many petrochemical companies have established themselves there, including Rallis, Gharda chemicals, Van Organics and National Organic Chemical Industries Limited (NOCIL), producing pesticides, fertilisers, paints and a variety of organic and inorganic chemicals. Like Vizag, the area has attracted the interest of these industries because of an abundance of cheap labour, bountiful natural resources and access to coastlines for the convenient disposal of effluent. Indeed, MIDC has explicitly invoked the availability of creeks for the disposal of treated effluent in campaigns to lure prospective investors (Anand 2002).

The third case centres on the mining industry and its relationship to tribal communities in and around Dumka, Jharkhand. It focuses on small-scale mining activity in Santal Pargana, particularly the 57 stone mines and associated stone factories in three villages of Dumka district. Though the Government of India has recognised the inalienability of tribal rights to land,[4] there is much evidence, including in this case, of their transfer to non-tribals. The incentives for land grabs, corruption and violence are high, since both the government and the private sector have a keen interest in gaining access to and control over the land the tribals occupy and its associated mineral wealth. The conflict is fuelled, as in the previous cases, by both the indiscriminate use of the Land Acquistions Act and pressures for regional commercial development, this time in the form of the World Bank/IMF-assisted Bihar Plateau Development Project, which have resulted in large-scale industrial, mining, irrigation and power projects being undertaken on tribal lands (Arjjumend 2004).

Differences between the three sites in terms of the nature of the companies involved and the responses of the affected communities generate interesting and important lessons about the possibilities and limitations of different accountability strategies. What is striking, however, is the very many similarities in terms of the ways in which decisions were made regarding the investments and the ways in which communities were both affected and sought to mobilise to defend their interests. The cases are used as a basis for identifying the key factors determining the conditions in which it is possible for communities to protect their interests through the construction of new mechanisms of accountability with the corporations they host. These are discussed in turn below. The issues raised by these case studies have a wider resonance than the regions or sectors to which they refer, as we see in Chapter 9 on environmental justice struggles in the United States. The challenges they imply are confronted by many communities around the world faced with similar dilemmas and engaged in struggles that might be advanced by an understanding of what has happened in these three locales in India.[5]

Limits of the law

Accessing the law and realising the rights it is meant to protect presents an enormous challenge for marginalised groups. At the centre of battles over land, livelihoods and compensation in the cases explored here is the Land Acquisitions Act of 1894, a remnant of colonial legislation which allows authorities to remove people from land according to some loose and poorly defined notion of the 'public interest'.

While some people receive compensation, many do not, and these cases suggest important limitations of viewing financial compensation as the ultimate goal of an accountability struggle or as an adequate substitute for political reform. In Vizag, while some families received compensation for their land at a rate above the commercial value of the land (at Rs225,000 or Rs2.25 Lakhs per hectare),[6] many receiving compensation were not entitled to any employment within the plant once constructed, jeopardising the employment opportunities of younger members of those families. Many of those most affected by the industrial development, such as landless labourers, do not have an entitlement to the land on which they work, and are therefore not able to receive any compensation. In Chiplun, for example, herders who grazed their cattle on land owned by the Maratha or Brahmin community got nothing, because the landowners sold it to MIDC (Anand 2002: 17). Community groups have demanded that the government secure compensation for these affected groups on the basis that the company has a 'social obligation' if not a legal obligation to pay for the damage it has caused. But most negotiations have resulted in a bad deal for the local communities and have taken place in private and with no formal records kept. Even where formal agreements have been reached, such as those between mineowners and landholders in Dumka, Jharkhand, none of the landholders who gave over land on mining lease have been given copies of the lease documents, despite having signed or thumbed those documents. None of the mineowners countersigned the settlements, leaving them unaccountable for their obligations (Arjjumend 2004).

An additional problem is that much land is not registered, as it was considered ancestral property and there are no village records, so no entitlement to compensation exists. Land acquisition officers in Hyderabad reported that the land around the NTPC site was 'wasteland', land that is not fertile or productive, so that all cultivation that has taken place on the land is illegal. It is perhaps unsurprising, therefore, that some community leaders accuse the government of 'behaving like monarchs' in driving people off what they perceive to be their land. This suggests the importance (in positive and negative terms) of property rights to the exercise of rights-based claims, either in clarifying the customary rights of communities or, more insidiously, in concentrating access rights in the hands of the powerful. The problem in realising rights, however, is brought out in the Jharkhand case, where 'when they saw the opportunity to gain economically and to get regular employment in return for foregoing their land rights, the tribal families engaged with the mining industry' (Arjjumend 2004: 77).

While maintaining scepticism about legally based accountability strategies, there are some cases of positive change. For example, in Chiplun, a petition was filed by a number of affected individuals against the State of Maharashtra, MIDC, the Collector and the Pollution Control Board (Anand 2002: 22). The High Court advised the appointment of a committee to examine the extent of land, water and air pollution, and the committee produced an extensive report. Though not all of the measures were implemented, it confirmed the extent of pollution and the Court ordered the provision of green belts, setting up effluent treatment plants, water and air monitoring centres and 'corrective measures for industries to prevent the pollution of the Dabhol Creek' (Anand 2002: 22). In the case of Jharkhand, too, organised NGOs have filed public interest litigation suits to contest the acquisition of land for mining and the degradation that has ensued from existing mines, but delays and the costs of the legal process, as well as 'threats' from powerful local figures, prevent many tribals from going to court (Arjjumend 2004).

Capital over community

It is has been common in India for large companies to buy up large swathes of land with the help of state governments and then sell it on at a higher price for a profit, without having delivered the promised industrial development in a region. This 'grab and run' strategy has been encouraged in the past by the use of subsidies and tax breaks by competing states in order to lure investors. For example, Jharkhand's State Industrial Policy of 2001 delivers commercial incentives and fast-track clearances in order to create 'a friendly business environment'. Towards this end, land has been made available at concessional rates, advances have been provided at favourable rates of interest and businesses have been offered nominal tax rates or in some cases relieved of a tax burden altogether. Additional promises to investors include reviews of forestry, mining and tenancy laws, priority supply of power and no 'unnecessary inspections' (Arjjumend 2004: 18). The use of such measures has been justified by the anticipated employment and broader developmental gains to be made by accepting a proposed industrial plant. Such justifications have also been invoked to secure community support for the developments.

One of the consequences of the 'grab and run' strategy has been that state governments have constructed programmes of infrastructure to accommodate industry's needs, which are either discontinued or not maintained when the investor moves on, so that the local communities do not even receive this 'knock-on' benefit. While some are happy to receive any infrastructure at all from governments that normally neglect them altogether, others express anger that their demands for these developments were only met when they coincided with a similar demand from a powerful industry. More controversially still, in Lote, the people are being asked to pay for a pump and pipeline to bring the water in from elsewhere since existing water supplies have been contaminated by industrial activity. In Vizag, promises to the communities included access to a supply of free power that has not been forthcoming, despite their proximity to the plant.

Contested science, contested impact

One of the key sources of grievance for communities is the negative effect on their health of living in close proximity to the industries in question. In Vizag, for example, communities report a number of complaints that they attribute to the plant, including illnesses associated with water contamination and respiratory problems such as coughing and throat infections.[7] Ranga Rao and Sampath Kumar note that 'The presence of upper respiratory infections as reported by the villagers has also been corroborated by the PHC [primary health care] doctors, who said that there has been a substantial increase after the establishment of STPP' (2003: 7). Establishing such connections in a way that would satisfy a law court is another matter, however, underlining again the limits of strictly legal strategies. For example, to make the case that it is the Lote industrial estates that are directly responsible for the damage to their health or their livelihoods means sending samples to laboratories in Mumbai for testing, yet many cannot afford the costs of sending such samples. The NGO PRIA has been able to provide communities with water testing kits to check themselves for levels of pollution.[8] The equipment required is often not very sophisticated: litmus tests to check for levels of acidity, for example. The pollution testing kits provide a useful means by which to challenge the Pollution Control Board's own pollution monitoring figures, nevertheless, which, according to their critics, routinely downplay and underestimate levels of pollution.

In Jharkhand, many of the key health impacts derive from the combined effect of water pumped from the mines being discharged into neighbouring croplands, streams and other water bodies. In Chitragarhia village an epidemic of water-borne diseases including diahorrea, dysentery, cholera and jaundice broke out in July–August 2002, claiming several lives. Dust generated by mining activity and exacerbated by the movement of trucks in and out of the quarries, has affected crops grown in nearby areas and human health. Environmentally, the forests that are traditionally home to many tribals have been devastated by the quarries and stone crushers (Arjjumend 2004: 62). In terms of regulation, it is claimed that the mineowners have not even registered their operations with the regional office of the Central Pollution Control Board, hence studies of the effects of stone quarrying in the area simply do not exist. Besides health and environmental impacts felt 'outside' these operations, occupational health hazards for those working within them are numerous given the nature of work employees are expected to undertake: boulder splitting, exploding, drilling and other heavy-duty extractive tasks.

Workplace conditions are hardly enhanced by the absence of running water and toilets. Minimum wages, insurance and health services, Arjjumend concludes, are 'distant dreams' (Arjjumend 2004: 60).

There have nevertheless been attempts to develop alternative methodologies to capture the disparate and multidimensional effects of the industrial plants in these areas, which are often overlooked in conventional environmental impact assessments. Anand, in her work in Chiplun (2002), encouraged people to identify 'key events' that depicted the impact of the industrial belt upon their lives. The Bhoi community, in particular, spoke of the how dead fish floated to the surface of the creek: 'due to a sudden release of toxic chemicals in the creek … the whole crop of fish died in one single blow' (2002: 18). Besides alternative ways of recording and gauging impacts, activists have also challenged the ways in which current assessments of social and environmental impact are made. For example, claims that rates of malaria have increased in the communities surrounding the NTPC plant were dismissed as ridiculous until people were able to show the relationship between the pollution of the water wells, the resulting stagnation, and the increasing numbers of malaria-carrying mosquitos attracted to the area.

It is indicative of the desperate situation that confronts several communities that many people we spoke to said they would tolerate these adverse human health impacts if they were to be offered some work as compensation. It is the sense that they are suffering the negative side of this industrial development without reaping any benefits that fuels their sense of injustice. One person declared angrily: 'We are being sacrificed for the national interest. We are the victims of this cause. What do we get in return?'[9] Often the absolute dependence created by the presence of an industry in a remote area serves to suffocate community demands for accountability. This is true of the struggle in Jharkhand. Tribal residents in Chitragarhia attempted to block the passage of trucks along the road through their village in protest at the health and environmental problems being exacerbated by the traffic to the mines. Yet 'when people saw their employment at stake, the last livelihood resort … they calmly withdrew the struggle for accountability' (Arjjumend 2004: 68).

Citizen action: barriers and opportunities

Having described some of the obstacles that stand in the way of justice for these communities, this section of the chapter analyses some of the strategies adopted within the community and civil society to contest these injustices and accountability deficits.

Local NGOs, supported by wider networks, have tried to advance the cause of these communities in a number of ways. In Vizag, Sadhana,[10] a Paravada-based NGO, has been the frontline organisation in the campaign around the NTPC plant. The group has conducted surveys of the villages most affected by the plant to compile data and evidence of the impact on their lives; it has also recorded their demands and how they would like to see them met. The findings from these surveys will be presented at a local *gram sabha* (local assembly) as well as at panchayat (village government) meetings, and will feed into the People's Development Plan to be presented at a public hearing.

Public hearings and People's Development Plans

In Vizag, there has been one public hearing so far. It is hoped that the second will provide both an important opportunity to reflect on the process surrounding the construction and development of the NTPC, and to identify necessary changes in time for the consultation process regarding the proposed 'Pharma Park' in the same area. Whereas a public hearing was not required for the NTPC plant, a decision was made subsequently that future developments required such a hearing. The challenge for concerned NGOs is to ensure that people get to know about the public hearing and are aware of the implications of the proposed development for their livelihoods. As things stand, a company is required to provide one month's advance notice of a public hearing. The notice must appear in one local English-language and one Telegu-language newspaper. Details are also meant to be kept at local Panchayat offices that people can visit to read the documents. Of course, many people in the area cannot read the documents and would not be aware of where they are being held because they cannot read the notices in the newspapers.

Activists also complain that, in the past, industries have deliberately placed announcements in the least widely read newspapers in the area (a discretion in their power) and often only run the announcement for one edition on one day, so that news of the public hearing is unlikely to spread very far. Given this, there have been calls to extend the time between the announcement of the hearing and the actual event, to allow people to discuss the implications and prepare submissions, and for NGOs and others to spread news of the meeting to a broad range of potentially affected constituencies, and to assist, for example, with their transportation to such an event.

Potentially, however, the public hearings provide an important opportunity to raise concerns, and to hold the company and government publicly accountable for their past track records regarding promises concerning employment, compensation and the like. Using the hearings effectively in such a way, however, requires significant advance preparation of materials and networking with other groups who have experience of previously affected communities in order to compile evidence and testimonies that can be used in the hearing. One of the key lessons from the NTPC experience has been that if bargaining takes place once the proposed industrialisation has the go-ahead or construction work has already taken place, the chances of getting the company to respond to demands and grievances are significantly reduced. This is why significant efforts are now being put into ensuring that the process surrounding the proposed 'Pharma Park' is more transparent and inclusive, and that concerns are raised early enough in the process to secure action.

Ensuring that companies such as NTPC will attend the proposed public meeting is a difficult task in itself, given previous refusals to attend.[11] Direct appeals for meetings from NGOs, on behalf of the communities, have been consistently refused or not acknowledged.[12] While the company claims not to have received correspondence, NGOs claim to have sent numerous letters requesting meetings and raising specific issues of concern. It is hoped that the company will view future hearings as an opportunity to clarify expectations regarding the scope of its obligations to the community. Often, of course, claims of abuse of due process are aimed at state bodies responsible for overseeing these investments. In the case of Jharkhand, land acquisitions are taking place without prior consultation with local people and the *gram sabhas* of concerned villages in direct contravention of administrative provisions for panchayats and other legislation (Arjjumend 2004: 21). Those public hearings about the mines that have been organised were conducted in a 'biased and discreet manner where the local administration, the statutory bodies for clearing the projects and the mining companies are in close collusion to ensure that there are no effective objections raised by the public' (Arjjumend 2004: 85).

Local NGOs in both Vizag and Chiplun, with the support of the Society for Participatory Research in Asia (PRIA), are also in the process of constructing People's Development Plans. These are constructed on the basis of the surveys conducted by NGOs and following extensive consultations with groups in the area over a number of months. The findings are compiled as a plan of desired development for the region: the types of industrial and other activities that people are willing to accept and would like to see, and those they want to avoid. There has even been some support from companies such as NTPC for the idea of a plan. The appeal for the company is the opportunity to receive a consolidated set of demands and ideas as opposed to a steady stream of disparate and bilateral demands from communities around the plant.

Working through the local NGO Parivartan, PRIA has also assisted in the development of a People's Development Plan and in establishing public hearings in Chiplun. The first public hearing was held in 1999. Many chemical companies operating in the area, such as Rallis, only undertook a full public hearing concerning their activities after they had been operating for seven years and after much of the environmental degradation had already been caused. In setting up the hearings the groups have relied, for example, on the assistance of local medics and union activists working in the area to provide inputs for the People's Development Plan, and have tried to facilitate communication between villages along the coastal industrial belt.[13] The public hearing organised by Parivartan was the first time that industries, MIDC and people came together face to face to air their views. One successful outcome was that industry accepted the major responsibility for setting up an effluent treatment plant (Anand 2002: 22).

The People's Development Plans that feed into the hearings provide an important opportunity for inter-community learning through knowledge sharing around their experiences with particular forms of industrial development. Such exchanges of experience allow communities faced with the prospect of a development in their area to inform themselves of the risks and benefits associated with the new investment by involving communities that have already been exposed to the same industries' activities. Having heard testimonies about the pollution of a creek which led to the death of cattle, water pollution has been a key focus of villagers' concern in Lote, for example.

Despite the many benefits of such informal tools, many communities continue to channel their concerns and grievances through state authorities. In the absence of corporate responsiveness, this makes some sense and mirrors the companies' own preference for operating through the state rather than talking to people directly.

NGO accountability

In addition, a key danger for NGOs adopting these strategies is that they become cast as the legitimate representatives of the community interest in dialogues directly with industry, either in the run-up to specific events or in ongoing bilateral discussions. Many affected communities are clear about their desire for leadership from groups with the perceived expertise, resources and networks to carry forward their concerns in seeking action from government and the company. The onus is then on the NGOs themselves to manage these expectations as best they can. NGOs such as Sadhana in Vizag are keen to see that the communities themselves take a lead on these issues with themselves in a supporting role, but it is clear from conversations with these communities that they do expect the group to play a leadership role.[14]

It may also be preferable from the company's point of view to engage with an articulate NGO that enjoys some credibility with the local community, rather than have to face the strength of feeling of the affected communities directly. But such arrangements inevitably raise issues of how adequately the interests of the community are being repre-sented and whether NGOs' own agendas are always consistent with the community's needs. In the Jharkhand struggle, only two of the four NGOs are from within the tribal community. Indeed, there are suspicions that the 'outsiders' were at least partly involved in order to seek material gain and personal benefits by negotiating with the mineowners (Arjjumend 2004: 67). There may also be a difference between communities being happy for NGOs to register their concerns with companies and governments and to use their expertise to 'validate' their claims, on one hand, and, on the other, their consenting to a process whereby an NGO brokers deals and negotiates terms with a company on their behalf. The consequences and the scale of the accountability challenge are certainly more significant in the latter case, where issues of trust and transparency are more critical.

Strategic alliances with the state

There have also been attempts by community activists to form strategic alliances with lower levels of the state such as mandals and panchayat rajs. Legally, panchayats can demand information from, sanction or even stop industrial operations in their jurisdiction. Nevertheless, while aware of the problems reported to them through NGOs, or directly by the villagers themselves, state officials at this level feel relatively powerless compared to the district government, which has greater powers; officials emphasise that they have no legal control over NTPC, for example, despite its being a government undertaking. P. Jagannadha Rao (MPP), local elected head of the mandal in Paravada, feels that decisions are being made above their heads. He said: 'We have no choice but to accept these investments: they are driven by the state governments; this is government policy.'[15]

It is difficult in such settings to differentiate between genuine incapac-ity on the part of the state to effect change and inaction justified by claims of limited power. In raising critical concerns about the direction of industrial development in the area, these government bodies would be pitting themselves against the strong state-level support for the NTPC plant as well as the proposed 'Pharma Park'. These projects form part of former AP Chief Minister Chandrababu Naidu's vision of constructing a 'new economic zone' in the Vizag area. It would be costly for local leaders to appear to be against these developments, especially when they are from the same political party – in this case Telegu Desam, the majority party in many mandals and panchayats in the Vizag area. That said, there are fractures within the local state that open up opportunities for new alliances. Some officers in the local mandal office, for example, express sympathy towards villagers' claims about the human health and environmental impacts of the NTPC plant.[16] The Medical Officer appeared in a video about the conflict supporting community claims that the plant's activities were damaging health.

Importance of the media

Given this failure of information flow, the media potentially play a key role in promoting accountability. Many journalists have taken a personal interest in the NTPC issue, for example, and are keen to work with activists to build coalitions around it. Following our meetings with the communities surrounding the NTPC plant, several journalists attended a press conference we hosted to discuss the issues raised by the visit and many published stories in influential newspapers as a result (*Deccan Herald* 2003; *The Hindu* 2003). Though downplaying their role in drawing the company into a public dialogue about its operations, activists are clear that it is negative publicity that has made the company more receptive to their demands for meetings and dialogue. *The Hindu* and *Deccan Chronicle*, two of the region's most widely read daily English-language newspapers, have started to publicise the issue, sparking debate within élite policy circles. When *The Hindu* carried a story about an information-sharing meeting organised by PRIA on the impact of the plant, the following day tests for water pollution were undertaken when the Pollution Control Board and district officials arrived. In addition, following media reports of security guards at the plant beating villagers climbing the walls of the plant to escape a fire sweeping across their villages, the company distributed 10 kilograms of rice to villagers in the immediate area to pacify anger about the incident.[17]

While publicity to the cause is welcome, there is concern that too much media attention could encourage the company to retreat from public debate. Once a level of trust between intermediary NGOs, such as

PRIA, has been achieved it may be counter-productive to continue to air grievances through the media, as the company may see this as a breach of trust. In the case of NTPC, proceedings have not got that far, and there is little discernible evidence that the company is as yet willing to involve the NGOs in its decision making or to partner them in exploring possible solutions of mutual benefit. In addition, the threat of negative coverage should the company fail to act and renege on its promises has to remain a plausible one to encourage compliance. The danger remains that media coverage serves to identify opponents of industry as a nuisance, inviting unwanted and potentially hostile action on the part of industry or the state.

Democratic space

At a basic level, citizen action for accountability is also affected by a culture of tolerance towards protest. While in theory this culture is an accepted feature of political life in India, in all these cases there have been complaints about the repression of protest activities. For example, there are allegations that threats of beatings were issued by the police when a community refused removal from their land in Vizag.[18] They refused to move on the basis that they had records of money paid to the government for the hire of the land for work, contradicting government claims that the land was not theirs. The law can also be used to break up protests that do take place. Protests of more than five people can be broken up and the people imprisoned under the colonial Criminal Procedures Act, on the basis that the protests constitute a public nuisance. The Act has been used in this way to disband protests over both proposed future petro-chemical investments in the Chiplun area and the controversial Daebol-ENRON project in the region (Mehta 1999).

Corporate responsiveness

Corporate responsiveness to citizen action, particularly in the absence of effective state action, is clearly also critical to the prospects of change. If answerability is one of the two pillars of accountability, it depends both on actors feeling obliged to justify their actions and to recognise that the accountability claims made of them are valid. NTPC, for its part, has denied allegations of human health impacts and environmental degradation resulting from its activities. It has, nevertheless, sought to defend its track record. The company's web site pronounces:

> As a responsible corporate citizen, NTPC is making constant efforts to improve the socio-economic status of the people affected by its projects. Through its

Rehabilitation and Resettlement programmes, the company endeavours to improve the overall socio-economic status of Project Affected Persons. (NTPC 2003)

Elsewhere, the company claims that its 18 power stations have received ISO14001 certification and proudly proclaims its membership of the UN's Global Compact initiative. The company also draws attention to its community development efforts, where Rs4 Crores (Rs40 million) have been spent over four years, according to the Resettlement and Rehabilitation Officer.[19] Displayed on the company office walls are photographs of family planning programmes, eye-testing clinics and water sanitation projects sponsored by the company.

In spite of company claims that its community development efforts are 'needs-driven',[20] it mainly funds projects tackling problems that do not implicate the company in any way. For example, clinics to test hearing, which many community members claim has been impaired by the noise the plant generates, would be useful – but would allow people to document damage to their hearing, for which the company might then be liable. The major environmental contribution that the company has made, and which adorns all its public relations material, is the plantation of 100,000 trees grown next to the plant to absorb the pollution generated by its activities and to 'offset' its emissions. This 'forest' is the source of many jokes in the communities, expressing cynicism about the green credentials of NTPC.

Again, we find competing notions of accountability at work. From the company's point of view, discretionary philanthropy is an adequate response to demands for accountability by the community. For the company, accountability is first and foremost to the state. In a typical response, one NTPC official said that the company's involvement in a public hearing would be conditional on the participation of the district collector. The challenge for PRIA and other groups working both in Chiplun and Vizag is to not only to get the state (re-)involved in such processes, but to expand the boundaries of what is up for discussion; to improve corporate responsiveness on livelihood issues such as land and employment; and to displace the more convenient and seemingly political neutral emphasis on 'soft responsibility', or philanthropic health and education projects which firms are happier to discuss.

While increasingly willing to engage in tentative discussions with groups such as PRIA, NTPC is unrepentant about the process to date: 'The past is past … there is no point having grievances,' one representative said to us.[21] Inevitably, with such a mega-project there are some 'adjustment' costs to be borne and a level of 'dislocation' that has to take place. The firm claims that all its actions are legal and were conducted with the acquiescence and support of the government. Its deal with the government was over land and no legally binding commitments were made regarding jobs and infrastructure. Indeed, it seems the government is equally to blame over the growth of misperceptions about the number of jobs that would be made available to the local community. Many villagers claim that it was the former Chief Minister Chandrababu Naidu who promised that 99 per cent of the jobs associated with the plant would be provided to local people. Equally, the company has no legal obligation regarding rehabilitation, despite having made efforts in this direction.

In Jharkhand, we find a more extreme case of reluctance on the part of the companies to engage in dialogue with communities affected by their activities. Negotiation through intermediaries has taken the place of direct dialogue, and companies employ influential staff members as 'diluting agents' or 'informers' to quell resistance and contain demands for change (Arjjumend 2004: 72). This is in addition to their use, noted above, of middlemen to broker deals needed to secure access to tribal land – despite legal protections, which are routinely overridden in the rush to claim property rights. Arjjumend cites the case of a village headman and supervisor in Madan Rathi's quarry. With little knowledge of local land or the leases held on it, and allegedly ignorant of customary norms, he supported mining interests by offering consent to the illegal and arbitrary transfer of lands for mining operations (Arjjumend 2004: 72).

Conclusions

This analysis highlights a number of key issues about the conditions which affect the ability of communities to secure accountability from key actors in these regions.

First, the importance of multi-pronged strategies: we saw above how media exposure, direct dialogue with companies and government officials, public hearings, and the law have been used to seek a fair deal for the communities that host these industrial projects. Often these strategies are pursued simultaneously and in ways that reinforce their impact. Decisions about which strategy it makes most sense to adopt at which time, and by whom, depend upon the nature of the change sought. At different times, these strategies have served respectively to expose, to embarrass, to engage and to seek redress. We have emphasised throughout the use of citizen-based methodologies of accountability. Citizen health monitoring, video, public hearings and People's Development

Plans have been among the tools employed to document concerns that have been overlooked, to give a platform to voices that have been ignored, and to generate new expectations about the conduct of powerful actors.

Second, mobilising early in order to shape discussions about a proposed investment is vital. This is the overriding lesson of the struggle around the NTPC plant that is now being applied in relation to the proposed 'Pharma Park' in the same region. Once land has been acquired and licences issued, it becomes increasingly difficult to raise objections or negotiate better terms for the communities that will host the project. Building an effective case requires sharing information and experience of communities that have hosted the same industry or even the same company. This issue emerges strongly from the Chiplun case study, where inter-community learning was used to feed into the development of a People's Development Plan and the public hearing – to hear testimony of the companies' conduct elsewhere, and whether promises made to other communities had been fulfilled.

A third key factor is the importance of rights (to land, compensation, and information). Much of the social dislocation caused by the Lote Industrial Area and the NTPC plant resulted from the fact that the poorest workers had no land entitlement and therefore were not in a position to receive compensation. Having rights is not enough, however. Being aware that you have those rights and knowing how to use them is what makes a difference. For example, many villagers affected by pollution from the NTPC plant were unaware that the information they need to support their claims already resides in the offices of the Pollution Control Board and that they are entitled to access it. In the Jharkhand struggle, people were unaware of the constitutional provisions pertaining to their land rights and process, and their decision-making rights with regard to consultation and participation. The barriers to realising those rights should not be underestimated, however, where governments systematically override legal obligations they have set for themselves, as they did with regard to tribal rights in Jharkhand.

A fourth factor that comes through strongly in the case of the NTPC plant is the importance of party politics and relations with the state in general. There has been systematic discrimination in favour of those villages that were under the control of the ruling party to the neglect of other villages, often those most affected by the plant. We noted how local panchayat and mandal officials felt relatively powerless in the face of strong state-level government support for the NTPC project, particularly from officials of the same political party. When the backing of state and federal government is so strong, strategies of negotiation are less likely to be effective. In the Jharkhand case, we saw how contests over tribal rights quickly became embroiled in broader party political struggles in which tribal communities were associated with the left and the communist parties in particular, an association which invited further marginalisation and repression from state officials (Arjjumend 2004: 72). We also saw (occasional) examples, however, of the potential for alliances with sympathetic elements within government able to lend their support and authority to community claim making.

Ultimately, these cases underscore the problem of reducing accountability to acts of corporate responsibility that rely on various forms of philanthropy. Such approaches assume not only a willingness on the part of the companies to engage in an open and public dialogue about their responsibilities, admit wrongdoing when necessary and take remedial action when negligence has occurred, but also a proactive approach to accommodating the needs of the communities with which they are working. This is particularly problematic for communities affected by irresponsible investment practices: they are rarely identified as legitimate stakeholders by business and lack sufficient influence within government policy making to articulate and defend their concerns. In this context, their resort to informal and often confrontational strategies can hardly be considered surprising. In this sense, the accountability struggles we describe here are a far cry from notions of corporate responsibility, which tend to confer on business the power to set the terms of its own conduct. The notion of accountability is more helpful in this context, for it lays bare the power relations that the seemingly benign language of 'responsibility' and 'citizenship' seeks to deny or transgress.

NOTES

1 We would like to thank Aruna Katragadda, Shagun Mahotra, Randeep Singh Saini, Shaikh Ismail and Ashok Kadam for help in setting up meetings with government and company officials, and for organising the visits to the villages that made this research possible. Thanks also to Jutta Blauert and John Gaventa for very useful comments on an earlier draft of this chapter. Some of the material in this chapter draws from Newell (2005a) and I am grateful to Ranjita Moharty and Rajesh Tandon for permission to reproduce it.

2 Representative from NTPC. Interview with Peter Newell, Aruna Katragadda and Shagun Mahotra, February 2003.

3 Villager from the area surrounding the NTPC plant. Village meeting with Peter Newell, Aruna Katragadda and Shagun Mahotra, February 2003.

4 These have been recognised in amendments to the Indian constitution in 1990, Provisions of the Panchayats Act, 1996, the Supreme Court judgement (Samatha),

1997 and the Environmental Protection Act of 1986.

5 The discussion of the case studies is based on two visits to the sites in Vizag (2002) and Chiplun (2001) in which meetings and discussions were held with affected communities, government officials, local NGOs and company officials (in the case of NTPC). It also draws on case reports by Anand (2002), Ranga Rao and Kumar (2003) and Arjjumend (2004). Recording and analysing the claims made by the different parties involved in these disputes should not be taken to imply that the authors endorse all reported claims and allegations.

6 The market rate for the land was said to be Rs45,000 per acre (*The Hindu* 22 November 2002). STPP officials claim that the land was worth between Rs40,000 and Rs100,000 (or Rs1 lakh).

7 Meeting with Peter Newell, Aruna Katragadda and Shagun Mahotra, February 2003.

8 The Society for Participatory Research in Asia (PRIA), an advocacy and research NGO (PRIA 2005).

9 Meeting with Peter Newell, Aruna Katragadda and Shagun Mahotra, February 2003.

10 The full name of the organisation is 'Visishta Gramodaya Swayam "Sadhana" Parishad'.

11 For example, prior to the construction and operation of the NTPC plant, unrecorded bilateral discussions took place between communities and individuals from the firm. Because there is no record of these meetings, promises made there have no legal standing.

12 Meeting with Peter Newell, Aruna Katragadda and Shagun Mahotra, February 2003.

13 Interviews by Peter Newell and Randeep Singh Saini with a number of activists, Chiplun, 2002.

14 Meetings with Peter Newell, Aruna Katragadda and Shagun Mahotra, February 2003.

15 Interview with Peter Newell, Aruna Katragadda and Shagun Mahotra, February 2003.

16 *Ibid.*

17 *Ibid.*

18 Meetings with Peter Newell, Aruna Katragadda and Shagun Mahotra, February 2003.

19 Interview with Peter Newell, Aruna Katragadda and Shagun Mahotra, February 2003.

20 *Ibid.*

21 Interview with Peter Newell, Aruna Katragadda and Shagun Mahotra, February 2003. ·

REFERENCES

Anand, V. (2002) *Multi-party Accountability for Environmentally Sustainable Industrial Development: the Challenge of Active Citizenship. A Study of Stakeholders in the Lote Parshuram Chemical Industrial Belt, Chiplun, Maharastra*, College of Social Work, Mumbai University, paper produced for Society for Participatory Research in Asia (PRIA) New Delhi.

Arjjumend, H. (2004) *Tribal Rights and Industry Accountability: the Case of Mining in Dumka, Jharkland*, New Delhi: Society for Participatory Research in Asia (PRIA).

Deccan Chronicle (2003) 'Acquisition Policy Draws Flak', 21 February.

Global Compact (2005) www.unglobalcompact.org, accessed 3 August 2005.

Mehta, A. (1999) *Power Play: a Study of the ENRON Project*, Hyderabad: Orient Longman.

Newell, P. (2002) 'From Responsibility to Citizenship: Corporate Accountability for Development' *IDS Bulletin* Vol.33 No.2 'Making Rights Real: Exploring Citizenship, Participation and Accountability' Brighton: IDS.

—— (2005) 'Citizenship, Accountability and Community: the Limits of the CSR Agenda', *International Affairs*, Volume 81, No. 3 (May), pp. 541–57.

—— (2005a) 'Corporate Citizenship and the Politics of Accountability: Communities and Companies in India', in R. Moharty and R. Tandon (eds), *Identity, Exclusion and Inclusion: Issues in Participatory Citizenship*, New Delhi: Sage.

NTPC (2003) http://www.ntpc.co.in/aboutus/rrpol.pdf, National Thermal Power Company website, accessed 10 January 2003.

PRIA (2005) www.pria.org, Society for Participatory Research in Asia website, accessed 9 August 2005.

Ranga Rao, A. B. S. V. and Sampath Kumar, R. D. (2003) *Multi-party Accountability for Environmentally Sustainable Industrial Development: the Challenge of Active Citizenship. A Study of Stakeholders in the Simhadri Thermal Power Project, Paravada, Visakhapatnam District, Andhra Pradesh*, Department of Social Work, Andhra University, paper produced for Society for Participatory Research in Asia (PRIA) New Delhi.

The Hindu (2003) 'Adverse Impact of Pharma City Feared', 19 February.

The Hindu (2002) 'Villagers Brood over a "Hazy" Future', 22 November.

CHAPTER 9

Environmental injustice, law and accountability

ROHIT LEKHI AND PETER NEWELL

> Poor people bear the brunt of environmental dangers – from pesticides to air pollution to toxics to occupational hazards – and their negative effects on human health and safety. At the same time, poor people have the fewest resources to cope with these dangers, legally, medically or politically. (Cole 1992: 620)

Work on environmental racism in the United States (US) shows that communities of colour are often targeted by firms engaged in the production of hazardous materials such as chemicals and toxics, because they anticipate a more compliant workforce that can be paid lower wages and where they expect political resistance to be less forthcoming. If these are the 'drivers' of environmental racism, its consequences include much higher levels of exposure to toxics and subsequently increased rates of illnesses related to exposure to these hazards among minority communities. Taking just one statistic to illustrate the point, the famous 1987 study by the United Church of Christ (UCC) Commission for Racial Justice found that three out of every five African and Hispanic-Americans live in communities with uncontrolled toxic waste sites (Commission for Racial Justice 1987).

Given the limitations of voluntary patterns of business-based self-regulation and state interventions to protect the rights of poorer communities – either excluded from mechanisms of corporate responsibility, or more often than not the victims of acts of corporate irresponsibility – there is growing interest in the role of community-based strategies for corporate accountability (Garvey and Newell 2005). Though it is often assumed that it is communities in the South that are more heavily reliant on strategies of self-help, in a prevailing context of a 'weak' state and a private sector not yet subject to the pressures and disciplines of corporate

186

social responsibility (CSR), we suggest in this chapter that important insights can be gained from the community-based struggles around environmental racism, principally in the US, which manifest many of the basic conditions confronting poorer communities the world over. Our aim is to review and consolidate insights emerging from these struggles in order to explore parallels with other campaigns for corporate accountability explored in this book (see chapters 8 and 10).

The purpose of this chapter is not to document the evidence of the poor being exposed to disproportionate levels of environmental degradation or to engage with debates that seek to establish whether the principal drivers of such patterns are race, class or some other hierarchy of social exclusion. Our enquiry is focused instead on the question of strategy: how poorer groups mobilise to defend their interests, to articulate rights claims and to secure a degree of accountability from the powerful economic actors that are located 'where we live, work and play', to borrow a phrase from the environmental justice movement.

Amid the many state-based, company-based and community-based factors that impinge upon the effectiveness of community-based strategies for corporate accountability, our enquiry centres on the potential and limitations of legally based strategies for corporate accountability. This reflects the fact that the strategic orientation the environmental justice (EJ) movement has been shaped, in large part, by the experiences of the civil rights movement. As a result, many of the strategies employed by EJ activists during the past three decades have sought to use and extend pre-existing frameworks oriented to addressing racial injustice. As a result, the EJ movement in the US has placed a great deal of strategic emphasis on the use of law as a primary mechanism for defending the interests and articulating the rights of poorer communities of colour.

This is not to suggest that the law is the only or even the best means of realising the rights of those communities, but rather that the orientation of the EJ movement has been shaped by the historic importance of the legal arena as the major location of challenges to racial discrimination in the US. Indeed, this emphasis on the law has generated numerous tensions within the EJ movement. As we note below, there are many within the EJ movement who argue that the limits of what can be realised through legal challenge necessarily requires an alternative strategic orientation towards grassroots mobilisation and the direct empowerment of local communities. Our aim in what follows is not to dispute that this may be the case. Instead, in seeking to analyse the use (and equally importantly, the limits) of law as a strategic tool, we hope to shed light on those alternative strategies that may be more appropriately employed when those limits are reached.

In pursuing this aim, we hope to identify parallels, lessons and insights that may resonate with struggles defined in opposition to similar patterns of injustice elsewhere. Lessons generated from the experiences of the environmental justice movement in the US cannot be unproblematically imported into other settings. Even work from outside the US, from South Africa for example, suggests the importance of studying the interface between race and environment in particular settings (Ruiters 2002). Nevertheless, the patterns of exclusion and inequality which define struggles for environmental justice in the US resonate strongly with the experience of poorer groups the world over, even if the contours of injustice and the forms of accountability politics express different histories, cultures and politics.

The first part of the chapter explores the historical, political and conceptual contexts that have shaped the development of the environmental justice movement in the US in order to better understand the origin and evolution of particular rights-based claims and their relation to broader accountability struggles. In the second part, we construct a framework for understanding the factors that facilitate or inhibit the success of community-based organising for corporate accountability, based on the experience of the environmental justice movement. In the concluding part of the chapter, we discuss how accountability struggles in the US share similarities with, and offer insights for, poorer groups engaged in similar struggles in other parts of the world.

The origins and development of the US environmental justice movement

Defining environmental racism

For many, the origins of the environmental justice movement in the US can be traced back to the protests that took place in 1982 against the decision to build a toxic waste landfill for PCB-contaminated dirt in Warren County, North Carolina, which is a largely African American and extremely poor area of the state. In the course of these protests, involving the arrest of both local people and high-profile civil rights activists, the relationship between race and environmental impact was given national prominence for the first time. 'While the protests did not succeed in keeping the landfill out of Warren county, an interracial movement was forged, linked to the larger civil rights and poverty movements, with the goal of empowering people to protect themselves and their communities from environmental harms' (Babcock 1995: 8). It was in the aftermath of the Warren County protests that the concept of 'environmental racism' was first advanced by the civil rights activist, Dr Benjamin Chavis. According to Chavis, environmental racism refers to:

> racial discrimination in environmental policy making and the unequal enforcement of the environmental laws and regulations. It is the deliberate targeting of people-of-colour communities for toxic waste facilities and the official sanctioning of a life-threatening presence of poisons and pollutants in people-of-colour communities. It is also manifested in the history of excluding people of colour from the leadership of the environmental movement. (Quoted in Sandweiss 1998: 36)

The idea of 'deliberate targeting' suggests, unequivocally, that the causes of environmental racism are intentional. However, as a basis from which to challenge inequitable distributions of environmental impact, the standard of proof required to demonstrate the existence of 'environmental racism' defined in this way has been notoriously difficult to establish – requiring as it does, *explicit* evidence of intent. Consequently, others have argued for a shift in the burden of proof required to establish the fact of environmental racism away from a notion of explicit intentionality to one premised on disparate outcomes or impacts of decisions. This can refer to policies, practices or directives (whether intended or unintended) that differentially affect or disadvantage individuals, groups or communities based on race or colour, or unequal protection against toxic and hazardous waste exposure and systematic exclusion of people of colour from decisions affecting their lives (Bryant 1995).

Whatever the precise nature of the mechanisms that generate specific inequalities in respect of environmental decision making, it is clear that an overt focus on causation has been unhelpful to the extent that it has deflected attention from the more important question of what to do about the inequalities (intentional or otherwise) that clearly do persist in respect of communities of colour and low-income communities – inequalities that include not just siting decisions but also standard setting, enforcement, clean-up, and opportunities (or the lack of them) to participate in regulatory processes.

From environmental racism to environmental (in)justice

The pursuit of remedial action in respect of such inequalities is represented in the shift in focus – both politically and conceptually – from environmental racism to environmental justice. If environmental racism is based upon problem identification, environmental justice is based on problem solving. For many social activists environmental degradation is just one of many ways in which their communities are under attack. Environmental racism, therefore, is often understood in relation to multiple forms of deprivation and exclusion experienced in daily life:

> Because of their experiences, grassroots activists often lose faith in govern-ment agencies and elected officials, leading those activists to view environ-mental problems in their communities as connected to larger structural failings – inner-city disinvestment, residential segregation, lack of decent health care, joblessness, and poor education. Similarly, many activists also seek remedies that are more fundamental than simply stopping a local polluter or toxic dumper. Instead, many view the need for broader, structural reforms as a way to alleviate many of the problems, including environmental degradation, that their communities endure. (Cole and Foster 2001: 33)

It is through this articulation of the problems to be addressed within the framework of EJ as, inseparably, those of racism *and* social justice that the environmental justice movement builds on the rhetorical legacy of the civil rights movement. Furthermore,

> The collective action frame of the civil rights movement – which emphasised such values as individual rights, equal opportunities, social justice, full citizenship, human dignity, and self-determination – provided a 'master frame' that legitimised the struggles of other disenfranchised groups. By framing the problem of disproportionate exposure as a violation of civil rights, the environ-mental justice movement was able to integrate environmental concerns into the civil rights frame. (Sandweiss 1998: 39)

This has allowed for a significant expansion of the civil rights movement into the environmental arena, bringing with it all the 'moral force, com-pelling emotion, dedication, activism, sympathetic response and relent-less commitment to the pursuit of rights that have characterised civil rights activism during the past 30 years' (Jones 1993: 28).

In order to operationalise its demands, the environmental justice movement has advanced two sets of rights-based claims (Pulido 1994). First is the demand for procedural rights to participate equally in the process of environmental regulation. This is seen as a primary mechanism to ensure that communities of colour and poorer communities are able to gain 'voice' in those fora where decision making occurs. As codified in the 'Principles of Environmental Justice' adopted by the First National People of Colour Environmental Leadership Summit, this is 'the right to participate as equal partners at every level of decision making including needs assessment, planning, implementation, enforcement and evaluation' (Bullard 1994: 274–5). However, in and of itself, the demand for equity in decision making around the distribution of hazards signals a clear limit in respect of the strategic goals that the environmental justice movement can hope to realise. As Heiman argues:

> Should the quest for environmental justice merely stop with an equitable distribution of negative externalities, business could proceed as usual. This time it would be with assurance from the Environmental Protection Agency (EPA) and other regulatory agencies that we will all have an equal opportunity to be polluted or – the flip side – protected from pollution, however ineffectively. Such assurance comes complete with procedural guarantees that we may participate in the equitable allocation of this pollution and protection, if we so choose. (Heiman 1996)

As a consequence, the environmental justice movement has also sought to advance a second set of rights claims. This is a demand for rights to live free from environmental hazard, not just to distribute that hazard more equitably. These substantive rights are oriented to the demand for preventative strategies to ensure that threats are eliminated before they create harm. As expressed in the aforementioned 'Principles' this is 'the fundamental right to clean air, land, water and food'.

Strategic orientation to realising rights: law vs activism

Within the environmental justice movement there are significant differences in respect of how these rights claims can best be pursued. Some argue that meaningful solutions can only be realised through the active intervention of federal government, and this requires a prioritisation of legislative/procedural strategies of reform (Ferris 1995). For others, grassroots mobilisation and the empowerment of local communities are the key strategic goals in any attempt to overcome environmental injustices (Schafer 1993; Bullard 1993a). For yet others, the meaningful realisation of procedural and substantive rights will only be secured through systemic changes in the very basis of economic production (Faber and O'Connor 1993).

As might be expected, given the framing of EJ issues in terms of civil rights, the use of constitutional and statute law features prominently in the tactical arsenal of the EJ movement. The first moves in this direction were to pursue EJ claims under the constitutional right to equal protection – the use of which had been pivotal in helping to secure African American civil rights during the 1950s and 1960s. The first EJ claim to be brought under these auspices was *Bean v. Southwestern Waste Management Corporation* in the late 1970s. This involved a challenge by local residents in Houston, Texas to the siting of a hazardous waste facility in a predominantly African American area. However, in this case – and in others brought subsequently under the auspices of equal protection – the US Supreme Court rejected the claim of unequal protection on the basis that it is necessary in such cases to show discriminatory *intent*.

Given the difficulties in establishing direct proof of intentionality in such cases, the EJ movement has sought to employ a civil rights approach that has been less onerous in the standards of proof demanded. Of greatest importance in this regard has been the use of Title VI of the 1964 Civil Rights Act, which prohibits racial discrimination in all activities and programmes in receipt of federal funding. Claims pursued under Title VI have sought to deny federal funds to those states that are involved in enacting discriminatory environmental decisions. In these cases, however, the standard of proof required is one of discriminatory outcome or impact rather than intent. Plaintiffs need only prove that the result of the policy or practice impacts disproportionately on (discriminates against) the community, not that it was the intent of policy or practice to do so.

However, the pursuit of legal remedies, while fostering some limited successes, is not the favoured strategic orientation of many EJ activists. As Cole and Foster (2001: 33) note,

> grassroots environmentalists are largely, though not entirely, poor or working-class people. Many are people of colour who come from communities that are disenfranchised from most major societal institutions. Because of their backgrounds, these activists often have a distrust for the law and are often experienced in the use of non-legal strategies, such as protest and other direct action.

Mobilisation

In pursuit of alternative strategies oriented to grassroots mobilisation as opposed to the law, the historical and strategic relationship of the civil rights movement to the EJ movement has again been crucial. According to Sandweiss (1998: 39), there are two aspects to this:

> First, environmental justice activists have been able to draw on the organizational resources and institutional networks established during the previous struggle for racial equality. Churches, neighbourhood improvement associations, and historically black colleges and universities have furnished the environmental justice movement with leadership, money, knowledge, communication networks and other resources essential to the growth of any social movement. Second, environmental justice activists have successfully borrowed many of the tactics associated with the civil rights movement to call attention to their demands – both direct action tactics, such as protests and boycotts, as well as more conventional activities, such as lobbying and litigation.

It was precisely these roots in civil rights and church-based advocacy that led to the UCC's landmark 1987 study, *Toxic Wastes and Race in the United States* and the 1991 First National People of Colour Environmental Leadership Summit (Commission for Racial Justice 1987). Both of these facilitated, for the first time, a national voice and national-level coordination of what until then had been largely localised struggles around specific instances of environmental injustice. The Summit itself, which brought together EJ activists from across the US and other parts of the world, also provided a platform for the first concerted attempt to articulate a coherent vision of environmental justice, embodied in its seventeen 'Principles'.

A further goal was to develop greater coordination of EJ activities at the regional level. In addition to the already-formed Southern Network for Economic and Environmental Justice (SNEEJ), further regional coordination was facilitated in the development of the Asian Pacific Environmental Network (APEN), the Indigenous Environmental Network (IEN), the North-east Environmental Justice Network; the Midwest/Great Lakes Environmental Justice Network and the Southern Organising Committee for Economic and Environmental Justice. These regional networks have played a crucial role in ensuring the coordination of activism and mobilisation, while at the same time recognising the diverse needs and concerns of specific ethnic and geographic communities (Pellow 2002: 77).

Accounting for mobilisation

Having provided an overview of the contexts in which the environmental justice movement emerged, this section organises insights regarding factors that impact upon the effectiveness of strategies employed by groups that are the victims of environmental racism. Given the many links, suggested above, including the forms of injustice and the ways in which these are contested, between the environmental justice movement and other forms of community-based activism for corporate accountability, we want to suggest there is a broad resonance in these insights that extends well beyond the contexts from which they are derived.

Planning, process and representation
Minority and poorer groups generally lack access to and representation within government, particularly at the national level (Babcock 1995). Beyond voice in areas traditionally considered to be environmental, lack

of representation in planning and zoning commissions is particularly relevant here. Bullard (1993: 23) suggests that 'Many of the at-risk communities are victims of land-use decision making that mirrors the power arrangements of the dominant society. Historically, exclusionary zoning has been a subtle form of using government authority and power to foster and perpetuate discriminatory practices.' Even accepting that state laws are to some extent not generating inequalities, Cole and Foster note that 'State permitting laws remain neutral or blind toward these inequalities; they therefore perpetuate, and indeed exacerbate, distributional inequalities' (Cole and Foster 2001: 75).

Corporate penetration of such decision-making processes further reduces their responsiveness to community demands. Discussing attempts by communities in Illinois to hold the company Clark Oil to account for its social and environmental responsibilities, Pellow (2001: 63) shows how the city council's environmental and industrial committee, charged with evaluating Clark Oil's health and safety record, included a former Clark Oil employee. These patterns of influence hint at deeper cracks in the democratic process and the inherent tensions faced by liberal democracies in balancing economic growth with democratic decision making. In this regard, Krauss (1989: 230) argues that 'The state must in one and the same moment achieve two conflicting aims: it must maintain the conditions for profitable capital accumulation and economic growth while legitimating its own power by appealing to the principle of democracy.'

Even where channels of representation within the state are made available, it is often very difficult for groups to make use of them. During the permit application process for the Genesee power station in Michigan, public hearings were held. However, community members were made to sit for hours while the committee undertook other business, and when the group finally got a chance to testify, 'the decision makers talked among themselves, laughed and paid little attention. Moreover, the hearing took place at a location more than an hour from the proposed site, forcing residents to rent a bus' (Cole and Foster 2001: 124). Citizen input is often seen as a nuisance and limited to a short period of time, signalling to residents (1) that they must make a quick decision; (2) that their input was deemed irrelevant during the planning phase of the proposal; and (3) that their input has been reduced to 'we want it' or 'we don't want it' (Allen 2003: 156).

It is predictable, then, that local authorities decide upon sites where residents are least likely to oppose such developments, which a 1984 report for the California Waste Management Board suggested would be 'rural communities, poor communities, communities whose residents have low educational levels ... and whose residents were employed in resource-extractive jobs' (Cole and Foster 2001: 3). The Cerrell report, a strategy manual for industries needing to set up polluting facilities such as incinerators, aimed to 'assist in selecting a site that offers the least potential of generating public opposition' (cited in Cole and Foster 2001: 71). Its recommendations were: (1) avoid middle- and higher-income neighbourhoods; (2) target communities that are less well educated; (3) target conservative or traditional communities, preferably with fewer than 25,000 residents; (4) target rural or elderly communities; and (5) target areas whose residents are employed in resource-extractive jobs like mining, timber or agriculture (Cole and Foster 2001: 3).

At the level of enforcement, there are also oversights, acts of negligence or patterns of exclusionary decision making that activists have sought to contest. Activism, in this sense, can serve to plug gaps in state enforcement of environmental regulations, highlighting both the limits of law and the reluctance of states to enforce it in circumstances in which private investors may be deterred from making further investments. Pellow suggests that corporate–community compacts and good neighbourhood agreements (GNAs) have become more common as a result of the weakening of state policy-making authority, as corporations have become both policy makers and the new targets of challengers (Pellow 2001). He defines GNAs as 'instruments that provide a vehicle for a community organisation and a corporation to recognise and formalise their roles within a locality and to foster sustainable development' (Pellow 2001: 55). They became more popular as a non-litigious method of dispute resolution among companies, workers, environmentalists and local communities in the wake of an increase in industrial disasters. Combating exemptions that allow corporations to keep certain information out of the public sphere, GNAs encourage broad disclosure so that communities and NGOs can play a role in the enforcement of codes of conduct. Even their proponents are clear, however, that GNAs are not a substitute for governmental regulation: they are simply a response to the lack of, and need for, such regulation.

Community activists often seek to address weaknesses in state-based processes through their own informal sanctions. Process requirements and resources available to corporate actors can make official sanctions difficult to impose, so that community groups adopt what Cable and Benson call (1993: 471) 'informal sanctions' (such as press conferences denouncing the company, pickets outside company offices, and attempts to attract media attention through rallies and protests). Informal sanctions are also important in incentivising the take-up of the sort of informal and 'soft' community-based policy tools described above.

Beyond drawing attention to an injustice through protest or media coverage, community groups have also sought to train and educate themselves, to find ways of exchanging experience about successful accountability strategies, and to build a degree of learning and reflection into their struggles. Activists, as well as setting up literacy programmes and field trips, have run programmes on participatory citizenship skills. Environmental justice clinics also play an important role. The clinics function, according to Babcock, 'as laboratories for exploring different ways to overcome legal and institutional barriers … and as catalysts for reforming the legal system' (Babcock 1995: 50). They provide high-quality legal services to communities at risk, including requests for disclosure of information and analysis and distillation of technical reports for local residents. As Babcock notes, 'Victories may be as seemingly insignificant as securing the release of information from a recalcitrant government official; however, even these exercises have led to changes in official attitudes toward public requests for information and reforms in their process of responding' (Babcock 1995: 56).

Law and its limits

These patterns of exclusion from decision making help to explain why legal battles to contest the outcomes of these processes have been commonplace. Allen argues that citizen groups end up with their complaints in the courts precisely because the legislative and executive branches have been co-opted by corporate lobbyists (Allen 2003: 90). She suggests that 'regulatory agencies such as DEQ are easily co-opted by industry because top-level officials often alternate between agency posts and positions in industry. The judicial branch is the last option for residents otherwise disenfranchised by the close liaisons between the chemical industry and their elected and regulatory officials.'

Nevertheless, legal strategies are seen as a key strategy by mainstream groups such as the Sierra Club, whose executive director of legal defence believes that 'Litigation is the most important thing the environmental movement has done over the past fifteen years' (quoted in Cole and Foster 2001: 30). However, there are many resource and procedural barriers to bringing, successfully pursuing and enforcing legal cases. Barriers for poorer groups are multiple and include: lack of legal literacy, lack of resources, distrust of the legal process, and inability to pay costs if the case is unsuccessful (Newell 2001). Babcock (1995: 22) notes that 'some members of a disempowered group may be initially hostile toward, or intimidated by, lawyers and the judicial process, or may have been trained in the confrontational tactics of the civil rights or poverty movements'. There are also process barriers to the successful pursuit of legal strategies, such as high demands for expertise required to engage the legal system effectively. Many environmental laws have 'created complex administrative processes that exclude most people who do not have training in the field and necessitate specific technical expertise' (Cole and Foster 2001: 30).

Besides these barriers and process issues, many environmental justice activists are wary of 'legalising' a problem. The concern, as noted earlier, is that legal strategies take the struggle out of the realm in which the community has control of it. Broader social justice claims get pressed into legally cognisable claims. In these instances, 'collective struggle is translated into an individual lawsuit with the result that the momentum of the community's struggle is lost' (Cole 1992: 652). Though successful in bringing attention to a case, the diverse and spontaneous forms of community organising that groups employ to contest their fate as victims of environmental justice are largely redundant within the legal process. Moral claims, the use of symbolic power and a variety of 'weapons of the weak' which poorer groups deploy to counter the structural and material forms of power that corporates benefit from become less visible and less relevant once a struggle is reframed in legal terms, shifting the balance of power towards those with resources, expertise and influence. Cole argues that 'Even if the law is "on their side", unless poor people have political or economic power as well, they are unlikely to prevail.... Tactically, taking environmental problems out of the streets and into the courts plays to the grassroots movement's weakest suit' (Cole 1992: 648, 650).

Beyond the limits of legally based strategies in general, there are also questions about the value of poorer communities seeking protection through environmental law. Because they are risk-oriented, environmental laws tend to support decisions as long as emissions comply with minimal state regulatory thresholds. As Cole notes (1992: 646), 'while we may decry the outcome, environmental laws are working as designed. Such a disproportionate burden is legal under US environmental laws.... Thus decisions to place unwanted facilities in low-income neighbourhoods are not made in spite of our system of laws, but because of our system of laws.'

The positive potential of the law

Our emphasis on the many limitations of legally based strategies should be tempered by an acknowledgement that cases can and have been won when the rights of poorer communities have been violated. Landmark legal settlements can pave the way for change. Allen (2003: 40) describes a court ruling in which it was determined that citizens' environmental protection must be given fair weight alongside economic and social factors. The groups bringing the case 'effectively changed the face of environmental planning in the state' according to Allen (2003: 40). Though enforcement remains a problem, following the ruling, chemical companies that sought to locate in the area had to prove that they had fully considered alternative sites and projects as well as environmental mitigation measures. In cases in Dallas and Alabama, out-of-court settlements have been achieved by communities affected by environmental racism, including, in the case of Olin Chemicals, an agreement to clean up residual PCBs and DDT, allocate money for long-term health care costs and pay cash settlements to individual residents.

Community groups have used to positive effect provisions that require the government to respond to each public comment on an environmental impact report, for example. In the case, *Pueblo para el Aire y Agua Limpio v County of Kings*, a community successfully filed a complaint against the environmental impact report on grounds of its inadequacy under the California Environmental Quality Act, and the court blocked the project. The legal challenge was based upon the principle of discrimination against Spanish speakers in the decision-making process, given the lack of Spanish translation in public consultation meetings and documentation.

Before they can locate a toxic waste facility in a community, companies have to obtain permits. Public notices of plans are issued, a comment period is allowed and public hearings are held where there is a significant degree of public interest, including published notices in area newspapers. In theory, if the content of the notice or the procedures for publicising it do not meet the regulatory requirements, a court may order the notice process to be repeated (Perkins 1992). While agencies are reluctant to deny permits, if an agency does issue a permit over community objection, administrative and judicial appeals are available, as with the case in California described above.

There are also community right-to-know laws, despite numerous attempts to revoke them. Some statutory schemes for hazardous waste siting have progressive potential. The Massachusetts scheme, for example, requires the hazardous waste developer to negotiate an approved siting agreement with the host community to offset any adverse impacts. State assistance is also sometimes available to the host community to obtain any technical studies and other material it needs to negotiate effectively

(Colquette and Robertson 1991). Provision of state legal aid can be important. Because they are free, for many people in low-income communities legal-aid services are the only option available and logically become 'part of the first line of defence for [those] facing environmental dangers' (Cole 1992: 656).

Beyond building legal capacity, the state can also facilitate less confrontational approaches to conflict mediation by initiating dialogues between companies and communities. Pellow and Park (2002) describe 'Project XL' under the Common Sense Initiative, a multi-stakeholder project aimed at reconciling the respective demands and expectations of companies and communities. The problem, however, was that rather than going beyond existing regulations, regulatory flexibility was traded in exchange for increased community involvement and concessions on improved environmental performance, worker safety and environmental justice criteria. In addition, companies have insisted that meetings would not be open, decisions would not be made by consensus and local stakeholders would not be able to veto the agreement or an element of the agreement.

Concessions to business are seen by community activists as part of a broader pattern of bias evident in the planning process. Allen (2003: 3) quotes a resident from Louisiana's chemical corridor complaining that while the Department for Environmental Quality spent 'hours and weeks with the applicant polluter to help them get their permitting applications legally and technically correct and to help the polluters stay in business ... the time for citizens just isn't there'. Cole (1992a: 1995) also takes issue with the presumption of state neutrality in such disputes:

> Increasingly, states have set up processes to site toxic waste facilities over local opposition – whether the opposition is by people of colour or not. Additionally, the US Environmental Protection Agency has threatened at least one state ... with loss of superfund monies if it does not site a toxic waste incinerator.

Far from being a neutral arbiter in such conflicts, the state is often aligned in direct opposition to those advocating environmental justice.

The purpose of this section has been to highlight the ways in which particular legal mechanisms and strategies can help to advance corporate accountability claims and the circumstances in which this is possible. In previous sections we noted the very many procedural barriers that make the legal process a difficult one for community activists to navigate, raising issues such of access, cost and representation. We have also emphasised the ways in which, by its very nature, the law validates certain forms of claim making and delegitimises others. This has important consequences for accountability struggles, which often aim at broader political change and seek to tackle the causes of injustice and discrimination – at times embodied by the law. It raises key dilemmas of strategy and brings to the fore awkward trade-offs between the prospect of short-term gains and the imperative of longer-term change.

Conclusions: parallels and insights

The parallels between what we have found here and other work documented in this book are striking. First, there is a sense in which the most controversial industrial developments are often located in the poorest areas of a country, whether it is areas in the US predominantly inhabited by black and Latino communities or the poorest states of India, where tribal communities are most likely to be victims. The pattern of privatising profit and socialising costs also appears to be similar. Just as Louisiana's cancer corridor has been described as a 'massive human experiment' and a 'national sacrifice zone' (Perkins 1992: 390), so poorer communities in India ask 'We are being sacrificed for the national interest. We are the victims of this cause. What do we get in return?' (Chapter 8). Often the target is a particular category of the poor, based on broader patterns of racial and social discrimination. In India, it is tribals, in the US native Americans have found themselves disproportionately exposed to toxic waste, while in South Africa forced relocation of poorer communities of colour was employed by the apartheid regime to make way for mining operations (Madihlaba 2002: 158).

Second, the luring of high-polluting industries as a state strategy emerges as a theme with global resonance. Just as an 'industrial tax exemption' has been used to attract the chemical industry into poor areas of the US, so it is has been common in India for large companies to be offered financial concessions in exchange for promised industrial development that is often not delivered. The importance attached to attracting chemical and pharmaceutical companies to the state of Andhra Pradhesh in India is seen by activists there as a constraint on state action and community mobilisation around claims of negligence.

Such trends serve to compound intra-state practices of 'economic blackmail', where companies threaten to relocate in the face of new labour or environmental legislation or when confronted by organised opposition. This creates extra challenges for community organising where capital mobility can have the effect of setting impoverished communities, in need of investment, against one another in the search for the least-cost and most trouble-free investment location (Gaventa and Smith 1991). Within the United States cooperative action between social justice and environmental groups has been seen as one of the best ways of weakening the hold of 'job blackmail' – threats of job loss or plant closure – on working-class areas and communities of color (Bullard and Wright 1990: 302). The immense structural advantage afforded to capital by its mobility clearly applies to some sectors more than others. As we shall see in Chapter 10 on the oil industry in Nigeria, the nature and availability of a resource, its materiality, shapes the options available to an industry in terms of where it operates and the form of politics which surrounds its exploitation, management and distribution. The industries discussed in this chapter have many more options open to them about where to locate, a factor that greatly enhances their bargaining leverage.

A third, interrelated, feature common to many of the situations we describe here is the conscious location of hazardous production activities in areas populated by groups from whom low levels of political resistance are expected. Impoverished communities generally lack the financial and technical resources necessary to resist environmentally hazardous facilities, as well as having less access to traditional remedies to ameliorate those burdens under environmental and civil rights laws. This is compounded by the lack of mobility of the poor in terms of employment and residence.

Fourth, the poorest groups in these conflicts are often the least visible. Migrant labour from some of the poorest states in India provides a pool of cheap and informal labour for industry. Even in high-tech sectors, immigrant populations face disproportionate exposure to toxic hazards (Pellow and Park 2002). Not only is mobilisation harder for migrant, transient populations with fewer resources and networks to draw on, but the often illegal nature of their work renders them less able to secure the forms of protection bestowed upon more formal types of employment. Inhabiting unregulated, unprotected spaces, immigrant, seasonal, temporary and child labour are most vulnerable to exploitation.

A fifth theme we have sought to highlight with global resonance is the importance of the law in both a positive and negative sense. Legal contests characterise many of the conflicts between communities, corporations and governments, raising issues of access and legal literacy as well as the enforceability of decisions and the regulations they invoke. While potential resides in existing state provisions for those that know about them and have the resources, time and confidence to make use of them, this positive potential is often diminished by deliberate oversight, manipulation of procedures by powerful interests or non-enforcement of the terms and conditions of regulations. Just as they did in Vizag, Andhra Pradesh, companies choose media with restricted reach to advertise hearings and notices of proposed developments. Residents of 'Chemical valley' in the US complain that public notices of siting decisions do not work because they 'can be placed anywhere in the newspaper – in the legal section, the classified and even the social section' (cited in Allen 2003: 36). Even far-reaching legal protection afforded to poorer groups is often bypassed in practice when the economic stakes are raised. Whether it is civil rights laws in the US or provisions for the protection of tribals in India, non-accessibility and the mobilisation of bias against poorer groups diminishes the utility of the law as a tool of accountability.

This is how what start as campaigns about particular siting decisions become struggles over decision-making processes that allocate risks in unjust ways. In this sense, Cole argues that 'many in the grassroots environmental movement conceive of their struggle as not simply a battle against chemicals, but a kind of politics that demands popular control of corporate decision making on behalf of workers and communities' (1992: 633). Anti-toxics activists, through the process of local struggles against polluting facilities, came to understand discrete toxic assaults as part of an economic structure in which, 'as part of the "natural" functioning of the economy, certain communities would be polluted' (Cole and Foster 2001: 23). This, in turn, raises many strategic questions, such as whether merely calling for environmental equity reproduces a naive faith in procedural justice and the ability of distributional notions of fairness to tackle the structural and institutional sources of injustice (Ruiters 2002: 118).

Our purpose in drawing these parallels is not to suggest that the settings are identical, permitting successful strategies to be exported to other locales unproblematically. How the factors are weighted in terms of political significance, and how they play out in practice, will always be context-specific – a function of the alliances between community, civil society and the state in any particular setting. And whilst we have suggested parallels with the insights emerging from work on environmental justice movements in the US, it is always important to bear in mind the ways in which accountability struggles are strongly defined by the context in which they emerge and the end for which they are employed.

REFERENCES

Allen, B. L. (2003) *Uneasy Alchemy: Citizens and Experts in Louisiana's Chemical Corridor Disputes*, Cambridge MA: MIT Press.

Babcock, H. (1995) 'Environmental Justice Clinics: Visible Models of Justice', *Stanford Environmental Law Journal*, Vol. 14, No. 3, pp. 3–57.

Bryant, B. (1995) *Environmental Justice: Issues, Policies and Solutions*, Washington: Island Press.

Bryant, B. and Mohai, P. (1992) *Race and the Incidence of Environmental Hazards: a Time for Discourse*, Boulder, CO, San Francisco and Oxford: Westview Press.

Bullard, R. D. (1990) *Dumping in Dixie: Race, Class and Environmental Quality*, Boulder, CO, San Francisco and Oxford: Westview Press.

—— (1993) 'The Threat of Environmental Racism', *NR&E*, Winter, pp. 23–6 and 55–6.

—— (1993a), *Confronting Environmental Racism: Voices from the Grassroots* (Boston: South End Press).

—— (ed.) (1994) *Unequal Protection*, San Fransisco: Sierra Club Books.

—— (1994a) 'Decision Making', in L. Westra and P. Wenz (eds), *Faces of Environmental Racism*, London: Rowman and Littlefied.

Bullard, R. D. and Wright, B. H. (1990) 'The Quest for Environmental Equity: Mobilizing the African-American Community for Social Change', *Society and Natural Resources*, Vol. 3, pp. 301–11.

Cable, S. and Benson, M. (1993) 'Acting Locally: Environmental Injustice and the Emergence of Grassroots Environmental Organisations', *Social Problems*, Vol. 40, No. 4 (November), pp. 464–78.

Cole, L. (1992) 'Empowerment as the Key to Environmental Protection: the Need for Environmental Poverty Law', *Ecology Law Quarterly*, Vol. 19, pp. 619–83.

Cole, L. (1992a) 'Remedies for Environmental Racism: a View from the Field', *Michigan Law Review*, Vol. 90, pp. 1991–7.

Cole, L. and Foster, S. (2001) *From the Ground Up: Environmental Racism and the Rise of the Environmental Justice Movement*, New York: New York University Press.

Colquette, K. M. and Robertson, E. H. (1991) 'Environmental Racism: the Causes, Consequences and Commendations', *Talane Environmental Law Journal*, Vol. 5, pp. 153–207.

Commission for Racial Justice United Church of Christ (1987) *Toxic Wastes and Race in the United States: a National Report on the Racial and Socio-Economic Characteristics of Communities with Hazardous Waste Sites*, New York: Public Data Access.

Faber, D. and O'Connor, J. (1993) 'Capitalism and the Crisis of Environmentalism', in R. Hofrichter (ed.), *Toxic Struggles: the Theory and Practice of Environmental Justice*, Salt Lake City: University of Utah Press.

Ferris, D. (1995), 'A Broad Environmental Justice Agenda', *Maryland Journal of Contemporary Legal Issues*, Vol. 5, No. 1, pp. 115–27.

Garvey, N. and Newell, P. (2005) 'Corporate Accountability to the Poor? Assessing the Effectiveness of Community-based Strategies', *Development in Practice*, Vol. 15, Nos 3–4 (June), pp. 389–404.

Gaventa, J. and Smith, B. (1991) 'The De-industrialisation of the Textile South: a Case Study', in J. Leiter, M. Schulman and R. Zingraff (eds), *Hanging by a Thread: Social Change in Southern Textiles*, Ithaca, NY: Ithaca Press.

Heiman, M. (1996) 'Race, Waste and Class: New Perspectives on Environmental Justice', *Antipode*, Vol. 28. No. 2, pp. 111–12.

Jones, S. C. (1993) 'EPA Targets 'Environmental Racism', *The National Law Journal*, 9 August, pp. 28, 34, 36.

Keeva, S. (1994) 'A Breath of Justice', *ABA Journal*, February, pp. 88–92.

Krauss, C. (1989) 'Community Struggles and the Shaping of Democratic Consciousness', *Sociological Forum*, Vol. 4, pp. 227–39.

Madihlaba, T. (2002) 'The Fox in the Henhouse: the Environmental Impact of Mining on Communities', in McDonald, D. (ed.), Athens and Cape Town: Ohio University Press and University of Cape Town Press, pp. 156–68.

McDonald, D. A. (ed.) (2002) *Environmental Justice in South Africa*, Athens and Cape Town: Ohio University Press and University of Cape Town Press.

Newell, P. (2001) 'Access to Environmental Justice? Litigation against TNCs in the South', *IDS Bulletin*, Vol. 32, No. 1.

—— (2005) 'Citizenship, Accountability and Community: the Limits of the CSR Agenda', *International Affairs*, Vol. 81, No. 3 (May), pp. 541–57 .

—— (2005a) 'Race, Class and the Global Politics of Environmental Inequality', *Global Environmental Politics* Vol.5, No.3, August, pp. 70–94.

Pellow, D. N. (2001) 'Environmental Justice and the Political Process: Movements, Corporations and the State', *The Sociology Quarterly*, Vol. 42, No. 1, pp. 47–67.

—— (2002), *Garbage Wars: the Struggle for Enivronmental Justice in Chicago*, Cambridge, MA.: Massachusetts Institute of Technology (MIT) Press.

Pellow, D. and Park Sun-Hee, L. (2002) *The Silicon Valley of Dreams: Environmental Injustice, Immigrant Workers and the High-tech Global Economy*, New York and London: New York University Press.

Perkins, J. (1992) 'Recognising and Attacking Environmental Racism', *Clearinghouse Review*, August, pp. 389–97.

Pulido, L. (1994), 'Restructuring and the Contraction and Expansion of Environmental Rights in the United States', *Environment and Planning A*, No. 26.

Ruiters, G. (2002) 'Race, Place and Environmental Rights: a Radical Critique of Environmental Justice Discourse', in McDonald, D. (ed.), Athens and Cape Town: Ohio University Press and University of Cape Town Press, pp. 112–27.

Sandweiss, S. (1998) 'The Social Construction of Environmental Justice', in D. Camacho, (ed.), *Environmental Injustice, Political Struggles: Race, Class and the Environment*, Durham: Duke University Press.

Schafer, K., with Blust, S., Lipsett, B., Newman, P. and Wiles, R. (1993) *What Works: Local Solutions to Toxic Pollution*, Report No. 2, Washington, DC: The Environmental Exchange.

Szasz, A. and Meuser, M. (1997) 'Environmental Inequalities: Literature Review and Proposals for New Directions in Research and Theory', *Current Sociology*, Vol. 45, No. 3 (July), pp. 99–120.

White, H. L. (1998) 'Race, Class and Environmental Hazards', in D. Camacho (ed.), *Environmental Injustice, Political Struggles: Race, Class and the Environment*, Durham: Duke University Press.

CHAPTER 10

Oil and accountability issues in the Niger Delta

OGA STEVE ABAH AND JENKS ZAKARI OKWORI

The politics of oil in Nigeria has attracted considerable activist and academic attention in recent years (Rowell and Goodall 1994; Okonta and Douglas 2003; Frynas 2000; Naneen 2004). Amid allegations of human rights abuses, environmental devastation and state corruption, the Niger Delta has come under increasing global scrutiny. Accountability in the region is intimately tied to the politics of resource extraction and the governance of abundance. The lack of accountability over how oil is extracted and who benefits in the Niger Delta has led to demands by many different community-based groups for their rights to the resource to be respected and guaranteed. They demand accountability from different actors, including the state and transnational corporations. The emergence of these community-based groups, especially youth organisations and women's groups, has resulted in the creation of new informal structures of governance.

The focus of this chapter is on community-level processes and politics as the site for accountability struggles, though these are linked to a wider context in which the state (federal and local), and transnational corporations are important actors. In order to understand how community-based politics relates to overarching questions of accountability and oil, this chapter draws on participatory research conducted using popular theatre, in which communities tell their own stories about rights and exclusion, and in this way identify for themselves where change is needed. Given the context of conflict and tension in the Niger Delta, drama is an important tool because it provides insights into the community-level politics of accountability, a topic neglected in many of the other studies on oil and politics in the region. The meanings and representations of oil at the local level challenge the idea of a 'resource curse' and open up the relationship between community-level politics and processes and the wider context of political and commercial interests.

Many studies on the Niger Delta, especially following the death of activist Ken Saro-Wiwa in 1995, have focused on the federal government and its failure to deliver development to communities in the region (see Johansen 2002; Ekeh 1999); even Shell's shortcomings are explained through the failure of the federal government to enforce rules and regulations. In contrast, our focus is on the accountability of other actors, including the private sector. To explore these issues, we begin with an overview of how the abundance of oil contributes to a lack of accountability in the Niger Delta. We briefly summarise the literature focusing on oil as a 'resource curse' that undermines the prospects for improving accountability, as well as on other contributory factors. We discuss the complex relationships between actors – including the government, transnational corporations (TNCs) and communities – and the accountability demands they make. The main focus of this chapter, however, will be community-level politics, explored through performance, drama and their relationship to state and corporate accountability.

The Niger Delta and the politics of abundance

The abundance of oil in Nigeria has made the country dependent on oil for revenue generation. Revenue from oil is controlled and distributed by the government. Corruption has made politics in Nigeria very lucrative, with politicians spending huge amounts to get into office. Once in office they and their business collaborators become the active beneficiaries of the centralised system of bureaucracy, through which they are then able to manipulate the distribution of the state's resources to enrich themselves through corrupt means. Since oil alone accounts for 80 per cent of Nigeria's budgetary allocations, there is a lot of wealth at the disposal of those in political office, which has led to capital-intensive projects in which overhead costs far outstrip actual disbursements to people-centred programmes (Mutizwa-Mangiza 1990: 43; Olowu and Wunsch 2004: 65). The crude oil output from Bayelsa and Delta states accounts for 90 per cent of Nigeria's foreign exchange earnings and over 80 per cent of its GDP (Okon 2003: 4). With each election, politicians promise to return more oil revenue to the communities from which it was derived, yet once in power these promises are largely unfulfilled and frustration mounts, often leading to violence.

The term Niger Delta refers to both the immediate area where the River Niger shreds into tributaries and empties into the Atlantic Ocean and the contiguous zones and communities that are geographically defined by the creeks that have formed as a result of the interaction of the Niger and the ocean. It covers an area of about 70,000 square kilometres extending from Akwa-Ibom State through Cross River, Rivers, Bayelsa, Delta and Edo to Ondo State. In its extended form it also includes Abia and Ebonyi states. The region is made up of several ethnic groups including Annang, Efik, Egi, Ibibio, Ijaw, Isoko, Ikwerre, Itsekiri, Ndokwa, Ndoni, Ogba, Oron,Urhobo, Ibo and Yoruba (Okon 2003: 1).

The people of this region are traditionally fishers and farmers. A large part of the population was also involved in trading, production of crafts, oil palm milling, timber extraction, boat building and local gin brewing. With the discovery of oil, there has been a remarkable shift from these means of livelihood to other sources centred on oil and oil exploration. In this sense, the production of oil has redefined livelihoods, the economy and politics in the region (Eson *et al.* 2004: 197). In comparison to other parts of the country, the region has inadequate infrastructure and high unemployment rates. There is, therefore, a correspondingly high level of tension and community-based conflict. Another effect of oil extraction and processing is the diminishing sustainability of livelihoods from forest products and marine resources due to environmental pollution and degradation caused by oil exploration activities.

At the same time, the advent of oil extraction has raised awareness among different groups of people in the area. Women's and youth organisations, as well as development unions and associations such as Ijaw national youth organisations (mostly formed after the discovery of oil), have become highly mobilized. This growing involvement in the politics of oil is informed by feelings of oppression and marginalisation, and alienation from the 'dividends' of oil manifested in an absence of education and employment. In turn, this contributes to a crisis of citizenship in Nigeria, where national citizenship has little meaning in comparison with other geographical and ethnic identities (Abah and Okwori 2005: 73).

There is consensus that a crucial way to address poverty, and the lack of accountability poor people experience, is to gain more control over resources, especially oil; people in the Niger Delta have been trenchant in calling for this (Eson *et al.* 2004). They believe that only through self-determination and direct control of the oil found on their land will they be able to use the revenue from oil to better their lives. The reality is that oil wealth is seen in Nigeria as a 'national cake' and politicians, the military and civilians scramble to get a slice of it.

Production from joint ventures (JV) accounts for nearly all of Nigeria's crude oil production. The largest JV, operated by Shell, produces nearly 50 per cent of Nigeria's crude oil.[1] The federal government generates revenues that it disburses to all states and local governments in Nigeria for development purposes. In doing this, it takes into account certain allocation principles, especially those of population, the need for equality between states, internal revenue generation, land mass and terrain. The current constitutional provision, however, is that the principle of derivation shall be constantly reflected in any approved formula as being not less than 13 per cent of the revenue accruing to the federation account directly from any natural resources (Udeh 2002: 3). This is in recognition of the need to compensate the oil-producing states for their contribution to wealth generation. Yet, despite the high levels of oil production from the Delta region, it remains one of the poorest in the country.

Given the pervasive and often perverse effects of oil on politics and development in Nigeria, it is important to highlight the contextual factors that contribute to the situation, including colonialism. There is also a growing body of literature exploring the idea that oil and other natural resources can constitute a 'resource curse' destructive of developmental and democratic prospects. The next section will summarise some of the key arguments from this literature, in order to contextualise the community-level perspectives on oil that will be the focus of this chapter.

Conflict and control: resource curse and neocolonialism

Neocolonialism
Scholars over the years continue to link the conflict in the Niger Delta region to British colonial arrangements and control of the Niger area. Agbonifo (2004) argues that Nigeria, from its inception, was treated as a business enterprise by British colonisers. Therefore, from the slave trade to the palm oil trade and subsequently petroleum, the terms of trade have always been unfavourable to Nigeria. He asserts that the discriminatory strategy of granting licences and leases to British subjects provided the basis for the entrepreneurial underdevelopment of Nigeria, and the entrenchment of the hegemony of foreign capital.

As argued by Akpobibio (2001), Alamieyeseigha (2002) and Ajakorotu (2004), ethnic competition laid the foundation for political and economic competition in the Nigerian state. They maintain that the division of the country into three regions and the subsequent linking of representational power to population size meant that minorities had little opportunity to demand access to resources or developmental projects in regional assemblies. In response, ethnic minorities in the region began to mobilise for self-determination. Against this backdrop, Ajakorotu insists that at the core of the Niger Delta crisis in the post-independence era has been the concentration of power and resources in the hands of the federal government through constitutions and decrees, making governments insensitive to the grievances of local people. Into this context of inadequate representation, and a history of exploitative resource extraction, came the discovery of oil and drilling on a large scale in 1958, creating the conditions for what has been described as a 'resource curse'.

Resource curse

The idea of the resource curse brings together political, economic, social and cultural dimensions of natural resource conflict and control:

> It is both difficult and artificial to distil out the narrowly defined biological and geophysical properties of 'crude' or 'raw' petroleum from the social relations (institutional practices, ideological associations and meanings, forms of extraction, production and use) of petroleum, a commodity not only saturated in the myths of the rise of the West but also indisputably one of the most fundamental building blocks of twentieth-century industrial capitalism. (Watts 1998: 2)

Work on the resource curse seeks to explain how abundance of natural resources can often stunt economic development, and contribute to a lack of accountability (Karl 1997; Shafer 1994; Sachs and Warner 1995). There are both economic and political explanations for this (Ross 1999). Some centre on the short-sightedness among policy makers that resource abundance produces (a 'get rich quick mentality'/'petromania'/'petro-fetishism'), while other accounts emphasise the way in which resource exports tend to empower sectors, classes or interest groups that favour growth-impeding policies. Another set of explanations focuses on the institutional weakness that derives from resource booms. Karl, for example, argues that 'dependence on petroleum revenues produces a distinctive type of institutional setting, the 'petro-state' which encourages the political distribution of rents' (1997: 16). In so far as state élites are able to accumulate revenues from resource exploitation without the need to raise taxes from citizens (who would then be entitled to a say in how those taxes are spent), they are able to insulate themselves from popular pressure. Rentier states 'are freed from the need to levy domestic taxes and become less accountable to the societies they govern' (Ross 1999: 312). This leads to poor governance in so far as state officials can use resources to meet unpopular, controversial or illegal objectives with low taxes and high patronage dampening pressures for democracy (Ascher 1999). Rentier states are able to concentrate wealth earned from resource extraction in activities that deepen and sustain their political power through economic pay-offs and military means. In many ways, this reflects the current situation in Nigeria.

The net effect of oil on Nigeria's growth, despite the ostensible wealth, is often negative. Sachs and Warner in their study on resource abundance and growth (Sachs and Warner 1995) show that states with a high ratio of natural resource exports to GDP in 1971 had abnormally slow growth rates between 1971 and 1989. Resource exporters are then left with resource enclaves that produce few knock-on benefits to other parts of the economy (Ross 1999: 302). Oil has been described as a resource curse because, despite its value, the effects of its extraction include increased violence, environmental degradation and loss of livelihoods, decreased economic growth, and a lack of accountability by governments and corporations to the people affected. As Watts notes (2003: 5089): 'oil capitalism produces particular sorts of enclave economies and governable spaces characterised by violence and instability'. Violence resulting from resource conflicts represents perhaps the most extreme expression of an accountability breakdown (Watts 2003; Dalby 2003; Collier 2000; Peluso and Watts 2001).

The value of resource extraction to companies, which determines where they can operate, means that they are often willing to tolerate adversarial operating conditions, conflict and even civil war. Though it is generally assumed that multinational companies prefer conditions of political and economic stability, Frynas suggests that, in certain circumstances, firms benefit from a lack of clarity about rules and expectations (Frynas 1998). Cultures of corruption can actually benefit those with the financial resources and political clout to secure deals to their advantage (Frynas and Wood 2001). It is not only in deals with government that financial resources are important. Our research has shown that funds from oil companies can contribute to inter-community divisions, which can lead to violence.

Firms, including Shell in Nigeria, have come under attack for encouraging the privatisation of security services, whereby state police services are supplied with arms to protect their investment sites or paid to see off attacks and acts of sabotage from those disputing their proclaimed right to operate in the area. Ross suggests that even when property rights are poorly enforced, 'resource extraction can still proceed since firms earning resource rents can afford to pay criminal gangs, private militias or nascent rebel armies for the private enforcement of their property rights while still earning a normal profit' (1999: 320). Contrary to popular assumptions, therefore, that investors tend to demand and benefit from good governance in the form of minimal corruption, transparency in transactions and respect for the rule of law and human rights, there is some suggestion that for some firms, weak forms of governance provide them with a degree of freedom of manoeuvre and discretion that would not otherwise be possible (Frynas 1998). In such contexts, claims by corporations to be uninvolved in politics ring hollow. For example, in the primary elections for local councils for the People's Democratic Party (PDP), Nigeria's ruling party, in Nembe in July 2003, 'officials of Shell and Agip were on hand to lend support to the governor.... Helicopters provided by Shell airlifted the cards and other electoral material from Creek House, to Nembe ... Agip also airlifted voting material directly to its own terminal in Brass instead of Twon, the local council headquarters designated by the party's national executive as the voting centre (Okonta 2004: 23–4).

Each of these dimensions serves to fuel the current conflict in the Niger Delta, sustained by people's feeling of dissatisfaction over the distribution of the resources accruing from the oil wealth of the Niger Delta (*This Day* newspaper, 29 October 2004: 2). In addition, each of the actors involved views the other as neglecting its role, or expecting too much of others. There is an overwhelming perception of corruption and mismanagement of oil resources involving the national, state and local governments. Our research in Bayelsa and Delta states also revealed that at the community level within the oil-producing communities, the chiefs, local élite and youth are thought to be caught up in corruption and mismanagement. Likewise, TNCs are perceived to be engaged in the intensive extraction of oil without adequate and commensurate attention to the protection of the environment and the communities it sustains.

Drama as a tool for researching rights and accountability

In circumstances of fear and lack of voice, drama becomes a vehicle to discuss the accountability failures, dilemmas and issues facing the community by creating linkages between different communities; to take forward actions discussed during meetings. Within the drama, community members would explore narratives about their experiences of accountability failures, recreating their stories through the lens of breakdowns in relationships with government and the oil companies.

Drama drew out a diversity of opinions and brought submerged perspectives into open engagement in public. It is a tool for generating information, engaging in analysis and eliciting community discussions. But it also allows groups to broach taboo issues, and to talk about issues without holding any one individual responsible for raising delicate subjects, especially those involving actors from government, TNCs and the militia. In addition to the drama, the Theatre for Development Centre (TFDC), a research unit of the Nigerian Popular Theatre Alliance based at Ahmadu Bello University, has also combined other research approaches such as participatory learning and action (PLA) in order to develop 'methodological conversations' (Abah 2003: 125) that help to democratise the research process.

This research has generated some key questions for accountability:

- What do we learn about accountability from working directly with community-based groups?
- What is the significance of oil at the local level and how is this represented through drama? Do these representations challenge or support the idea of oil as a 'resource curse'?
- What is the relationship between community-level politics and processes and the wider context of political and commercial interests?

Community perspectives on the politics of accountability

All over the Niger Delta region, oil exploration and exploitation activities have adversely affected the environment and human welfare. The issues and problems range from environmental pollution, unemployment and the lack of potable drinking water to the absence of health facilities and an overall lack of say in the control and use of the natural resources from the region.

The drama in Otuegwe chronicles the story of two brothers pitted against each other in a fight to the death because oil had been found on land that belongs to one of them. Out of jealousy, the one without oil on his farm fights the other and kills him. In the midst of the brothers' mortal conflict the oil rig bobs up and down irreverently, ceaselessly. The constant refrain of *'Na wetin de happen here?'* (What is going on here?), demonstrates the agony, the frustration and confusion of the community. The drama may also have been forward-looking in warning against the kind of greed and conflict that the presence of oil in a community could cause without effective management. The paramount chief in Otuegwe said: 'I know there is a problem with oil everywhere. Nevertheless, I believe that oil in itself is not the problem. It is the way it is managed.' These issues were interrogated in the drama performances, articulating a critique of TNCs and government for unmet responsibilities and offering suggestions for action beyond the drama.

The Sanubi drama titled 'Unfulfilled Promises' was a performance that rolled together several issues from denial of rights through to collusion, corruption and violence. In the drama, oil is found on the farm of one of the community members. The chief tries hard to deny him the compensation money on the grounds that his forefathers were slaves and therefore he could not claim to be indigenous to the place. The women and the youth are excluded from discussions with Shell and therefore denied some of the benefits that should accrue to them. When the Shell contractors destroy farms to lay pipes, hell breaks loose. The women and the youth join forces declaring "Shell o! Emo! Emo!" (Shell o! It is war! It is war!). What these dramas show is that oil is linked to accountability in complex ways within particular communities. Inter-community and even inter-family divisions are part of the experience of lack of accountability. Indigeneity and citizenship also appear to shape rights claims and the demand for accountability.

A resource curse? Meanings of oil at the local level

We heard from people in the communities that agricultural production has diminished significantly as vegetation cover and soil have deteriorated since drilling began. In Samagidi, Ethiope East Local Government, for instance, the thick vegetation cover has been replaced by a scanty vegetation of trees and certain species of weeds which the people now refer to as 'Shell'. Residents also complained of dwindling marine resources. Fish have either migrated or have been badly depleted by oil spills. Although the group we worked with acknowledged that there is, in general, an increase in capital inflow to the community, funds go mainly to the village élite.

Other concerns as expressed in Otuokpoti, Nyambiri and Tuburu included lack of proper transportation to and from the village. The boats are few and irregular; they are overcrowded; very often they sink and passengers drown. There is no potable drinking water in the village. The creek water is used for drinking, for washing and for waste disposal, including human waste. In the words of one of the community elders, 'We are not known by government here. The many young people here have nowhere to go.' The elders argued that this explains why they are very restless and get involved in violent acts.

The community also accused Shell and other TNCs of differential treatment and marginalisation. Leaders argued that while Shell pays monthly fees to elders and youth in Isoko, Itsekiri and Ijaw communities, they are refused such benefits. According to Samagidi elders, 'oil wealth is not in the hands of Samagidi sons and daughters because our children are not employed in the oil industry, except in menial jobs'. They cited the example of Shell Petroleum Development Company (SPDC), where no local people are employed.

In contrast to this catalogue of complaints, Shell paints a picture of its good environmental record, which contradicts the reality of the oil communities' lived experiences. According to Chris Finlayson, Chairman of Shell in Nigeria, the corporation has 'continued to work to mitigate the impact of our operations on the environment. Five years ago, the company began voluntary certification to international standards through the ISO 14001 process. All our major facilities are now independently certified' (SPDC, *People and Environment Report*, 2003). He goes on to say that Shell has a major commitment to end gas flaring by 2008, but then ends by saying that it was not feasible. He acknowledges that the volume of associated gas flared in 2003 was 700 million standard cubic feet per day over and above previous volumes. He acknowledges that, 'oil spills remain a persistent cause for concern, damaging the environment, posing health hazards, and disrupting production'. In 2003, there were 221 such incidents, in which a total of some 9,900 barrels of oil were spilled. He blames two-thirds of the spills on wilful damage to facilities, however, suggesting that Shell is 'particularly concerned about the high proportion of incidents that are caused by theft, or motivated by the prospect of compensation payments and/or employment opportunities in the resulting clean-up' (SPDC, People and Environment Report, 2003: 7–8).

However, the reality from the field, also documented by other research, tells a different story that does not tally with Finlayson's claims. According to the Executive Governor of Bayelsa State, Chief Diepreye Alamieyeseigha, (2004)

> the atrocities of oil companies have reached scandalous proportions. There has been systematic violation of environmental safety laws especially as relates to pollution. One good illustration of this is the volume of natural gas flared in the country. The average rate of gas flaring in the world is about 4 per

cent. In Nigeria, over 70 per cent of associated gas is flared. Nigeria has the notorious record of 25 per cent of all gas flared in the world.

In addition, community members deny the location of blame for most of the spills on theft and sabotage. They argue that pipeline vandalism requires expert knowledge of petroleum technology, which is beyond the capacity of ordinary people. They charge that vandalism and spills are done at the insistence of, or in connivance with, oil officials who stand to benefit from monies allocated for cleaning and repairs.

Changing livelihood and altered community ethos

Oil has contributed immensely to the rural–urban divide because of the destruction of rural and community livelihoods arising from exploration and mining, as well as the job prospects offered by oil operations. On one hand, the discovery of oil in the Niger Delta enhanced the status of several urban centres where the oil company's major operations are based or headquartered. On the other hand, it has altered livelihoods and community life in significant ways. Many young people drifted into cities, notably Warri, which employed thousands in the construction industry. When construction eased in the early 1970s, however, a deluge of unwanted labour remained. Today, many of them are in the 'militia industry'.

Additionally, oil workers introduced new modes of consumption and altered social life and behaviour within the communities. Where in-kind contribution was common, cash has replaced traditional systems of exchange in a context in which every facet of life has become monetised. This has reduced and diminished the value of communality and hard work, and set the stage for a culture of greed to flourish around the unbridled quest for money. A local prayer in Urhobo that captures the new culture is very telling: 'May your workload lessen while your money triples.' While some degree of commodification of work is inevitable as a result of these changes, a key accountability challenge is how to manage it in a productive and positive way.

A resource can sometimes be a curse when its abundance breeds complacency instead of the creativity that scarcity seems to elicit. In Nigeria, resource abundance has produced a culture of rent seeking. In order to protect the rent, the rent seeker must ignore some unaccountable practices and human rights abuses in the bid to keep the tenant engaged. The materiality of the resource in this sense, and the incentives to exploit it, constitute a serious constraint on efforts to hold corporations to account. The lack of ownership and control of the structure of oil production also mean that the Nigerian government cannot monitor the activities of TNCs effectively. The concentration of knowledge about production rests in the hands of non-Nigerian entities, in turn creating a dependency which undermines prospects for accountability. Such regulations as do exist are often not enforced because of the power the oil companies wield. In addition, the boundaries between the state and the private sector are often unclear when the latter, as in the example above, is involved in providing logistical support to government campaigning. There are, nevertheless, trends in the Niger Delta towards increased agency and action by excluded groups, even if it is currently of an *ad hoc* and temporary nature.

From community politics to accountability

In this section we argue that the discovery and extraction of oil in the Niger Delta have altered community life and ethos in ways that impact upon accountability relations.

The politics of abundance and who benefits, particularly those communities that live in the oil producing areas, are critical issues. The social costs of development were sharply brought to the attention of the youth groups at the time of the 'Million People march in March' for Abacha's self succession campaign in 1999. At this time the gap between the wealth accumulated in Abuja and their own experience of rural deprivation became clear raising questions about how revenue earned from oil was being allocated.

The close collaboration between governments and TNCs in profit-sharing and the TNCs' support of the government's political activities have compromised the government's ability to hold TNCs to account. The operations of the TNCs have also affected traditional systems of accountability at the local level through chiefs and elders, and led to new formulations of rights (such as the right to control natural resource extraction) and contestation for those rights. Power has shifted away from a culture of respect centred on the authority of chiefs to a culture of greed in which people increasingly seek direct access to resources through the state and corporations. As a result of the failures of government and traditional institutions, other 'governance' structures have emerged. Some of these are independent, while others are set up by government as a way of promoting participation and giving voice to the people in the development of their areas.

Community-based groups and accountability
There are different types of community-based groups. There are the umbrella organisations such as the Ijaw National Youth Organisation,

which has formed itself into an umbrella body under which various groups in the Ijaw diaspora operate, from Bayelsa through Delta and Rivers to Ogun states. There are also other ethnic groups, such as the Ogoni, Urhobo and Itsekiri. In addition to these groups, there are a plethora of community organisations and women's groups. The Ogulaha Development Council (ODC) and the Niger Delta Women's Association in Warri are examples.

These ethnic, youth and women's groups have emerged for a number of reasons. First, the breakdown in governance results from the government's failure to provide basic social development in terms of education, employment or infrastructure. In response, women's and youth groups have been created, seeking to be heard and respected in community affairs. Second, these groups have a sense that they are not benefiting from the proceeds of natural resource extraction. Third, there is a lack of trust in the elders and chiefs to do business on their behalf, because they are seen as complicit in corruption. Finally, there is a strong feeling that the government does not care about their loss of livelihood. The perception of these groups is that the different tiers of government, from federal through state to local, have become highly unaccountable and dysfunctional.

In cases of perceived breaches of agreement by TNCs or the government, the groups may press their cases through protest. Examples of such protests include the Niger Delta Women for Justice protest (January 1999), Kenyabene Women Action (10 June 2002), Ugborodo Women's Action (July 2002), and the Ekpan Women's blockade (30 July 2002). In all of these instances, groups demanded, among other things, the provision of basic social services and employment. In some cases, it is claimed women were shot at, beaten up and injured by state armed police officers and security personnel from TNCs (Okon 2003: 10). This is one of the many reasons different communities are hardly able to separate the government from the TNCs. They see them both as collaborators in undermining accountability. These new groups see their role as (informal) law enforcement to ensure transparency and accountability. On this basis, they now engage in negotiation with government and TNCs on behalf of their communities. They also monitor the award of contracts and the employment of workers in the oil sector, functioning as watchdog pressure groups. The informal practices produced by this action may not give rise to governance in a formal sense, but these groups have been able to produce a certain form of order. They have been able to undertake a critical analysis of their own predicament and given voice to many groups previously ignored by government. They have also been able to develop and take actions to address this situation. Whilst not all of these contributions may be deemed positive, they do nevertheless provide forms of governance or social regulation in the absence of government responsiveness.

However, in addition to these apparently altruistic motives, some of the groups have agendas of personal enrichment. The militias fall into this category, despite their rhetoric of fighting for the welfare of the Niger Delta people. Initially, the militias were instruments for claiming from the oil companies and the Nigerian government what the communities perceived to be their entitlements from oil, but which they had been denied. It was soon realised, however, that they could also be used to extract concessions for personal and group enrichment.

This interest has since taken on new dimensions in which different communities have armed factions that war against each other for traditional chieftaincy titles. The rivalry over chieftaincy is explained by the fact that to control oil-bearing land and access to the oil companies is to be wealthy and powerful. This generates intra-and inter-communal conflicts as local élites jostle for access to the resources. Such dynamics explain the apparent contradiction between promoting the interests of the community and seeking law enforcement and the conflicts generated by these intra- and inter-communal conflicts, which produce more short-term and self-interested strategies.

A large number of unemployed youths, already alienated by their own social condition and with very little hope for the future, have become the crack troops of ethnic-based conflicts in the Delta (Naanen 2004: 5). Some of the wars are exacerbated by the way the oil companies allocate wells and pipes to communities. During field research in Odovie and Samagidi, we heard from youth groups that oil companies sometimes deliberately label the wrong communities on well or pipe sites, provoking conflict where they are the beneficiaries because common platforms of complaint become harder to articulate. We also heard how the oil companies employ the services of the militias to protect their installations, encouraging inter-militia conflict. A study commissioned by Shell supports the idea that TNCs are heavily implicated in the security crisis of the Niger Delta: 'It is clear that SCiN (Shell Companies in Nigeria) is part of the Niger Delta dynamics and that its social licence to operate is fast eroding', that Shell uses 'a quick-fix, reactive and divisive approach to community engagement expressed through different areas of policy, practice and corporate culture' (SPDC, Peace and Security in the Niger Delta (PaSS), December 2003: 5).

In staking their rights to control the resource found on their land, the groups breed abuses of other kinds of rights. The different levels of conflict that exist between the various groups in the communities are caused by the fact that the élite members of the community, as well as chiefs or leaders who represent the communities before the TNCs and or government, negotiate for themselves instead of the communities. The self-seeking attitude of persons in positions of power was reflected in the Eku drama, *If You Give Even a Madman a Hoe and Tell Him to Farm, He Will First Till the Soil Towards Himself!* The struggles for accountability can also produce their own accountability problems: groups that set out to fight for rights and accountability have ended up being unaccountable in their operations and activities, pursuing shorter-term material gains over broader community concerns. Demanding accountability can itself reveal accountability deficits.

Conclusions

What the above discussions demonstrate is the strong link between the nature of oil as a resource and the lack of accountability in the Niger Delta. The problems of accountability produced by resource abundance are compounded by cultures of corruption and a lack of transparency. Many people do not know how much oil is extracted and how much money the state earns from this. The refusal of the government to make this clear is related to how much profit is being made. Transparency about this would reveal what was earned and the government could then be held to account for its (lack of) expenditure on development. Lack of clarity allows the Nigerian government maximum discretion over how to use the resources.

What we observe is an accountability culture defined by corruption and patronage. We noted above how the activities of the youth groups, for example, help to create new structures of governance, but do so in ways that we would not usually associate with practices of governance. Yet, the degree of organisation of the youth groups makes them attractive to politicians, who usurp them for their own ends. Nonetheless, the youth group discourses of emancipation, enfranchisement and control now shape the conduct of politics and the terms of debate in the Niger Delta. While rights and responsibilities are in theory defined, they are often not enforced in practice; it is difficult for meaningful accountability to be established when transparency is lacking and rights and responsibilities are contested. There is a gap between the rhetoric of corporate citizenship and the local reality of poverty, conflict and failed expectations in which companies are implicated. This seems to reflect more fundamental conflicts within communities and between communities, the state and TNCs over who should be accountable, to whom, and for what.

The federal government is torn between protecting and fending for its citizens in the Niger Delta and ensuring an enabling environment for business to earn revenue. So far, the balance is lacking and the government is, in general, viewed by citizens in the Niger Delta as choosing to protect business. The Niger Delta, therefore, continues to be an area where contestation over resources and conflict over rights and responsibilities will remain unresolved for some time yet.

When all of these events and facts unfold in the dramatic performance, they suggest a need for action. This action is situated in the afterlife of both the drama and the research. However, the links between the immediacy of the events in the performance and the action afterwards are many: the performance has identified gaps and established a basis for further dialogue; eventually leading to a congruence of concern between community members, a common agenda and the will to act.

The research process democratises in three ways. It creates a space in which people can speak and bring issues forward for discussion. It allows them to make suggestions about what is to be done. It challenges power relations within the community, creating a space to question roles and hierarchies within the community. Yet, while individual actions can be questioned, the positions of traditional rulers cannot be challenged, and therefore only certain relations of power are subject to scrutiny through drama. The limitation of drama as an accountability strategy is that inevitably it only reaches a limited number of people at any one particular time. It is harder to engage higher levels of decision making. The challenge, therefore, is to connect these local experiences of accountability failure, as explored through drama, with the politics of state decision making.

NOTE

1 The state-owned oil firm, Nigerian National Petroleum Corporation (NNPC), has a 55 per cent interest in the Shell JV. NNPC also has 60 per cent stakes in JVs with ExxonMobil (US), ChevronTexaco (US), ConocoPhilips (US), Eni SPA (Italy), and Total SA (France). (see 'Country Analysis Briefs' 2004).

REFERENCES

Abah, O. S (2003) 'Methodological Conversations in Researching Citizenship: Drama and Participatory Learning and Action in Encountering Citizens', in Oga S. Abah (ed.), *Geographies of Citizenship in Nigeria*, Zaria: Tamaza Publishing Company Ltd., pp.114–43.

Abah, O. S. and Okwori, J. Z. (2005) 'A Nation in Search of Citizens: Problems of Citizenship in the Nigerian Context', in Kabeer, N. (ed.), *Inclusive Citizenship: Meanings and Expressions*, London, Zed Books, pp. 71–84.

Agbonifo, J. (2004) 'The Colonial Origin and Perpetuation of Environmental Pollution in the Postcolonial Nigeria State', pp. 4–5, available at http://www.lilt.Ilstu.edu/critique/fall2002docs/jagbonifo.pdf, accessed 8 December 2004.

Ajakorotu, V. (2004) 'Oil Minorities and the Politics of Exclusion in the Niger Delta of Nigeria', p. 11, available at www.sidos.ch/method/RC28/abstract/Victor per cent200jakorotu.pdf-similar, accessed 8 December 2004.

Akpobibio, O. (2001) 'Sustainable Development as a Strategy for Conflict Prevention: the Case of the Niger Delta', pp. 6–8, available at http://www.waado.org/NigerDelta/Essay/resourceControl/Onduku.html, accessed 8 December 2004.

Alamieyeseigha, D. (2004) 'The Environmental Challenge of Developing the Niger Delta', p. 6, available at http://www.newsAfrica.net/article.php?section=9 , accessed 8 December 2004.

—— (2004a) 'The Niger Delta and Youth Restiveness: a Way Forward', paper presented to the Nigerian Union of Journalists, Abuja Chapel, 16 September 2004.

Ascher, W. (1999) *Why Governments Waste Resources: the Political Economy of Natural Resource Policy Failures in Developing Countries*, Baltimore: Johns Hopkins University Press.

Collier, P. (2000) 'Economic Causes of Conflict and their Implications for Policy', paper for World Bank, 'The Economics of Crime and Violence', online research project.

Country Analysis Briefs (2004), pp. 1–2, available at www.eia.doe.gov/emeu/cabs/nigeria.html, accessed 1 January 2005.

Dalby, S. (2003) 'Environmental insecurities: Geopolitics, Resources and Conflicts' *Economic and Political Weekly*, Vol. 38, No. 48, pp. 5073–9.

Ekeh, P. (1999) 'What the Federal Government of Nigeria is Doing in the Niger Delta is Wrong', available at www.waado.org/.../BayelsaInvasion/EkehWritesToPresidentObasanjo.html

Eson *et al.* (2004) 'Contesting Control of Resource Allocation: Power Relations, Actors and the policy process in Bayelsa State, Nigeria' in K. Brock (ed.), *Unpacking Policy: Knowledge, Actors and Spaces in Poverty Reduction in Uganda and Nigeria*, Kampala: Fountain Publishers, p. 197.

Frynas, G. (1998) 'Political Instability and Business: Focus on Shell in Nigeria', *Third World Quarterly*, Vol. 19, No. 3, pp. 457–79.

—— (2000) *Oil in Nigeria: Conflict and Litigation between Oil Companies and Village Communities*, Hamburg, New Brunswick NJ and London: LIT/Transaction.

Frynas, G. and Wood, G. (2001) 'Oil and War in Angola', *Review of African Political Economy*, Vol. 28, No. 90, pp. 587–606.

Johansen, B. E. (2002) 'Nigeria: the Ogoni: Oil, Blood and the Death of a Homeland. Indigenous Peoples and Environmental Issues: an Encyclopedia', available at www.ratical.org/ratville/IPEIE/Ogoni.html, accessed 25 June 2005.

Karl, T. L. (1997) *The Paradox of Plenty: Oil Booms and Petro-States*, Berkeley: University of California Press.

Mutizwa-Mangiza, N. D. (1990), 'Decentralization and District Development Planning in Zimbabwe', *Public Administration and Development*, Vol. 10, No. 4, pp. 355–72.

Naneen, B. (2004) 'The Political Economy of Oil and Violence in the Niger Delta',

Association of Concerned African Scholars (ACAS) Bulletin, No. 68 (Autumn), pp. 4–9.

Okon, E. J. (2003) 'Women's Issues and Women's Action in Claiming Citizenship Rights in the Niger Delta', Zaria: Theatre for Development Centre (TFDC), pp. 1, 10.

Okonta, I. (2004) 'Death-Agony of a Malformed Political Order', *Association of Concerned African Scholars (ACAS) Bulletin*, No. 68 (Autumn), pp. 23–9.

Okonta, I. and Douglas, O. (2003) *Where Vultures Feast: Shell, Human Rights and Oil in the Niger Delta*, London: Verso.

Olowu, D. and Wunsch, J. S. (2004) *Local Governance in Africa: the Challenges of Democratic Decentralization*, Boulder, Colorado: Lynne Rienner Publishers.

Peluso, N. and Watts, M. (2001) *Violent Environments*, New York: Cornell University Press.

Ross, M. (1999) 'The political economy of the resource curse', *World Politics*, Vol. 51, No. 2 (January), pp. 297–322.

Rowell, A. and Goodall, A. (1994) *Shell-shocked: the Environmental and Social Costs of Living with Shell in Nigeria*, Amsterdam: Greenpeace International.

Sachs, J. D. and Warner, A. (1995) 'Natural Resource Abundance and Economic Growth', Development Discussion Paper No. 517a, Cambridge: Harvard Institute for International Development.

Shafer, D. M. (1994) *Winners and Losers: How Sectors Shape the Developmental Prospects of States*, Itacha, NY: Cornell University Press.

SPDC (2003) *People and Environment Report*, Shell Petroleum Development Company, http://www.shell.com/static/nigeria/downloads/pdfs/2004rpt.pdf.

SPDC (2003a) *Peace and Security in the Niger Delta (PaSS)*, Shell Petroleum Development Company, December, http://www.shell.com.

This Day newspaper (2004) Vol. 10, No. 3476, 29 October, pp. 1–2.

Udeh, M. (2002) 'Petroleum Revenue Management: the Nigerian perspective', available at www.earthinstitute.columbia.edu/.../Nigeria/Nigeria%20petroleum%20Revenue%20Management%20UdehPaper.pdf, accessed 4 January 2005.

Watts, M. (1998) 'Some Notes on Petro-violence', paper prepared for the workshop on 'Environment and Violence', University of California, Berkeley, 24–26 September.

—— (2003) 'Economics of Violence: More Oil, More Blood', *Economic and Political Weekly*, Vol. 38, No. 48, pp. 5089–99.

CHAPTER 11

Compliance versus accountability: struggles for dignity and daily bread in the Bangladesh garment industry

SIMEEN MAHMUD AND NAILA KABEER

> The women workers in the Bangladesh garment industry have had more public attention to their rights than any group of workers in the entire history of the country. (Journalist, Development Research Centre (DRC) Inception Workshop on Inclusive Citizenship, Bangladesh, 2001)

> I believe that the 'culture of compliance' is far ahead in the garment manufacturing sector and changes in the RMG [ready-made garments] sector are dramatic compared to other sectors. (Director, Labour Department, Bangladesh, 2004)

The process of globalisation has brought workers in the poorer countries of the global South into direct competition with workers in the wealthier countries of the global North, exposing the stark inequalities in the conditions under which they work to the full glare of international publicity. Trade unions, the media, human rights activists and others in prosperous Northern countries have made consumers aware as they never were before about the conditions under which some of their regularly purchased consumer items are made. The international garment industry is one that has consistently attracted the attention of these groups and given rise to various campaigns, including Students against Sweatshops, the Clean Clothes Campaign and OXFAM's Make Trade Fair (See Luce, Chapter 12).

The working conditions of Bangladeshi export garment workers, predominantly women, have featured regularly in these campaigns: the absence of written contracts, long working hours, delayed payment of wages and routine violations of health and safety standards. Since working conditions in the garment industry are no worse, and generally are considered to be better, than those prevailing in the rest of the economy, the intense concern with garment workers' rights, referred to in the first quote above, reflects both the publicity generated by international campaigns as well as the unusual visibility of its largely female workforce in a society in which women have historically been regarded as a vulnerable group, in need of protection and hence confined to the shelter of the home. Currently the export garment industry employs 1.8 million workers, of whom 1.5 million are women. The mass entry of women workers into a sector hitherto dominated by men dramatically changed the character of the urban manufacturing labour force in the span of a few years[1] and explains some of the attention they receive domestically.

The second quote comes from the Director of the Labour Department, the government department responsible for ensuring that workers' rights are upheld. It testifies to one of the consequences of the intense public scrutiny on the working conditions prevailing within the export garment industry. This is the proliferation of codes of conduct imposed by the various international buyers operating in the export garment sector and anxious to avoid adverse attention from their consumers at home. The Director pointed out that the attempt at self-regulation on the part of garment manufacturers reflected the fact that non-compliance with basic labour standards in this sector carried real penalties in the form of lost orders from their international buyers.

It is worth noting that these observations were couched in the language of 'compliance' and that the compliance in question was to a voluntary code of conduct drawn up by the affected section of the private sector. He was not referring to compliance with national labour laws drawn up by the state to set out the rights of all citizens of Bangladesh, including its garment workers. There is clearly a gap between compliance of the kind the Labour Director is referring to and the kind of accountability that this book is about.

As we saw in Chapter 2, there are two key elements to the concept of accountability: *answerability*, the right to make claims and demand responses; and *enforceability*, the mechanisms for ensuring that answers are backed by actions and for sanctioning non-responsiveness. Accountability thus gives 'teeth' to the concept of rights and hence is indispensable to the status and practice of citizenship. A 'culture of compliance', on the other hand, refers to the willingness to abide by a given set of regulations (whether laws or codes). It is not the same as a culture of accountability, but it need not be incompatible with it, and may even contain the seeds from which such a culture can emerge. Whether it has done so or not in Bangladesh is a matter for empirical investigation, one that will be addressed in this chapter. We will be basing our analysis on in-depth interviews with 20 garment workers, with relevant officials of the Department of Labour, employer representatives and factory managers, with trade union officials and NGO workers. The chapter also draws on previous research carried out by the authors as well as media reports and the secondary literature. In the next section, we sketch out the context in which our analysis is located.

The context: poverty and patriarchy in a labour-surplus economy

There are a number of features of the Bangladesh context which represent 'the initial conditions' from which cultures of compliance and accountability have had to grow. Bangladesh was, and remains, a poor, largely agrarian economy, with 45 per cent of its population below the poverty line; it is one of 49 'least developed countries' in the world, according to the United Nations (2002). Although industrialisation dates back over a hundred years, it has been very narrowly based, confined largely to the processing and manufacture of jute, until recently its main export. The spread of market relations and infrastructural development has led to increased rates of economic growth and a small but steady decline in poverty over the 1990s. However, growth in agriculture has not been sufficient to absorb this annual increment and there has been increasing diversification into off-farm activities in rural areas, partly assisted by the spread of microfinance activities, and migration into urban areas.

Bangladesh was, and remains, a society that continues to be largely governed by patron–client relations. The intersection of patron-clientelism and a modern state apparatus with monopolistic control over rules and resources created a particular type of patrimonial ruling élite in Bangladesh (Khan 2001), whose search for political power and personal profit is pursued through the granting of special privileges to politically influential actors – including industrialists and trade unions – in return for their support at national and local level.

Finally, Bangladesh was and remains an extremely patriarchal society, with strict cultural constraints on women's participation in the public sphere and their confinement to reproductive work and the domestic domain. Socialised into this role from an early age, denied independent access to economic resources and defined as life-long dependents of male breadwinners and guardians, women occupy a subordinate position within the family as well as the wider society. Women have consequently constituted a significant proportion of the country's pool of 'surplus' labour, particularly in more close-knit communities in rural areas, where gender-specific constraints on their ability to take up paid work are more severe.

The expansion of export-oriented garment manufacturing in Bangladesh coincided with a period of radical economic reform. Under the aegis of the World Bank/IMF, the Bangladesh government had undertaken a series of measures since the late 1970s to move away from a strategy of protection for import-substituting domestic industry towards a more liberalised, open and export-oriented economy. Various incentive schemes channelled domestic investment into the export sector so that around 95 per cent of garment factories in the country are owned by local private capital (Kabeer and Mahmud 2004a). However, foreign direct investment was also encouraged through the establishment of export processing zones (EPZs) outside Dhaka and Chittagong, where the country's few joint ventures are located.

The dramatic expansion of the export-oriented RMG sector has also seen a substantial expansion of its workforce from a few thousand workers in the early 1980s to around 1.8 million workers in recent years, of whom 80 per cent are women (Kabeer and Mahmud 2004a). There has been a gradual growth in the share of knitwear to woven garment manufacturing and here there is a somewhat higher percentage of men. Although the export garment sector is, strictly speaking, in the formal economy and hence subject to national labour legislation, it is characterised by informal economy characteristics: easy entry and exit, an absence of written contracts, irregularity of payments, violations of health and safety regulations, long hours of overtime, low levels of unionisation and high rates of turnover in the workforce. The main exceptions to this are to be found in the country's EPZs, where more formal conditions exist, but these account for a very small proportion of total garment employment.

These working conditions, which are not unique to Bangladesh but prevail to a lesser or greater degree in export garment factories across the world, have led to various campaigns by coalitions of trade unions, students, NGOs and consumers including the living wage campaign described in Chapter 12. Faced by the threat of boycotts of their goods, the major buyers in the global market for clothing have adopted codes of conduct to regulate the conditions under which those goods are produced.

The question we are addressing in this paper is the extent to which the proliferation of these codes in the Bangladesh garment industry have brought about a 'culture of accountability'. Their adoption is only the beginning of a process of translation, and a variety of different actors have a role to play in ensuring that the translation does indeed occur. Along with the buyers who draw up the codes and the employers who are responsible for their implementation, there is the state, which has overall responsibility for upholding the rights of workers; the trade unions, who are considered to be the organised voice of workers; and, of course, the workers themselves, who have most to gain from the growth of a culture of accountability. We will consider the views and roles of each group in turn.

Monopoly power and consumer clout in buyer-driven global value chains

Competition in the clothing market revolves around prices and brand names. The major clothing retailers are constantly driven by the need to respond to fashion-led fluctuations in the demand for clothing at increasingly competitive prices. The fact that it is a highly labour-intensive industry means that this price competition has revolved to a significant extent around the cost of labour. The production process lends itself to subdivision into an increasing number of routine tasks, each of which can be carried out by increasingly unskilled, and hence increasingly cheaper, labour.

The increasing divisibility of the production process allows different stages of garment manufacturing – from design to delivery – to be located across the globe on the basis of comparative advantage, giving rise to an internationally networked production system in which the same item of clothing may be designed in one location, cut in another, assembled in another and delivered for final sale in yet another. The producers of garments, particularly those involved in its labour-intensive assembly stages, are mainly based in the low-wage countries of the South, so that these countries enter the production chain as providers of cheap labour, competing with each other for orders from buyers of clothing in the international market for garments.

The restructuring and concentration of the clothing retailers over time mean that today buyers are operating in a buyer-driven commodity chain in which large numbers of producers compete for orders from a relatively small number of transnational volume retailers. They are consequently in a position to use their monopolistic power to threaten to withdraw orders from a factory or a country and to dictate conditions to producers. At the same time, their drive to reduce costs continuously has led them in search of ever-cheaper labour working in ever-more exploitative conditions.

However, this footloose strategy and its consequences have attracted the attention of trade unions, consumers and labour activists across the world. As a result of the threat of adverse publicity and consumer boycotts exercised by their campaigns, most of the major garment retailers now espouse the principle of 'corporate social responsibility'. They have drawn up their own codes of conduct regarding the conditions on which they are prepared to place orders, and have set up departments and full-time staff to promote the socially responsible face of their business.

The state and public policy in an era of deregulation

While the interest of the buyers is focused on profits and working conditions in the export sector of Bangladesh, the state is, in principle, responsible for promoting the economic growth of the country and the welfare of its citizens. The pursuit of growth and foreign exchange explains why the state played an extremely active and innovative role in the promotion of the export garment industry from its inception. The fact that many of those in government own garment factories may have also contributed to their active engagement.

The New Industrial Policy of 1982 introduced various incentives to encourage local entrepreneurs, including tax concessions and special duty-free import facilities. However, as far as the interests of its workers are concerned, the state has displayed an attitude of apathy bordering on indifference. The Bangladesh constitution, adopted in 1971 after independence from Pakistan, spelt out the fundamental rights of its citizens and asserted the state's responsibility for emancipating 'the toiling masses' from their exploitation. In reality, however, less than 3 per cent of the workforce is protected by the existing legislative framework (Mondol 2002: 121). Instead, labour legislation in Bangladesh both reflects and reproduces a dualistic economic structure in which a small formal sector coexists alongside a large and growing informal economy.

A great deal of existing labour legislation is inherited from the period of colonial rule in the subcontinent, when it was formulated for the benefit of workers in the urban industrial sector who had the potential to make trouble for their rulers. In the Bangladesh context, this was largely confined to a small number of textile and jute-related manufacturing units. At present there are 51 labour laws in existence: while only 13 of these were actually passed in the colonial period, most of the others draw on rules and regulations which originated in that period (Mahmud and Ahmed 2005). Today they mainly benefit the urban, male workforce employed by the public sector and a tiny formal private sector found in financial services and larger-scale manufacturing. The vast majority of the workforce – which is employed in agriculture, services and cottage industry, the informal or so called 'unorganized' sectors[2] – has little or no legal protection.

Labour legislation in Bangladesh not only excludes the majority of workers in Bangladesh, but also fails to protect those it formally includes. There is an elaborate and hierarchical infrastructure for ensuring compliance with national regulations within the labour ministry, also inherited from the British period, which exists only on paper.

Because the number of inspectors is far lower than is required, there is an implicit institutional bias in the inspections carried out in favour of more dramatic accidents and 'dangerous occurrences' at the expense of the routine violations of labour rights that the more vulnerable sections of the workforce are likely to face. And a blind eye is often turned to those violations that do come to the attention of inspectors if factory owners obtain necessary clearances through the payment of bribes to poorly paid and generally overworked inspectors. Finally, officials interviewed for the research suggested that penalties for non-compliance with the existing laws were not severe enough to act as a deterrent. The flaws in the procedures for enforcing labour legislation are evident from the fact that over 10,000 court cases are pending and collection of fines in the last 10 years has been miniscule (personal communication with Director of Labour Department, Bangladesh, 2004).

The government took a decision in the early 1990s to reform its labour laws in order to bring them up to date to deal with the challenges of the contemporary economy. A high-powered commission was set up in 1992 with a view to dropping or modernising old laws, introducing new ones and developing a unified labour legislation that would cover workers in both formal and informal sectors. A draft code was drawn up in 1994, but with changes in governments has yet to be finalised and adopted. There has been a long process of consultation around these changes and unprecedented participation by different sections of civil society, including the trade unions. The next challenge, of course, is to get the law finalised and, even more challengingly, implemented. The country's track record on implementation does not inspire optimism: in the words of a senior official from the Department of Labour, 'We will need a law to implement the new law.' However, one of the new trade union federation leaders was hopeful:

If the new Labour Code were passed, it will improve the situation a great deal. The New Labour Code has had much more airing than any other. There was a tripartite consultative committee, and workers had more input. If this code is passed, we can make more reasonable demands – demands that we can stand by.

Employers' strategies and the informalisation of the labour contract

The initial emergence of the export garment industry in Bangladesh was almost accidental, a product of the search by East Asian firms using 'quota-hopping' strategies to bypass the Multi-Fibre Arrangement (MFA) regulations in the late 1970s. The subsequent adoption of a more liberal trade regime brought into existence a number of domestic entre-preneurs, many with no previous experience of running industry but who were able to take advantage of the opportunities available in a largely informal economy with a large pool of cheap and already 'flexible' female labour. Despite its *ad hoc* beginnings, however, it became clear early on to the garment employers that they needed to organise themselves to deal with the challenges of operating in the global economy.

The Bangladesh Garment Manufacturing and Exporters Association (BGMEA) was established in 1987. While it began by lobbying with government for the interests of the industry, inevitably it has been drawn into international controversies about labour standards and played an increasingly proactive role in this issue, undertaking various social pro-grammes in collaboration with the International Labour Organisation (ILO), the United Nations Children's Fund (UNICEF) and various national and international NGOs. In 1998, it set up procedures for arbitration between workers and management in collaboration with the leading trade union federations in the garment sector in order to avoid time-consuming processes of resolving these through the labour courts. As many as 10 federations of garment workers, representing several thousand union and even more 'non-union' members, are institutional partners in these procedures. Disputes frequently go in favour of workers, primarily because employers have been accustomed to violating workers' rights with impunity and, therefore, do not take precautions to disguise their actions. Evidence that they now search for pretexts to sack 'troublesome workers', or seek to make their lives so difficult that they leave of their own accord, suggests that the threat of immediate arbitra-tion is having some effect.

With the proliferation of codes of conduct among the international buyers, the BGMEA has also taken on the task of developing a uniform code of conduct as the basis of future contracts in the industry. The BGMEA has thus become a key actor in developing institutional mechanisms for establishing responsibility for labour standards. This role did not emerge out of sudden conversion to the principles of corporate social responsibility, but out of the recognition that, in a ruthlessly competitive market, demonstration of compliance was becoming a source of competitive advantage. Employers have thus gone through a process of education about the nature of global competition in their sector. As the Managing Director of V Apparels commented: 'In the beginning it was beyond the imagination of factory owners to provide such facilities for the workers. But now owners believe that without compliance it is not possible to stay in this highly competitive business. So there is no alternative.'

However, while employers have formalised their relationships with each other and with the government, their relationships with their workers, and their attitudes towards them, remain rooted in the mindset of the informal economy. Interviews with 13 employers carried out in the late 1980s concluded that they could be positioned on a continuum extending between those who viewed their workers as commodities to be exploited as ruthlessly as possible and those who viewed them in clientelist terms, to be treated with benevolent paternalism (Kabeer 2000). None saw their workers as citizens with rights and obligations.

Little has changed today. There is a new breed of employers who have been shamed by the negative image that the industry has acquired in the international arena or influenced by the rising tide of women's activism in the country, and made considerable efforts on their own initiative to improve working conditions in their factories. However, they remain a minority. Of the rest, there is at best paternalism and, at worst, ruthless commodification. Some employers present themselves as responsible for the welfare of the young girls from the countryside who have left their parents and their homes to work in the city: 'they are like my daughters'. Others regard their workers as little more than bonded labour, hired to provide maximum labour at minimum cost. Some expect gratitude and loyalty in return for the privilege of a job, other use threats and coercion to impose discipline.

Such attitudes serve to reproduce and justify the informalised labour practices of employers. Some employers thought workers behaved like workers in the informal economy, coming and going as they pleased, and neither expected nor deserved to be treated like workers in the formal sector. This construction of garment workers as lacking 'professionalism' and hence undeserving of formal treatment is evident in the description provided by one managing director interviewed: 'Actually they don't like to work under any rules. They work for some days, if they need to go home they leave without any notice and come back to join another factory.'

From the perspective of most employers, the imposition of codes of conduct by buyers is seen as simply another set of conditions (along with meeting their deadlines and observing quality control) that have to be met in order to stay in business. Consequently, working conditions have improved over time in their factories, most visibly in the EPZs, but also in factories which deal directly with buyers rather than on the basis of subcontracted orders. Improvements relate mainly to paid leave, maternity leave, overtime pay and medical care. However, there were two telling indicators of the limits of what company codes achieve: less than 5 per cent of the garment workers reported a presence of a trade union in their workplace (none of the workers outside the export industry did so) and only around 20 per cent had heard of the country's labour laws (Kabeer and Mahmud 2004b). Codes thus appear to have more impact on workers' welfare than their rights.

It could be argued that since Bangladesh generally lacks a culture of rights, these employers are simply reproducing the attitudes of their society. However, these employers as a group have also benefited from state largesse a great deal more than their employees or, for that matter, employers in other sectors. An equally persuasive counter-argument might be that they owed a great deal more by way of social responsibility to their workers than the simple generation of jobs. Company codes of conduct could thus be seen as the attempt by international buyers to enforce this social responsibility, given the failure of employers to do so voluntarily and the state to compel them. On the face of it, therefore, codes of conduct may indeed be planting the seeds of a culture of accountability within the corporate sector in Bangladesh.

Unfortunately, there is a great deal of well-founded scepticism on the part of Bangladeshi employers towards these codes, which somewhat undermines this interpretation. Many see them as a public relations exercise on the part of international brand name companies, concerned about their public image, to maintain a facade of social responsibility with their consumers while covertly passing the cost of compliance to their producers. A number of employers complained with bitterness about the double standards of these companies, who combined their demands for increasingly onerous and expensive quality and labour standards with a steady reduction in the prices they offered to their producers. One employer who has been in the industry for many years commented: '

We follow factory laws which say that after three months, you have to make your workers permanent, that if we sack a worker, we have to 'show cause', have an enquiry. But our factory laws are not enough for US buyers. They each have their own codes – how many square feet per workers, how much light, how high the fire extinguisher should be. [...] Still I am prepared to comply with all their codes if they increase the price they give me. Smaller factories are closing down because prices are falling.

Another employer pointed to the implications of flexible business practices:

There is no such thing as a permanent contract in this business. None of the buyers will give you a permanent contract and say okay, we have booked orders with your factory for at least the next two years.... They will work from contract to contract and demand shorter and shorter delivery times.

Thus, if garment producers profit from keeping their relationships with their workers as informal as possible, using the threat of dismissal to discipline their workers, international buyers in turn use their monopoly power in the global market for clothing to keep their relationship with their producers as informal as possible, using the constant threat of relocation to create a permanent condition of insecurity among their suppliers across the world.

Trade unions and the politics of collective action

Although not all buyers include the right to organise in their codes, international campaigns to promote improved working conditions in the export garment industry have placed particular emphasis on this. Trade unions are seen as the concrete expression of this right. Both law and constitution in Bangladesh recognise the right of workers to freedom of association, to join unions and, with government approval, to form unions.[3] Unions in Bangladesh are enterprise-based and registered with the Ministry of Labour if 30 per cent of workers in the enterprise become members. These unions form the basis of larger federations which tend to be organised by sector.

However, trade unions are virtually absent, not only from the garment industry, but from the economy at large. Our recent survey found that only 5 per cent of EPZ garment workers, 1 per cent of export garment workers outside the EPZs and none of the non-garment informal-economy women workers reported the presence of a trade union at their place of work (Kabeer and Mahmud 2004b). One important factor has been the hostility of employers. Unions were generally regarded as troublemakers. Some used paternalistic relationships to ensure worker loyalty, the rest resorted to a variety of coercive tactics, having workers beaten up or arrested, lodging criminal cases against them, and so on. There is therefore a high cost associated with exercising the right to organise in Bangladesh.

However, the problem also lies with the trade unions themselves. They tend to be associated in the public mind with confrontational struggles in pursuit of their own interests by a privileged and protected minority of workers. Trade unions have a history of aggressive politics towards employers, because prior to Bangladesh's independence in 1971 most employers were non-Bengalis, reinforcing the nationalist case that Bengalis faced discrimination in their own country (Mondol 2002). Nationalisation of major banks and industries, after Bangladesh's independence meant that most trade unions have been confined to public sector administration, banks and industries where units are larger and easier to organise, but which are also among the better-paid sections of the workforce. Trade union membership thus accounts for less than 3 per cent of the total workforce and only one-third of the formal workforce (Mondol 2002: 121).

In addition, all the major unions are affiliated to political parties. Consequently, they tend to represent the competing political agendas of their parties rather than the interests of their members. During periods of political unrest, quite frequent in Bangladesh, union federations organise on partisan lines, calling for nation-wide stoppages and strikes –which, of course, lead not only to the well-publicised losses of the country's industrialists, but also to the less well-publicised loss of income of the working poor, including their own members, across the country.

There are currently about 14 federations of garments workers unions working in the country, but some exist in name only and are not registered with the Directorate of Labour (Khan 2001). They do not have a great deal of incentive to be accountable to their membership because their bargaining power with employers comes from their party-political affiliation and is largely independent of their membership base. Some factory owners describe union leaders as 'brokers' who 'milk' both sides. They allege that, in times of industrial conflict, federations take money from owners in order to 'buy off' prospective troublemakers. At the same time, federation leaders take money from their largely female membership by promising protection from the police or the employers' musclemen (Khan 2001).

The lack of accountability to their membership on the part of the federation leaders also reflects the social distance between the two. The leadership is almost overwhelmingly male and drawn from activists in political parties or former student leaders who have had very little previous involvement with the garment sector or its workers. They tend to blame the workers themselves for their lack of unionisation. Many have a university degree and view the passivity of female garment workers as the product of their rural backgrounds, their illiteracy and their general backwardness: 'Since the women are illiterate they do not understand what a labour union is and that we are trying to improve their working conditions. We visit them but they hardly listen to us because they cannot grasp the idea of solidarity and unity' (Dannecker 2002: 222).

Workers in turn do not appear to have much faith in unions. They spoke of past betrayals, of collusions between union leaders and management either because of shared political affiliation, in which case management is given an easy ride, or because they have been bought off. They complained that federation leaders were only visible when some factory conflict or agitation captured the newspaper headlines, but had little to do with the everyday demands and struggles of workers. As one male factory leader observed: "During our agitation, I saw lots of federations. I don't know why they all came here, however, they don't come here now. I can't say why they don't come [...]'

However, not all attempts to organise workers can be dismissed as politically motivated machinations on the part of union leaders. As the importance of the industry has become established, as the slow but steady rise in female labour force participation across the economy has become evident, and as human rights activism has grown across the country, some of the more progressive parties have begun to devote more attention to the challenge of organising women workers and addressing their grievances.

The Textile and Garment Workers' Federation, for instance, has been active in the industry since 1990 and has around 6,000 unionised members who pay dues and 40,000 'non-unionised members' in those workplaces where employers do not recognise unions. The latter pay a fee when they join but do not pay dues. Most of their members are in the larger factories, as they find it too difficult to organise the workforce in the small subcontracting factories. The federation is moving towards a more formalised mode of representational politics in place of the adversarial politics which has been the hallmark of employer–union relations so far. As one of its leading representatives put it:

> Unions are a right under the ILO, but they are also the law of the land. I recognise why employers won't want a union, but the government sides with the employers. I am much more angry with the government about this than

with employers.... We have agreed on procedures for negotiation. When we agree on a demand, we sign, but the employers gradually violate the agreement. The government should enforce this. ... I favour social monitoring systems – civil society, unions, workers – to pressure the government to enforce laws.

The Bangladesh Independent Garment Workers Union Federation (BIGUF) was founded with United States Agency for International Development (USAID) funds and supported by the Solidarity Foundation in the US, an affiliate of the American Federation of Labour–Congress of Industrial Organisations (AFL–CIO). It has also been extremely active. It calls itself 'independent' because it is not affiliated to any political party, although of course in the view of some of the labour activists, it is seen as dependent on the goodwill of USAID and the AFL–CIO. However, its leadership is made up of active, rather than token, women members who were themselves once garment workers, in contrast to the middle-class origins of most other union leaders. It pursues a variety of strategies to organise garment workers, visiting them in their homes, organising cultural programmes to motivate them, encouraging them to engage in collective bargaining with management and providing legal education as well as legal support in disputes with management.

Kormojibi Nari (Working Women) is the other federation led by a woman. Founded in 1991, it is affiliated to the leftist Workers' Party, and partly financed by more progressive international NGOs like War on Want. It has also opted for neighbourhood-based organisation of women workers and the provision of legal education and support but, unlike the BIGUF, it focuses its efforts on all women workers, not just those involved in the export garment sector:

> First, we have to organize the women, then we promote the union. We work by forming cells.... In Dhaka, we work in 12 areas: *bidi*, shrimp, construction, home-based work, industrial, digging for construction, handicrafts, printing and dyeing. Half our membership is from the informal sector .... Trade unions are very important – *true* trade unions. Those that are working to implement laws, enforce workers' rights. Those that are truly in support of the workers. You can't solve any problem if workers have no union of their own. Even the health and safety laws – you can have the law, but only the workers can enforce it.... Ours is a culture of favours.... We say, don't go asking for favours: demand your rights!

There are, along with trade unions, a range of other civil society organisations which focus primarily or exclusively on issues related to rights. Prominent among these is Ain O Salish Kendra (ASK), which has been working on legal issues since 1994. Initially it worked with two trade unions to provide training to garment workers on labour law and trade union rights. However, it found that workers tended to turn to them for advice on family-related rather than work-related problems. Workers were not interested in forming trade unions or in taking legal action against their employers. They preferred to change jobs if they had a grievance against an employer. The initiative closed down but the organisation continued, in collaboration with a number of NGOs, to provide legal support and education to workers through its six legal clinics in Dhaka. Discussing the culture of accountability within the industry, one ASK representative felt the problem lay partly with the nature of the workforce, who 'haven't developed any kind of professionalism yet. Most of them do not think of this job as a career.' He believed that women workers took on these jobs temporarily, that many would not continue to work after marriage and that, in any case, the levels of exploitation in the workplace ruled out working for more than a few years. However, he also believed that training succeeded in bringing about some change in the attitudes of workers, giving them greater self-confidence and the willingness to challenge exploitative practices at work, something that had been almost unheard of in the early stages of the industry.

Women workers and the struggle for dignity and daily bread

As we have seen, women workers have been variously constructed by employers as unprofessional and lacking in workplace discipline; by trade union leaders as illiterate, backward and rural, and unable to grasp concepts of unions and solidarity; and by other civil society actors as 'temporary' workers, likely to leave once they get married. These negative stereotypes are not devoid of an element of truth. Certainly the vast majority of garment workers are young women, socialised into docility and subservience to authority, mostly illiterate or with very low levels of education. They have migrated from the countryside, where notions of workplace discipline, trade union organisation and worker solidarity have little purchase.

What is also relevant, however, is the fact that these women come from poor households, with few options in the labour market and only their family as a safety net to fall back on should they lose their jobs. Such factors would tend to constrain militancy on the part of any worker. But additionally, in an economy in which women historically have been confined to a limited number of economic activities and where there is an apparently unlimited supply of female labour in search of jobs in the garment sector, women with jobs are particularly likely to be cautious about making demands or taking stands that might jeopardise their employment. Thus, while their illiteracy, gender and origins may play an initial role in explaining women's reluctance to protest their conditions, it is the larger structural constraints on their capacity to act on their own behalf, and the costs they may incur if they were to try to do so, that prevent the majority of women workers from standing up for their rights.

However, like other actors in the economy, women workers have not remained untouched by the forces of change in the larger society. Intense media coverage of their working conditions, increased attempts to mobilise them and the involvement of a wider range of actors than traditional trade unions have all served to raise their knowledge and awareness of their rights. How has this affected their capacity to take action?

Statistics on trade union membership and knowledge of labour laws may underestimate the actual degree to which workers know about their rights and are willing to take action to claim them. Time, both personal and historical, emerges as a key factor in the evolution of workers' consciousness. Each young woman who arrives fresh from the country-side needs time to adapt to the very different rhythm of work in the urban factories compared to the rural economy, and she also needs time before she understands what her entitlements are. Recent cohorts of workers may be coming into the factory with a different level of consciousness than earlier cohorts, however. People in the countryside are now better connected with what is going on elsewhere in the country than they were in the early years of the industry because of improvements in transport, communications and media, while rising levels of female education mean that recent garment workers are at least more aware of what is going on around them. According to Shefali, a female garment leader,[4] NGOs have also played an important role in disseminating information about workers' rights:

> Earlier it used to be much more difficult to make the workers understand different issues. But now they understand the importance of organisations, when a worker loses their job but eventually gets it by filing a case through the labour court they stand to gain much…. Now they understand about the ILO convention and the law, and they ask for information.

Workers may also have become less willing to put up with instances of injustice in the workplace. Many take action as individuals. Resigning from the factory is still the most frequent individual response to injustice, a silent form of protest, and one that women resort to more frequently than men, but there were also instances of workers taking a more collective approach to dealing with problems, such as staging walk-outs or threatening the manager. From our interviews, it was clear that many women are learning the principles of collective bargaining. There were a number of cases when workers got together, sometimes spontaneously, sometimes in a planned and co-ordinated way, to undertake factory-wide protests which often spilled out onto the streets. Most of these protests revolved around issues of wages and overtime rather than workplace conditions, because, as workers themselves said, 'getting paid their wages on time is the biggest problem of garment workers'. These incidents are often reported in newspapers. In one case, workers agitating over three months' wage arrears were arrested on charges of assault: 72 of them, all women, were given bail but 13 were taken into custody (*Daily Star*, 12 November 2004). In another case (*Daily Star*, 5 September 2004), women workers took to the street in support of a male worker who had been struck by his manager for demanding workers' overtime dues. The management later fixed dates for settling the workers' dues in phases.

Accounts of such spontaneous street-level protests make two points clear. First of all, women workers are active participants in many of these protests. The second point is that, perhaps predictably, the protests are generally led by male workers. One female worker explained male leadership partly in terms of their greater physical strength – which meant they were better able to look after themselves in a confrontation – as well as their greater knowledge of their rights. Another pointed to the importance of women's earnings for their families and their fear that they would not easily find another job. Clearly greater activism among women suggests they have been able to overcome some of the fears and inhibitions associated with being women – but not all of them.

Finally, there were examples of more organised forms of collective action by garment workers that provide insights into some of the potentials and limitations of workers' struggles in the garment sector in Bangladesh. One example of organised collective action came from Alam, who had had long-standing connections with a union federation. He had participated in the campaign when a number of federations got together and put five basic demands to the BGMEA: recognition of the right to organise; maternity leave; an appointment letter; a weekly holiday; and a minimum wage. His view with regard to a strike he had led in 2001 against an employer who did not observe the five demands was that although they did not win their demands, the day-to-day abusive behaviour towards workers decreased:

Certainly our agitation had an impact in reducing the verbal abuse of workers. Due to the agitation, they saw that the workers had become united, if they continued their agitation, it might get spread throughout the country and in that case the buyers would also create a fuss.

There is thus no linear story of progress that emerges out of these accounts, of victories gained leading on to further victories. Some workers felt that conditions had improved after a protest, some felt they had worsened. Employers made promises in order to quell a disturbance, but used every pretext subsequently to victimise or get rid of the leaders. However, changes in consciousness were often permanent and the leadership that developed did not simply fade away when a struggle was lost but went on to other factories to start the job of organisation once again.

Compliance and accountability in Bangladesh

The question that we set out to answer in this chapter is the extent to which the emergence of what a government labour official described as a 'culture of compliance' within the export garment sector in Bangladesh has contributed to the growth of a culture of accountability. We have described some of the elements in the process by which this perceived 'culture of compliance' came into existence. We noted that efforts of trade unionists, students, consumers and human rights activists to exert pressure on buyers to take greater responsibility for working conditions have resulted in the proliferation of codes that garment manufacturers now have to accept before they can win an order from these buyers. Indeed, the BGMEA, at least (though not necessarily all its members), has realised that compliance with codes holds the key to future survival in the post-MFA competitive environment. As a result, there has been a marked improvement in health and safety standards in the major factories as well as a range of other benefits, such as payment on time, proper overtime rates, maternity leave, and so on.

The setting up of arbitration procedures by the BGMEA has reduced the employers' prerogative of sacking workers and also given rise to some degree of cooperation between the BGMEA and unions, in place of the relentless confrontations of earlier encounters. Representatives of both workers and management have come to recognise that submitting to a joint process of conflict resolution is likely to yield longer-term gains for both parties outweighing any short-term defeats. From the point of view of the federations, having a place at the negotiating table has opened up a novel way of recruiting members, by responding to their most pressing everyday concerns (being paid on time, getting proper overtime, increasing their wages) rather than relying on the promise of political patronage. For women workers in particular, the former is a far more appealing incentive to join unions than the latter.

While these various developments are certainly steps in the right direction, do they constitute evidence of a 'culture of compliance' within the garment sector? There is certainly evidence of greater compliance in the garment sector than in other industries, as asserted by the Director of the Labour department, but this is primarily because other sectors are not under the same external pressures to comply. It is thus the vulnerability of the export garment producers within a buyer-driven global value chain which has led to 'compliance' on their part.

The concept of a *culture* of compliance, by contrast, suggests the internalisation of the norms embedded in the codes of conduct, so that they become a routine and accepted part of the way that business is done. We did not find widespread evidence that this is the case in the garment industry. Despite the fact that higher labour standards did prevail within the industry, and that some garment employers have clearly embraced the principles of corporate social responsibility, we found persistent attempts by many, perhaps most, employers to evade their responsibilities. Many sought to comply only with the more visible aspects of the codes while they reneged on the less visible, some of which were of greater importance for their workers. Moreover, the codes are not applied to the smaller factories, which are not members of BGMEA and deal only indirectly with the buyers.

While many workers expressed the belief that buyers were their allies against the owners, since they had introduced the codes of conduct, it was clear from the employers' accounts that they had a less benevolent view of buyers for very good reasons. If most Bangladeshi employers have not internalised the concept of corporate social responsibility, neither have most of their buyers. Consequently, employers sought to comply with buyers' codes of conduct in response to the threat of withdrawal of orders, while buyers sought to impose the codes in response to the threat of negative publicity and the accompanying loss of sales. Although they made sure that their suppliers were monitored for code compliance, they generally used the threat of withholding orders rather than any positive incentives to promote compliance. In fact, their demands for compliance have been accompanied by the demands for shorter delivery times and lower unit prices. Not surprisingly, employers in Bangladesh do not generally view codes of conduct as a manifestation of social responsibility on the part of international buyers, but as a cynical marketing strategy which allows the latter to keep their brand image with their consumers 'clean' while passing on the costs of maintaining this image to the former.

From this perspective, it is difficult to describe changing practices on the part of employers in the garment industry as evidence of a culture of compliance, although there is certainly evidence of the enforcement of compliance. To what extent, then, has the enforcement of compliance led to a growth in the culture of accountability? A similarly qualified response is required. There is certainly a greater willingness on the part of many workers to make claims and demand responses from employers, while the adoption of the arbitration procedures by the BGMEA has also certainly contributed to the enforceability of some of these claims. However, changes in the visible segments of the garment industry should not be conflated with changes in the entire industry.

The reality is that many of the workers in the export garment sector are to be found in small units in the informal economy, beyond the reach of buyers (and their complicated codes of conduct), the BGMEA and the major trade union federations. Furthermore, the vast majority of workers in the country are not in the export sector at all. For them, the new accountability structures of the garment industry have very little relevance. Of greater relevance to them are the activities of the government and of organisations prepared to represent their interests. For this larger and generally poorer work force, there are a number of developments, directly or indirectly triggered by the rise of the export garment industry, that could have positive future implications. First of all, the new labour code is a step in the right direction – but getting the law right is, of course, only a first step in changing the reality.

Second, there are proposals to reform the trade unions themselves. The widespread politicisation of trade unions in Bangladesh is a product of the structure of political parties in the country rather than of the nature of trade unionism itself. Not only have the political parties failed to curb the rent-seeking activities of trade union leaders, but they have actively benefited from their partisan activities. It is, therefore, the responsibility of the political leadership in Bangladesh to transform their relations with the trade union movement in such a way that they can perform their function of representing the interests of their membership and ensuring that employers are held accountable. Such reform is difficult but essential if an environment is to be created that will allow a genuine workers' movement to flourish.

Finally, and most hopefully, in spite of the unpromising political situation in Bangladesh, we may be seeing the emergence of a 'new' form of trade unionism that is more responsive to the needs and interests of its membership, and to its women members in particular. These new forms of labour organisations are seeking to reach out to women workers who have been bypassed by both development NGOs and by trade unions. Like women workers all over the world, women workers in Bangladesh need organisations that address their needs and interests as women as well as workers. These new organisations provide hope that a genuine labour movement may yet emerge in Bangladesh, one that is more closely aligned to the interests of the workers that make up its membership. They appear to be far more cognisant of this than the older, male-dominated unions, indeed, some are led by articulate and experienced women activists. Furthermore, a number of these organisations have moved beyond the focus on codes and conditions in the export garment sector, which has been the sole preoccupation of global campaigns for labour standards, to organising all women workers, both within the export sector and outside it, both within the formal economy and outside it. It is in this willingness to take on the challenge of organising those who are most vulnerable within the economy, who have little strategic importance internationally because they do not earn the country's foreign exchange or compete with workers in the North, but who nevertheless make up the majority of the working poor in the country that we may find the seeds of a genuine culture of democratic accountability being sown.

NOTES

1 The percentage of working women in manufacturing rose from around 4 per cent in 1974 to 55 per cent in 1984–5, while urban female labour force participation rates rose from around 12 per cent in 1883–4 to 26 per cent in 1999–2000 (Kabeer and Mahmud 2004a).

2 In 2000 three-quarters of the workforce was employed in the informal sector (calculated from the 1999–2000 Labour Force Survey, 2002).

3 The exceptions are government civil servants and security-related employees who are forbidden to join unions. Until recently, unions were banned in the EPZs. Under pressure from the US government, limited trade unionism will be allowed in the EPZs from 2006.

4 We use the term 'garment leaders' to refer to those who are active within their own units but may or may not have connections with any of the larger federations.

REFERENCES

Dannecker, P. (2002) *Between Conformity and Resistance: Women Garment workers in Bangladesh*, Dhaka: University Press.

Daily Star, 5 September 2004.

Daily Star, 12 November 2004.

Kabeer, N. (2000) *The Power to Choose: Bangladeshi Women and Labour Market Decisions in London and Dhaka*, London: Verso.

Kabeer, N. and Mahmud, S. (2004a), 'Rags, Riches and Women Workers: Export-Oriented Garment Manufacturing in Bangladesh', in *Chains of Fortune: Linking Women Producers and Workers with Global Markets*, London: Commonwealth Secretariat.

Kabeer, N. and Mahmud, S. (2004b), 'Globalization, Gender and Poverty: Bangladeshi Women Workers in Export and Local Markets', *Journal of International Development*, Volume 16, Issue 1, pp. 93–109.

Khan, S. I. (2001) 'Gender Issues and the Ready-made Garment Dector of Bangladesh: the Trade Union Context', in R. Sobhan and N. Khundker (eds), *Globalisation and Gender. Changing Patterns of Women's Employment in Bangladesh*, Dhaka: University Press.

Bangladesh Bureau of Statistics (2002) *Report of Labour Force Survey Bangladesh 1999/2000*. Dhaka: Ministry of Planning, Government of the People's Republic of Bangladesh.

Mahmud, S. and Ahmed, N. (2005) 'Workers Rights' and Working Conditions in the Export Garment Sector in Bangladesh: A Review', Draft, Bangladesh Institute of Development Studies (BIDS), Dhaka, March.

Mondol, A. H. (2002) 'Globalisation, Industrial Relations and Labour Policies: the Need for Renewed Agenda', in M. Muqtada *et al.* (eds), *Bangladesh: Economic and Social Challenges of Globalisation*, Geneva and Dhaka: International Labour Organisation and University Press.

Personal Communication (2004) Director of Labour Department, Bangladesh.

UN (2002) *The Least Developed Countries Report 2002. Escaping the Poverty Trap*, New York: United Nations.

CHAPTER 12

Accountability begins at home: the living wage movement in the United States

STEPHANIE LUCE

This chapter deals with mobilisations around the right to a living wage in the United States. This implies a form of accountability politics that is at once global and local, public and private. The outcomes of the living wage movement demonstrate that accountability cannot be assumed, but must be fought for by stakeholders, through a variety of means. This case study highlights the importance of accountability processes and the contested relationship between rights and standards, and provides an exploration of the relationship between the rights of capital and the rights of labour. It engages with the themes explored in the previous chapter on workers' rights in the garment sector in Bangladesh, showing how workplace and national labour struggles connect to global commercial and political arenas. If working conditions in Bangladesh have become the *site* of global scrutiny, this chapter shows how US campaigns on these issues have become a *source* of global scrutiny.

The US struggle for a living wage, which developed in the 1990s as a local struggle, emerged parallel to a global debate about international labour standards. In labour and policy circles, much attention was focused on apparel industry employers that violate domestic labour law or international labour codes. As manufacturing facilities proliferated in the global South, NGOs and Northern unions raised awareness around their working conditions, building up a moral outrage by consumers and students who viewed large retailers as exploiting children and young women to produce garments and other items for export. From this grew the so-called 'anti-sweatshop movement'. The idea of an anti-sweatshop movement itself is not new: similar campaigns have been waged in various countries at various times for more than a century. But the current campaign differs in that it has focused largely on an effort to hold transnational corporations (TNCs) accountable to their workers as they move around the globe.

There is a growing body of literature on the global anti-sweatshop movement, such as the work of Armbruster-Sandoval (2005), which examines cross-border organising campaigns in the US and Latin America, and the work of Esbenshade (2004), which examines efforts to monitor factories for compliance with labour standards.[1] Recent work by Elliot and Freeman (2003) and Fung, O'Rourke and Sabel (2001) engages in debate about whether international labour standards should be included in trade agreements and international institutions like the World Trade Organisation, or whether other mechanisms would be more effective at improving wages and working conditions.

These scholars, along with anti-sweatshop activists, saw that it was hard enough to hold corporations accountable within one country, let alone across borders. For this reason, activists have looked for various points of leverage that could be used in the absence of binding international law. One such point of leverage was universities. Students came together to pressurise their universities to adopt codes of conduct regarding the purchase of apparel and goods with the university logo. These campaigns were relatively successful in getting universities to adopt the codes and join international monitoring agencies (such as the Worker Rights Consortium). Soon, these students began to realise that sweatshop conditions prevailed in garment factories at home as well as abroad. In addition, they saw that workers in the university towns, and indeed, on the university campuses themselves, often suffered similar conditions as the garment workers in other countries: low wages, little job security, and resistance to unionisation efforts. Eventually, college sweatshop activists began to get involved in 'living wage' campaigns in their cities and on their campuses.

Living wage campaigns are part of another social movement that arose in the US around the same time as the anti-sweatshop movement. Rather than mobilising pressure in the North to affect working conditions of TNCs in the South, the living wage movement began by looking for leverage to affect corporate behaviour and local government spending in the US. While the approach of the living wage movement is different from the anti-sweatshop movement, and there are some important differences between the two struggles, the living wage movement can offer valuable lessons for those searching for ways to hold corporations accountable to their workforce and host communities. The processes of privatisation, deregulation and deunionisation that are central to the emergence of the living wage movement can be found in many parts of the world. The movement provides findings useful for understanding the relationships between processes of accountability, rights and resources. In particular, it has discovered that it is not enough to vote in legislation that specifies the right to a living wage. Because low-wage workers have few resources and little power, they must find ways to hold those with greater resources and power – employers and governments – accountable for enforcing those laws.

Living wage supporters have also found that processes can be as important as outcomes. Specifically, processes that create conditions for implementing laws – including mechanisms for workers to file complaints about non-compliance and to form unions – may matter more in the end than setting a particular wage standard. This chapter examines the US living wage movement to draw out these lessons for other movements for worker rights.

The material presented here is based on research conducted by the author over the past eight years. This includes reviews of city documents, surveys of employers and employees, and over 100 interviews with living wage advocates and opponents, city council members, city administrative staff, researchers and journalists.[2]

Context and background

The US labour movement fought hard to win certain gains for workers over the past century. These include the establishment of state-provided services and public sector employment to provide those services; a federal minimum wage law passed in 1938, which set a mandated hourly wage;[3] and the 1960s–1970s wave of unionisation of many public sector jobs that created good wages, benefits and job security.

However, by the late 1970s and 1980s, the rise of a neoliberal agenda began a backlash against these gains. Congress failed to pass regular raises to the minimum wage (which is not adjusted automatically with inflation), and by the mid-1990s the real value of the minimum wage was 30 per cent below its 1968 peak value and far below the hourly amount needed to raise a worker with a family to the federal poverty line. City managers pursued an agenda of privatisation of public services, which resulted in an attack on public sector unions and savings based on reduced wages, benefits and job security. They also pursued a 'business climate' model of economic development, using tax breaks and economic subsidies to lure firms to their region (and to retain existing firms).

One result of these trends was a sharp decline in the real wage for the average worker, as well as those at the very bottom. Although the US is the richest country in the world, there are a substantial number of people who can be considered the 'working poor': those who do not earn enough to meet the federal poverty lines despite having jobs. In 2003, approximately a quarter of all US workers did not earn an hourly wage high enough to meet the poverty threshold for a family of four (Mishel, Bernstein and Allegretto 2005).

At the same time, a fall in unionisation density rates and union power took away one avenue for raising wages. This was compounded by an unfavourable political climate at the national level. Even after Bill Clinton was elected in 1992, ending twelve years of Republican rule, there appeared to be little political commitment to raising the federal minimum wage.

By 1994, pastors in Baltimore, Maryland observed that a number of the people coming for free food from their churches were people who had jobs yet did not earn enough to feed themselves and their families. For the previous few decades, city leaders had persuaded citizens that if they supported the city's economic development plans ('revitalising' the downtown), jobs would follow. While some jobs did come, the bulk of these were low-wage and non-benefited, resulting in a growing population of the working poor. The pastors, members of a faith-based community organisation, joined forces with a local public sector union to demand that city leaders respond to this problem.

The end result was a 'living wage ordinance': legislation requiring that any private sector firm providing city services pay its workers an hourly wage high enough to meet the federal poverty line for a family of four. Although this would only raise wages for a small percentage of all workers in the city, the policy was an initial step toward making the city accountable to low-wage employers for its decisions to privatise city services.

The Baltimore ordinance inspired activists in other cities to pursue living wage campaigns. Soon, activists were looking to expand coverage of the ordinances. In addition to covering firms providing city services, some ordinances also included firms receiving economic development financial assistance (tax breaks and subsidies), firms operating on city property (such as retailers and restaurants in airports and sports arenas), and direct city or county employees. By 2004, three cities even passed city-wide minimum wage laws, establishing higher wages for most workers working within city borders.[4] Many of these ordinances include automatic indexing for inflation, correcting for the weakness in the federal minimum wage. In addition to higher wages, some ordinances began to require that employers provide health benefits, paid overtime and paid days off.

After five years, over 40 ordinances have been passed in cities and counties. The campaigns turned into a social movement, with coalitions developing at the grassroots around the country. After ten years, more than 120 ordinances had been passed in cities, counties, universities, school boards and other agencies.

The right to a living wage?

Living wage campaigns were so successful in part because the language used resonated strongly with the public. Since the federal minimum wage was established, the US population has favoured the idea that the rate be raised regularly.[5] The idea of a fair wage for work is supported perhaps in part because the idea of work has powerful moral and social connotations in the country: people are often judged by whether they have a job and what kind of work they do. In addition, despite its wealth, the US has always had a relatively weak welfare state. Those without access to jobs that pay a fair wage will likely live in poverty. Work is not only one of the few avenues for subsistence, but it is also a crucial means of achieving full citizenship. For example, many US cities have outlawed homelessness (vagrancy laws) and asking for money (anti-panhandling laws). There are few and dwindling government resources available to help the poor.

Despite this, no one has the 'right to work' in the US.[6] In fact, courts have interpreted the law in such a way that jobs are seen to be the private property of employers, not employees. As Michael Yates points out so clearly in *Naming the System: Inequality and Work in the Global Economy*, no capitalist economy ever has solved the problems of unemployment and underemployment (Yates 2003). This means that there are never enough jobs that pay a living wage, and that people must compete for those jobs that do exist. Competition over living wage jobs occurs within countries and, increasingly, between countries. Despite spot shortages in particular occupations and countries, there exists an excess supply of labour in the global labour market. In this context, even if a laws exists giving workers the right to a living wage, the conditions of globalisation make it almost impossible to realise this in practice.

But this raises a larger issue around the idea of labour standards and labour rights. Some scholars point out that there is an important distinc-tion between rights and standards: for example, the right to organise, the right to collective bargaining, the right to be free from danger and dis-crimination, versus standards that may vary from country to country, such as the minimum wage level. Labour rights may be about processes, while standards are about outcomes. This means that labour rights, such as the right to organise unions, create a *process* by which labour market *outcomes*, such as wage levels, are determined. Some suggest that rights should not vary from country to country, whereas standards might.[7]

Elliot and Freeman (2003) add that there is a difference between standards that are relatively free or low-cost and those that cost money, or 'cash versus non-cash' standards. They suggest that the main concern of labour activists should be to win the right to collective action. Once workers have the right to unionise, they have a mechanism to bargain over other standards, such as wages. Robin Broad echoes this, writing that focusing on basic rights, such as the right to freedom of association, 'avoids a major pitfall: having to determine which standards are appropriate for which corporations or which levels of development – a potentially messy judgment call' (Broad 2001: 44).

While focusing on the right to organise seems a possible solution to improving conditions of work, there are critics of this approach. Some proponents of labour standards say that the right to organise is not enough. For example, Heintz (2004) argues that within the current global commodity chain structures, workers simply do not have enough power to bargain over wages. Indeed, even a large swath of unionised workers in the US find themselves relatively powerless to bargain wages upward – let alone keep their jobs. While stories of mass outsourcing are mostly exaggerated in terms of their impact on total jobs in the US, a recent study found that in the first quarter of 2004, 39 per cent of all jobs leaving the country were unionised jobs (compare this to a national private-sector union density of only 8 per cent) (Bronfenbrenner and Luce 2004). Clearly, simply having a union does not provide workers in global industries with much bargaining power.[8] In these cases, labour standards advocates argue that it is necessary to establish wage standards that serve as a floor, preventing a 'race to the bottom' in wages even when unions are present.

Esbenshade raises another important point concerning the difference between rights and standards. She argues that the anti-sweatshop movement's 'focus on working conditions rather than rights put the movement in a vulnerable position' as it allowed corporations to make minor changes in working conditions and declare the problems fixed (Esbenshade 2004: 202). The focus on working conditions also ignores the crucial fact of worker rights. Labour is a unique 'input' into production precisely because there is a 'non-cash' element involved in human labour.

The living wage movement has provided an interesting twist to this debate. Some of the ordinances have worked to include labour rights or processes in the ordinance: for example, some include protections for workers trying to form a union or organise around wage issues. Many include specific language giving workers the right to file charges of non-compliance against employers without risk of retaliation or job loss. Yet the living wage campaigns have also tried to make the living wage itself – a labour standard – into a right. In particular, the campaigns declare that a living wage is at a minimum a moral right, which should be made into a legal right. Clergy members have been active in campaigns, citing scripture to argue that all humans do, in fact, have the 'right' to a living wage in return for their work. For example, in 2000 the United Methodist Church passed the following resolution: 'The United Methodist Church recognises the responsibility of governments to develop and implement sound fiscal and monetary policies that provide for the economic life of individuals. Every person has the right to a job at a living wage.' (United Methodist Church 2000: 55.) Catholics point to several teachings in their tradition that call for a living wage, such as Catechism of the Catholic Church 2434: 'A just wage is the legitimate fruit of work. To refuse or withhold it can be a grave injustice. In determining fair pay both the needs and the contributions of each person must be taken into account' (United States Catholic Conference 1997).

The campaigns are also often posed as a counter to the expanding rights of capital to relocate, privatise, and control the terms of debate. Indeed, the Montgomery County, Maryland living wage campaign quotes President Franklin D. Roosevelt, who stated in 1933: 'No business that depends for its existence on paying less than living wages has any right to continue in this country ... and by living wages I mean more than a bare subsistence level. I mean the wages of decent living' (Progressive Maryland 2005). In some cases, living wage supporters frame their campaign as being about the right of municipalities to attach standards or requirements to private companies that receive economic development subsidies or contracts for performing city services. In this way, citizens have mobilised to struggle for what they considered a right of workers and governments against the rights of capital.

The campaigns have involved a mix of 'inside' and 'outside', or formal and informal strategies, to get the laws passed. The outside strategies include building coalitions of sympathetic organisations, public education on the issues of wages and inequality, public rallies and protests designed to get media and public attention, and, at times, tactics such as marches and civil disobedience. The inside strategies involve developing alliances with city leaders and staff, and direct lobbying of and negotiating with city council members and mayors. Throughout the campaign activists emphasize a range of arguments in favour of the living wage, but particularly underline the idea of the living wage as a right.

Implementation struggles

Using the argument that working people have the right to a living wage, the movement saw considerable success throughout the 1990s. But, as new campaigns continued to emerge, the original activists turned to the question of implementation. The challenge was how to hold governments and employers accountable: to ensure that employers were paying the mandated living wage, and that the city governments were taking the necessary steps to monitor workplaces and enforce the law.

In almost no city has the city, left on its own, pursued strong enforcement of the living wage ordinance. While city councillors subject to re-election are sensitive to voters' wishes to pass ordinances, city administrators are not as eager to enforce laws that they see as running counter to the dominant neoliberal economic development paradigm that suggests cities need to focus on creating a positive business climate in order to grow. In other words, passing and enforcing regulations on businesses is seen as having a negative impact upon the business climate. In this case, there may be *ideological opposition* or resistance to reform.

Even where city staff may be personally committed to enforcement, either due to personal sympathies with the law or simply the desire to do their jobs well, cities are not likely to devote many resources or much staff time to monitoring and enforcement. Often, reluctant to hire new staff to implement laws effectively, the city merely adds the job of enforcement to the workload of existing personnel. This means living wage enforcers are overworked and stretched between multiple tasks, revealing a *lack of state capacity* to enforce the laws.

The accountability issues were not confined to a vertical demand of activists against the state and employers, however. Living wage advocates had to hold themselves accountable to make implementation a priority. The fact is that, in most places, the workers who were to be covered by the ordinances were not the main activists involved in passing the ordinances. Rather, the coalitions comprised representatives from labour unions, community organisations, faith-based groups, student groups, women's groups and others. To be sure the workers eventually got the living wage, living wage advocates had to themselves pursue avenues to monitor compliance. For example, after getting the ordinance passed in Baltimore, activists soon turned to efforts to organise the covered workers into a new organisation of low-wage workers called the Solidarity Sponsoring Committee (SSC). SSC organisers went to bus yards to talk to school bus drivers and monitors covered by the Baltimore living wage law. They soon found workers who did not know about the ordinance, and who were not receiving the higher wage. SSC helped the workers file complaints with the city. They then launched a public pressure campaign, holding rallies and getting large crowds to turn out for city hearings, in order to force the city to implement the law. Eventually, the city ruled in favour of the workers and ordered the bus companies to raise the wages and give back-pay to their employees.

In addition to the efforts in Baltimore, activists in other cities had similar concerns about implementation. However, in Los Angeles living wage coalition members realised that in order to ensure more systematic enforcement they would need to find ways to institutionalise their role in implementation. After the city council passed the ordinance, coalition members worked with their allies on the council to write the regulations and include the right of non-profit organisations to provide training to covered workers to educate them about the living wage policy. This provision allowed living wage advocates regular access to covered workers, greatly improving the chances of successful implementation. The coalition also pressured the city to hire an adequate number of staff to enforce the law, including Spanish-speaking staff that could answer workers' questions and complaints.

Activists in Boston, Massachusetts went one step further. They got the city to pass regulations establishing a Living Wage Advisory Board, comprised of government, business, union and community members, which would meet every month to review contracts covered by the ordinance, examine complaints of non-compliance, and oversee general implementation. This Advisory Board has since recommended revisions to the ordinance which were passed by the City Council and mayor, substantially expanding coverage and raising the wage. The Advisory Board has also played a key role in reviewing the applications for exemption submitted by employers. In almost every city, the living wage ordinance includes language that allows for 'hardship waivers': employers who claim that they will suffer undue economic harm from paying the higher wage are allowed to request exemption. In many cities these requests are granted with little investigation, but in Boston the Advisory Board has been strict about requiring employers to open their books and prove their case of hardship. The Advisory Board has turned down a number of these requests, even from non-profit child care agencies.

Another important tactic pursued by some living wage coalitions was to include language in the ordinances giving citizens the 'right to know'. This means that the ordinances specifically state that cities must make public information about their contracting and economic development, and/or that firms receiving service contracts or economic development

assistance must make their payroll records available. In some cases, the disclosure provision is the one that employers fight most vigorously. For example, the Toledo Chamber of Commerce did not put up much resistance to a general living wage ordinance: rather, they put their energy into keeping the disclosure provision out.

The battle over disclosure can be found in other labour standards struggles as well. In the anti-sweatshop movement, students quickly found that it was not enough to pressure large retailers to improve their labour conditions, since they would just say that they had subcontracted all their manufacturing work to other firms all over the world. Therefore, the students had to develop ways to get the TNCs to disclose the location of their factories. This access to information was a crucial first step to determining whether the factory owners were complying with labour codes. Disclosure has also been an issue in the movement for corporate accountability in the US, around the issue of 'corporate welfare'. Activists have pressured their local and state governments to disclose details about the subsidies that they give out to corporations.[9] This is a key lesson for accountability struggles: stakeholders must have equal and reliable access to information in order to assess implementation progress and outcomes.

Civil society involvement: inside and outside strategies

The above examples highlight the various mechanisms that living wage advocates have used to improve implementation outcomes. Parallel to the strategies used initially to pass the ordinances, inside and outside strategies have been utilised in implementation struggles as well. In Baltimore, activists relied on outside strategies: applying public pressure to force the local government to enforce its law. In Los Angeles and Boston, activists used inside strategies: establishing mechanisms to institutionalise their role in the implementation process and work from within the state. Including disclosure provisions in ordinances also helps systematise the implementation process, as it allows an opening for citizens to get information to which they would not otherwise have access.

Relying solely on outside or inside strategies has limitations. In Baltimore, public pressure resulted in a victory for bus drivers and monitors. However, in 2003 the union which represents the food and beverage workers at the city sports stadium discovered that the employer, Aramark, had not been in compliance with the overtime provision of the ordinance. The union filed complaints with the city and, again using public pressure and media attention, was able to get the city to force the employer to comply and provide back-pay for the unpaid overtime. These examples led to successful outcomes, but they suggest that, without systematic scrutiny, there may be many other workers not receiving the mandated living wage who are in fact entitled to it. Organisations with the motivation to do so, investigated conditions for the workers they were trying to organise or already represented, but what about the other workers? The city expended few resources to implement the living wage, and did not conduct its own workplace investigations.

In Los Angeles and Boston living wage advocates were able to have greater systematic monitoring. Yet this did not solve all implementation problems. While advocates had won a place in the monitoring process, they did not have the power to enforce. In both cases, the city council and mayor had the final say over all implementation issues. This meant that, in a few cases, employers resisted compliance with the ordinance.

For example, the Los Angeles living wage ordinance was intended to cover the airport, but employers at the airport – restaurants as well as airlines – claimed that the law did not apply to them. In this case, the Los Angeles living wage coalition resorted to 'outside pressure' tactics in order to pressure the city council to amend the ordinance and close loopholes, making it explicit that the ordinance did in fact cover the airport employers.

In Boston, KTI, the firm holding the contract to provide recycling services to the city, announced that it would not comply with the ordinance. The Advisory Board told KTI that it needed to prove its case that compliance would cause a hardship, but the firm refused. The Advisory Board recommended that the city not grant a waiver, but the mayor did not accept that ruling. Instead, he has been granting temporary contract extensions to the firm for several years. Living wage advocates have resorted to outside strategies: leafleting the public to call the mayor, and working with advocates in nearby cities where living wage ordinances also covered KTI to develop strategies to get the company to comply. Although these efforts have not yet resulted in victory, they have raised awareness in the community about the living wage issue. A major city newspaper that had initially opposed the ordinance came out in favour of the city denying the KTI waiver.[10]

These examples provide several important lessons. Whether due to ideological opposition or lack of state capacity, cities are not enforcing the ordinances on their own and holding employers accountable to pay the living wage. Living wage advocates must work to hold the state accountable for implementing the laws. This can be done by outside tactics – 'protest politics' – which can improve the chances of enforcement. At the same time, these outside tactics often fail to result in systematic changes in the implementation process, such as increased numbers of city personnel to monitor worksites.

In Los Angeles and Boston, living wage supporters pursued inside strategies that institutionalised improvements and enhanced state capacity. At the same time, because this still did not give the advocates decision-making power, they needed to maintain their ability to utilise pressure politics when necessary. This outside pressure is important for keeping the public educated and engaged on the issues, and to demonstrate that city officials must remain accountable to the citizenry that demands living wages. Outside pressure is also important because it can give city staff the political cover they need to make demands of powerful employers. Finally, maintaining the avenue for outside pressure is important to ensure that individuals or organisations serving in formal Advisory Boards are not 'co-opted' by employers or city officials. These individuals may also benefit in the same way that city staff do: outside pressure gives them political cover to stick to their demands for strong enforcement.

Although civil society participation can lead to more accountability from governments, one cannot assume that it will solve all implementation problems or replace the state as the chief implementation agent. Community organisations are subject to some of the same constraints as states – for example, they too may have weak capacity or the social movements they are a part of may fade away over time. As mentioned above, individual activists are subject to 'capture', much like government officials.

In addition, many of the organisations involved in the campaigns lack a direct incentive to monitor the ordinances. It is not enough for cities to create the space for community involvement: those actors must be motivated to do an effective job. For example, in Cleveland, although there were two seats for union representatives on the living wage task force, one member never came to meetings, and the other attended but offered little input. Apparently, according to Policy Matters Ohio researcher Dave Focareta, the union representatives had little or no incentive to put time into living wage enforcement. This may be because they did not see the connections between the living wage and organising opportunities for their union, or because they saw living wage enforcement as a low priority compared to other tasks they had to do. In contrast, activists in Baltimore, Boston and Los Angeles saw specific connections between living wage enforcement and representing or organising workers. We cannot assume that all civil society organisations will possess similar incentives to monitor the ordinances. Because they face numerous constraints on their own ability to do the work, and they do not have the force of law behind them, they should only be seen as a complement to state enforcement, not a substitute. The issue of motivation to monitor, and to hold governments accountable is key, and one that deserves further attention.

Conclusion

The living wage movement highlights the fact that accountability should be understood as a process rather than an outcome. While activists had won certain struggles to prioritise workers' rights, particularly in the 1930s–1960s, employers and the state failed to maintain their commitment to these gains. Instead, power shifted in favour of capital and against workers, leading to a situation where many were denied access to jobs that paid a living wage.

In response, activists mobilised at the local level, where they felt they had greater resources *vis-à-vis* capital. Successful in these efforts, they got cities to pass local living wage ordinances. But as Kerry Miciotto, an organiser in the Baltimore campaign, notes, 'It takes one kind of power to get a law passed. Getting it enforced takes a whole other kind of power.' The lessons of the struggles to implement living wage ordinances highlight the fact that passing laws alone is often not enough to improve conditions for workers, or those without power. Top-down legislative strategies will not address power imbalances. Laws can give workers points of leverage, but it takes work to enforce them. Living wage activists have found a combination of inside and outside (or formal and informal) strategies are needed to provide the best chance of enforcement.

In addition to these lessons about accountability, the living wage movement also demonstrates that workers in the global North often experience the same kinds of challenges faced by those in the global South: poverty-level wages, lack of benefits, work insecurity, and attacks on any gains won, such as unionisation. The 'business-climate' model used to lure investors with tax relief and other financial incentives is similar to that employed by state governments in India, discussed in Chapter 8. The struggle for US-style living wage ordinances has emerged in other Northern countries (such as the UK and Canada), but, certainly, general living wage struggles can be found in the South as well as the North. South Africa was home to an active campaign for living wages in the 1980s. According to the Congress of South African Trade Unions (COSATU), that campaign was aimed at uniting workers across sectors under some common goals. Some of the demands were then adopted under the new regime, but the living wage campaign re-emerged in the late 1990s. COSATU General Secretary Zwelinzima Vavi noted that the executive committee met in 2002 and 'agreed that the struggle for a living wage must be at the core of creating a better life for all South Africans'.[11] As a result, COSATU has made a demand for a basic income grant that all citizens would receive.

As mentioned in the introduction, the United Students Against Sweatshops (USAS) have also linked their anti-sweatshop campaigns to local living wage campaigns. On some campuses, members of USAS began to realise that garment sweatshops were not only found in the global South, but in the US as well. Furthermore, the conditions faced by workers on their own campuses were often poor. Many universities were also privatising services, attacking unions, and paying low wages. In some cases, students launched campus-based living wage campaigns to fight for better conditions for the janitors, food service workers and housekeepers at the university. In other cases, students linked up with local living wage campaigns aimed at the municipal government. And in a few cases, students realised that they themselves were workers who deserved better wages and working conditions. In 2002 undergraduate students working in the dormitories at the University of Massachusetts-Amherst formed their own union to bargain for better working conditions. The focus on labour issues prompted graduate students working as teaching assistants at several public and private universities to undergo unionisation drives.[12] Today, USAS considers campus-based workers' rights movements and living wage campaigns to be a core part of its work. This story shows how students began with an effort to hold corporations accountable for their wages and working conditions in factories in other countries, but soon began to see connections between the working conditions of garment workers in the global South, gatekeepers on their campus, and even themselves as workers. This also involved a realisation that 'accountability begins at home'.

There are at least two important questions that remain unanswered. The first involves the relation between the local and the global. If a living wage is a right in the US – if activists succeed in passing ordinances in most cities that declare this – what does this mean for workers in other countries? Specifically, if the US living wage ordinances declare that employers have the responsibility to pay their workers enough to live on, shouldn't that responsibility apply to the employer no matter where they are located? Or if the right to a living wage is attached to the worker, should that worker not be entitled to that right no matter where he/she is located? Although the rhetoric of the living wage movement calls for a universal right to living wages, the ordinances provide only an opening to attach a right and responsibility to worker and employer in a particular relationship (employment in a given city, or under a given contract). In this sense, there is a disconnect between the rhetoric of the campaign and the outcomes. However, this raises interesting questions about the relationship between rights and accountability. The discussion of the difference between rights and standards brought this out clearly, where rights may deepen accountability means or processes, guaranteeing representation, association and freedom of speech, for example, while standards specify accountability outcomes or ends in a material sense. The relationship between the two and the ability of one to reinforce the other is not always clear-cut, however.

The second question is related to the first. To what extent can living wage ordinances really bring about change? Activists have found mechanisms to hold their local governments more accountable for enforcing living wage ordinances, and to hold certain employers accountable for complying with the law. But there is a widespread problem of accountability when it comes to enforcing labour law in the US, which stems from a gross imbalance of power and a system of labour law that privileges capital over workers. Living wage enforcement can be improved to achieve marginally better outcomes, but can it alter the balance of power between employees and employers? In order for living wage activists to win real rights, and the real ability to hold corporations and governments accountable, much more fundamental changes are needed. So far, the movement has enjoyed success in part because it does not always have to address deeper ideological debates. Some living wage advocates are business leaders who see higher wages as compatible with healthier markets. Some are trade unionists that like to hark back to a New Deal economy, or advocate a 'high road' solution. But as the living wage opponents themselves realize, living wages are ultimately not sustainable under an economic system that has built-in business cycles and a permanent pool of unemployed workers. This remains the next challenge for the living wage movement: shifting the terms of debate so that it confronts the real ideological battles at the core of the issue: should governments make decisions based on the right to profit-maximization, or based on human needs as the utmost concern?

NOTES

1 There are many more books on the topic, such as R. J. S. Ross, 2004; A. Ross, 2004; A. Ross 1997; Bonacich and Appelbaum 2000; and E. I. Rosen 2002.

2 Further description of the research methods and data can be found in Luce (2004).

3 The minimum wage was part of the Fair Labour Standards Act of 1938. Not all workers were covered, although over time Congress amended the law to expand coverage.

4 Whether a city government has the right to pass a city-wide minimum wage law differs by state: only those states with 'home rule' allow cities to pass laws of this kind. Currently, San Francisco, California, Santa Fe, New Mexico, Madison, Wisconsin, and Washington, DC are the cities with city-wide minimum wage laws. Voters passed a city-wide minimum wage in New Orleans, but the state legislature passed a law overriding home rule in the case of minimum wages.

5 Polls have tended to show widespread and consistent support for raising the minimum wage in the US. Data shows majority support for raising the minimum wage for most years since 1945 (Waltman, 2000 p. 50). As inequality continued to rise through much of the 1990s, even with a booming economy, public support for 'economic fairness' increased. See, for example, a 1998 Gallup Poll, 'Have and Have-Nots: Perceptions of Fairness and Opportunity'. A number of measures in this poll suggest that Americans generally support a 'reduction in the degree of economic inequality' in the US (Meyerson 1999).

6 In fact, the term 'right to work' in the US generally refers to state legislation that limits the ability of trade unions to require workers to join a union in a worksite covered by a collective bargaining agreement. In this sense, 'right to work' is used to mean 'right to hold a job and not have to join a union'. Unionists counter this by referring to these laws as 'right to work for less'.

7 Guy Standing of the ILO argues that 'In developing a strategy [for labour standards], you need to identify a core of standards that are a floor of human decency; then practices that accord with a country's capacities and a firm's size and structure; and then standards that are reasonable aspirations.' (Standing 2001: 72).

8 It is not only in mobile industries that unions suffer from weak bargaining power. Even in industries such as retail, janitorial services, daycare and hotels, workers do not always see significant increases in pay with the presence of a union. In fact, in a few places unions that have been unable to win significant wage increases through bargaining have supported local living wage ordinances as a way to raise union members' wages through legislation.

9 According to the research organisation Good Jobs First, the states of Minneapolis and Maine have the 'cadillacs' of disclosure laws. These states require state and local agencies to name the companies that receive subsidies, along with the dollar value of the subsidy, the number of jobs expected to be created/retained, the wage and benefit levels of those jobs, and this information must be available to the public in a centralised location and on a regular basis (LeRoy and Hinkley 2002).

10 Editorial, Boston Globe, 'Recycling Wages', 22 February 2003, p. A14. The editorial states, 'Though the company [KTI] has a right to charge what it wants for its services, Boston has an obligation to recognise where there is economic room for higher wages.'

11 Editorial, COSATU Weekly, 7 June 2002. http://www.cosatu.org.za/news/weekly/20020607.htm. Accessed 20 March 2005.

12 Graduate students had already unionised at a handful of campuses, starting with the University of Wisconsin-Madison, in 1966. However, the resurgence of interest in labour issues led to an upsurge in graduate student unionisation efforts in the 1990s.

REFERENCES

Armbruster-Sandoval, R. (2005) *Globalization and Cross-Border Labor Solidarity*, New York: Routledge.

Bonacich, E. and Appelbaum, R. (2000) *Behind the Label: Inequality in the Los Angeles Apparel Industry*, Berkeley: University of California Press.

Broad, R. (2001) 'A Better Mousetrap? A Response to "Realizing Labor Standards"', in A. Fung, D. O'Rourke and C. Sabel, *Can We Put an End to Sweatshops? A New Democracy Forum on Raising Global Labour Standards*, Boston: Beacon Press.

Bronfenbrenner, K. and Luce, S. (2004) 'The Changing Nature of Corporate Global Restructuring: the Impact of Production Shifts on Jobs in the US, China, and Around the Globe', Washington, DC: US–China Economic and Security Review Council.

Elliot, K. A. and Freeman, R. (2003) *Can Labour Standards Improve under Globalisation?* Washington, DC: Institute for International Economics.

Esbenshade, J. (2004) *Monitoring Sweatshops: Workers, Consumers and the Global Apparel Industry*, Philadelphia: Temple University Press.

Fung, A., O'Rourke, D. and Sabel, C. (2001) *Can We Put an End to Sweatshops? A New Democracy Forum on Raising Global Labour Standards*, Boston: Beacon Press.

Heintz, J. (2004) 'Globalization and Sweatshops, Comments', MacArthur Research Network on the Impacts of Inequality on Economic Performance, Sloan School of Management, Massachusetts Institute of Technology, 8–10 October.

LeRoy, G. and Hinkley, S. (2002) 'No More *Secret* Candy Store: a Grassroots Guide to Investigating Development Subsidies', Washington, DC: Institute on Taxation and Economic Policy.

Luce, S. (2004) *Fighting for a Living Wage*, Ithaca: Cornell University Press.

Meyerson, H. (1999) 'Gray Davis Takes Over', *LA Weekly*, 15 January, p. 15.

Mishel, L., J. Bernstein and S. Allegretto (2005) *The State of Working America 2004/2005*, Ithaca: Cornell University Press.

Progressive Maryland (2005) 'Introduction to Living Wages', Webpage. http://progressive-maryland.org/page.php?id=148, accessed 27 May 2005.

Rosen, E. I. (2002) *Making Sweatshops: the Globalisation of the US Apparel Industry*, Berkeley: University of California Press.

Ross, A. (2004) *Low Pay, High Profile: the Global Push for Fair Labor*, New York: New Press.

Ross, A. (ed.) (1997) *No Sweat: Fashion, Free Trade, and the Rights of Garment Workers*. London: Verso.

Ross, R. J. S. (2004) *Slaves to Fashion: Poverty and Abuse in the New Sweatshops*, Ann Arbor: University of Michigan Press.

Standing, G. (2001) 'Human Development: a Response to 'Realising Labour Standards,'' in A. Fung, D. O'Rourke and C. Sabel, *Can We Put an End to Sweatshops?: A New Democracy Forum on Raising Global Labour Standards*, Boston: Beacon Press.

United Methodist Church (2000), *Book of Resolutions*. Washington, DC: The United Methodist Church.

United States Catholic Conference (1997), *Catechism of the Catholic Church*. Washington, DC: United States Catholic Conference. http://www.usccb.org/catechism/text/pt3sect2chpt2art7.htm, accessed 27 May 2005.

Waltman, J. (2000). *The Politics of the Minimum Wage*, Urbana: University of Illinois Press.

Yates, M. D. (2003) *Naming the System: Inequality and Work in the Global Economy*, New York: Monthly Review Press.

Index

Abacha, Sani 216
Abia State 207
Abuja 216
accountability, active and passive 55;
administrative 51, 54, 65, 118,
136-8; alternative forms of 54-5; as
answerability and enforceability 7,
13, 15, 17, 28, 39, 41-2, 46-7, 50,
76, 90, 140n, 146, 151, 164, 167,
189-90, 195, 198, 201, 224, 242,
247, 252-9; auditing the auditors
52; and citizenship 28, 144-60,
166-7, 179, 181, 213, 224, 231,
254; and civil society 44-50, 53-5,
115-19, 146, 149-51, 155-60, 165,
173, 229, 236, 254, 256; and commodification 14, 82, 215, 227, 231;
and community, 8, 10, 18, 32, 45,
72, 102, 112, 114-16, 119, 164,
205, 212, 216-17, 252, 256; and
'compliance' 223-4, 231, 240-3;
and conflicting rights 25, 60, 63,
90, 104-5, 110-19; conceptualising
28, 39-40; consumers and 26, 40,
63, 223-4, 226-8, 232, 240, 242,
245; corporate 42-4, 47, 51-3, 163-
5, 166-83 (India) 186-8, 193-4,
199, 206, 210, 214-16, 228, 231-2,
241; cultures of 21-2, 83, 90, 96,
119, 159, 165, 219, 224, 227, 232,
237, 240, 242-3; and democracy
28, 41-2, 45-6, 55, 146, 149-50,
157-60, 179, 194, 243; and development 21, 39, 52-3, 101-2;
dynamic relationships with rights
and resources 4-13; and the environment 12, 81; financial accountability 50-3, 137, 146-8, 150-1,
153-4, 163; four key questions
about 4, 37-8, 56; gaps in 43-4, 81,
116, 164, 173, 224; and globalisation 8, 11, 13, 22, 163-5, 230-1,
241, 243, 245, 249-50, 254, 257-8;
as a grammar of conduct and performance 39-40; and indigenous
people 213; institutional aspects of
1, 11-13, 20-4, 29, 46, 48-50, 87-
97, 104, 115, 117-19, 122-40, 145-
6, 157, 159; and investment
globally 9, 27, 43, 163, 166-9, 171,
175-7, 179, 182-3, 195, 200-1,
210-11, 226, 257, 226, 257; and
law 6, 13, 16, 26, 47, 50, 135, 148-
9, 164-5, 169, 181, 186-202, 247-
8, 252-9; and markets 42-4, 165,
231; measurement of 23; and
media 14, 18-19, 46, 48-9, 127-9,
167, 174, 178-9, 181, 195-6, 202,

262